CO-APQ-900

K23
S5
1974

Crime and Compromise

Crime and Compromise

Janos Kadar and the Politics of Hungary Since Revolution

by
William Shawcross

E.P. DUTTON & CO., INC. | NEW YORK | 1974

Library of Congress Cataloging in Publication Data

Shawcross, William.
  Crime and compromise.

  Includes bibliographical references.
    1. Kadar, Janos, 1912–   2. Hungary—
Politics and government—1945–   I. Title.
DB950.K23S5   1974   320.9'439'05 [B]   73-15503

Published simultaneously in Canada
by Clarke, Irwin & Company
Limited, Toronto and Vancouver
ISBN: 0-525-08735-4

"Now, Comrade Kadar, perhaps you could tell us your opinion."

"Thank you, Comrade Chairman. Well, Marx once wrote . . ."

"Yes, Comrade Kadar, we know what Marx wrote. It's your opinion we want."

"Of course, of course, Comrade Chairman. Well, according to Lenin . . ."

"Please, Comrade Kadar, please; your own thoughts please."

"Oh, very well, Comrade Chairman, of course comrade, but before I state my own opinion I should like to make very clear in advance that I do not agree with it."

Budapest joke

Acknowledgments

The material for this book was collected during frequent trips to Central and Eastern Europe over 1970–72. The book could not have been written at all but for the aid my friends in Hungary gave me in making an assessment of Kadar and his work: I owe them all enormous, though unattributed, thanks. Outside of Hungary itself I must thank Paul Ignotus, William Robinson, Francis Miko and especially George Schöpflin for reading various stages of the manuscript and making invaluable criticisms; my newspaper, *The Sunday Times* of London for allowing me the time to write the book; William Robinson, again, for permitting me to read and quote from the preliminary work for his excellent book *The Pattern of Reform in Hungary* (published by Praeger in March 1973 and undoubtedly the most informative work on Hungary since the Revolution); Radio Free Europe for the unlimited use of its unique, excellent library and research material, which cover every conceivable aspect of East European history, life, and politics; and Tony Godwin, Hal Scharlatt, Elaine Greene, and especially Marina for their grace in tedium.

Crime and Compromise

One

In the darkening afternoon of November 1, 1956, Kossuth Lajos Square in Budapest was deserted save for a few weeping old women who crossed themselves and stuck candles onto the pavement under the walls of the mock Gothic Parliament. All day long conflicting reports of Russian troop movements in the country had been telephoned through to the nineteenth-century palace which squats on the cold, gray, dirty bank of the Danube, and in his office, Prime Minister Imre Nagy—later to be executed—was now confronting Soviet Ambassador Yuri Andropov—later to become head of the KGB, the Soviet Secret Police.

The Russians had sent their tanks into Budapest seven days before, on October 24, to try and put down demonstrators who demanded the overhaul of the system of government which Hungary had suffered ever since 1948 when the Communists, under their Moscow-trained leader Matyas Rakosi, had usurped total power in order to Sovietize Hungary according to the example and the orders of Stalin. In the last eight years thousands had lost their lives or at least their livelihoods and a special feature of this Terror was the persecution of communists as well as non-communists: many of the Party's most important servants were arrested and some of them, including its wartime leader, Laszlo Rajk, were executed.

Like the revolt in Poland, the 1956 Hungarian uprising was precipitated by Khrushchev's denunciation of Stalin in February that year. The little Ukrainian-born Russian had demanded an end to some of the stark methods by which Stalin and his admirers had governed the Soviet Union and Eastern Europe. In Hungary people took this as carte blanche for the removal of all the men and the methods associated with the last eight years.

The character of the people's demands was at first anti-Stalinist rather than anticommunist and its hero was the mild-mannered, walrus-mustached, Moscow-trained communist, who looked like a retired and benevolent family grocer, whose name was Imre Nagy.

In July 1956 Rakosi was finally removed from power but his position was given not to the reformist Nagy but to a Stalinist colleague, Erno Gero, a man closely associated by all Hungarians with the horrors of the last eight years and therefore almost as unpopular as Rakosi himself. It was to demand, among other changes, Gero's dismissal and his replacement by Nagy that the students demonstrated on October 23, 1956. They clashed with the secret police and the Russians immediately ordered the Red Army mobilized.

But the cry for change was taken up by Hungarians of all classes and ages, and despite the menacing prowl of the Soviet tanks, Nagy did replace Gero as prime minister. He began to plan some of the reforms the people demanded.

The Russians seemed to dither. While their soldiers camped in the suburbs of Budapest and around all Hungary's major cities, Khrushchev's envoys, Anastas Mikoyan and Mikhail Suslov, discussed the crisis with the new prime minister. On October 30 they promised him that they had decided to withdraw their troops, confident that the Hungarians could resolve the situation for themselves. But to many Hungarians it seemed that the Soviet soldiers were taking an unconscionable time striking their camps, packing their tents, and turning their lorries, their armored cars, and their tanks back toward the east.

On this very morning, November 1, Ambassador Andropov had come to assure the worried Nagy that, whatever the appearances, the withdrawal was still proceeding "as normal." If that was so, he was asked, what was the meaning of the reports from villages all along Hungary's northern and eastern borders that some seventy-five thousand soldiers and twenty-five hundred tanks were moving into the country? How could Andropov explain the telephone messages from confused, frightened local officials and peasants who quoted Red Army privates declaring that they had been summoned by the Hungarian government to put down the fascist counterrevolutionaries? Andropov couldn't. At lunchtime, after the ambassador had left, the Executive Committee of the Communist party, which had just been reformed in an attempt to appease some of the popular demands for its abolition, met to discuss just how it should now deal with its Soviet comrades. Among them was Imre Nagy himself, one of the few Communists the people had trusted at all over the past eight years; there was

Ferenc Munnich, a straightforward Party functionary
who had done service to the cause since the First
World War, always obediently, rarely with distinction;
there was Janos Kadar, tall, spare, looking far older
than his forty-four years, not well-known in the
country but, where he was known, recognized as a vic-
tim of the Stalinist trials and as such relied on as an
opponent of Stalinism—a reasonably popular if un-
tried new Party leader; and, lending counsel of moderation in his clipped, modest, and soft old voice,
there was the gray-haired, thin-faced, thin-bodied
George Lukacs, certainly the most important philosopher Hungary had produced for a century.

Together these men and their colleagues agreed
that Nagy should give the Soviet ambassador an ul-
timatum: unless the Red Army really did leave and
was actually seen to leave straightaway, then Hungary
would at once declare its neutrality and withdraw
from the Warsaw Pact—tne fraternal links which had
bound Hungarians so closely to Moscow since 1948
would be broken. It was a courageous and an enormous decision for such lifelong communists to
make—as difficult for them as for Catholic priests to
deny the authority of the Pope—but only George
Lukacs and one other member, not Janos Kadar, opposed it.

That afternoon more reports from border villages
and from ground staff at many of the country's
airfields, from railway officials and from Hungary's
own army officers showed that, far from withdraw-
ing, the Red Army was reinforcing, maneuvering into
better positions, digging in, preparing to do battle in
the country.

Nagy and his colleagues stood by their threat. At
5:15 that afternoon the lights of a black Soviet-made
limousine circled Parliament Square in the dusk and

Yuri Andropov stepped again into the palace to hear what the Hungarian leaders had to tell him.

First Nagy informed the ambassador of his government's decision, and then his principal cabinet colleagues added their verbal support. Almost all were calm as they did so. But, when his turn came, Janos Kadar stood up in front of Yuri Andropov and, to the amazement and concern of his comrades, shouted with barely controlled fury: "I am a Hungarian and I will fight your tanks with my bare hands if necessary." Yuri Andropov said nothing, left the prime minister's office, joined his aide outside the door, walked downstairs, pulled his coat around him and drove in his official car back to the Soviet Embassy.[1]

A few hours later, Nagy broadcast the declaration of neutrality to the people, and at 9:50 that same evening, on Radio Free Kossuth, Janos Kadar declared, "In their glorious uprising our people have shaken off the Rakosi regime."

Over the next week it became quite clear that Kadar's outburst with Andropov reflected faithfully the emotions of his fellow Hungarians and when the Soviet tanks entered Budapest finally to crush the Revolution on the morning of November 4, thousands of citizens did take to the streets to fight with their empty hands and anything they could fill them with. At 5:08 that morning Nagy announced the attack by declaring over the radio: "This is Imre Nagy speaking, the President of the Council of Ministers of the Hungarian People's Republic. Today at daybreak Soviet forces started an attack against our capital, obviously with the intention to overthrow the legal Hungarian democratic Government. Our troops are fighting. The Government is in its place. I notify the people of our country and the entire world of this fact."

At almost exactly the same time as Nagy was broadcasting, another voice came over the airwaves from a Soviet-controlled radio somewhere east of Budapest; it was that of Janos Kadar. For him the "glorious uprising" had very quickly become incipient counter-revolution. He declared that a new self-styled Hungarian Revolutionary Worker-Peasant Government, "acting in the interests of our people, our working class and our country, requested the Soviet army command to help our nation in smashing the dark reactionary forces and restoring order and calm to the country." And it happened just like that. Very bloodily.

Kadar returned to Budapest in a Soviet-armored car on November 7. By then the Red Army had destroyed most of the revolutionaries: his task was to abort the embryo reforms of the short-lived Nagy government and to restore Hungary to the narrow mold of Soviet orthodoxy. There have been few national leaders in this century so hated by their people as was Janos Kadar after those euphoric and bitter days of autumn 1956.

But it's almost impossible to believe it today. He is now the most popular leader in the Warsaw Pact. Out of the rubble of the Revolution which he himself had razed, he has somehow managed to construct one of the most reasonable, sane, and efficient communist states in the world. Hungarians now speak, not only ironically, of their country as the "gayest barracks in the socialist camp" and praise Kadar for making it so. It is a not unremarkable feat: from being almost universally loathed as the betrayer not only of his people but also of his best friend, Laszlo Rajk, he is now highly regarded not only by that friend's friends but by his people too.

The development of Kadar's political personality

and the reasons for the change in the Hungarian people's feelings for him can best be shown through study of some of the important aspects of Hungarian life today. For, even if it is incorrect to say that Kadar *is* Hungary today, it is certainly true that Hungary today is personified by Kadar and that many Hungarians are convinced that without him their country would be a very different and probably far worse place to live.

To show the sort of place it has in fact become I have looked at a very few features of Hungarian society—among them the development of "socialist-democracy" and the changed role of the Party this implies, the influence of the economic reforms introduced in 1968, the place of culture, the freedom of the press, and the attitude of the young toward the "Kadarization" of their country.

This profile of modern Hungary I have tried to present within the scheme of a profile of Janos Kadar himself, for the simple reason that his is such a superb story. In 1958 he was the antihero of a play by Robert Ardrey, which Peter Hall produced at the Piccadilly Theatre in London. Called *Shadow of Heroes,* it was a good play and still today it describes well the anguish and the dismay, the aspirations, the disillusions, and the betrayals endured by Central European Communists after the last war, as their beloved but unknown leader, Jozsef Stalin, imposed his will upon them.

Shadow of Heroes seeks to explain Eastern European communists of the fifties in the same way as *Darkness at Noon* had described the thought processes of Soviet party members in the thirties. It does it well not just because the play is cleverly written but because of Ardrey's choice of subject: Kadar. In Kadar's life and work can probably be found more tragedy, more despair, more dilemmas, more hatred, and more suffer-

ing than in those of any other East European communist leader.

But the details of that life are curiously hard to discover in Hungary today. Hungarians are eager to
express their admiration of him, but when questioned
they admit that they know almost nothing about him.
Is he married? "I think so." Where does he live? "I'm
not sure." When is his birthday? "I've no idea." Does
he have children? "I don't think so, but perhaps."
What are his hobbies? "Well, I think he likes walking
or reading. I expect so, anyway." This ignorance is
partly explained by the fact that Kadar hates personal
publicity. His official biographies (never more than a
few hundred words long) have always declared that
his parents were "poor cotters" or peasants or "land
workers." In the late 1940s these biographies stated
that he was born in a small village near Lake Balaton.
Since then there has been a subtle change of format:
they now say simply that he spent his childhood there,
and suggest only by omission that that was also where
he was born. By omission also they fail to disclose that
there was anything unusual in the way in which he
was brought up or that his parents' relationship was
other than normal and happy. In fact the circumstances of Kadar's childhood, discovered now for the
first time, are rather extraordinary and go far toward
explaining some of the intricacies of his character.

As for his later life, the Party will say officially only
that he joined it when still a youth, fought valiantly
against the Nazis, was imprisoned in 1951 "on
trumped up charges under the Stalinist regime of
Matyas Rakosi" and that in November 1956 "he
helped to thwart the counter-revolution and led the
struggle for the renewal of the Party." [2]

That, so far as the Party is concerned, is all that is to
be said about Janos Kadar. On my first visit to

Hungary I was informed that if I hoped to return I must not try and write about him. As a result I have had absolutely no cooperation from Party or government officials in doing so. I was told, very politely, that the archives of the Party's Historical Institute contain no biographical information on Kadar; his colleagues in the Party and government today claim they know nothing at all about his past. He himself gives only one interview a year to a selected Western journalist; he has not chosen me and to those reporters to whom he has spoken he has never revealed much of himself.

Loathing the Stalinist cult of the personality which his predecessor Rakosi practiced to excess and which glorifies the leader rather than the Party, Kadar has studiously sought to cloak himself in the disguise of anonymous apparatchik or bureaucrat. A gray man in a gray suit, leading his Party and his country through the uncertain shadows of communist reform, he stands behind the light and turns his face away. Conscious that there are incidents in his past of which he is perhaps ashamed and which anyway he would certainly rather not now retell, many Hungarians respect both his personal and political motives for secrecy and even private citizens who once knew him in whatever capacity will not now talk about him. But from what one can see through the Party darkly, and after extensive researches along the back streets of Budapest, the shores and villages around Lake Balaton, and the coast of Yugoslavia, it seems that Kadar's twisted, tragic life and personality mirror almost exactly the complicated relationship between the Hungarian Communist Party and the people it has for fifty years sought to control and represent.

Two

I wanted to be happy but not, like a hamster,
alone.

> J. Kadar, on his youth
> May 11, 1957

Some time during the hot dusty Central European summer of 1910, a young Slovak peasant girl left her home and set off south to seek perhaps her fortune and almost certainly a better way of life. For her home was in the scruffy little village of Ogyalla, some forty miles north of the Danube town of Komarno, beside the railway line which leads from Budapest into Slovakia and into what were then the farther reaches of the vast and ramshackle empire of Austro-Hungary, which had sprawled so long and to such debilitating effect over Central Europe. Ogyalla was an impoverished agricultural community with only two claims to attention, none to fame.

First, it was the birthplace of Arpad Feszty, whose huge circular painting of the discoverer and founder of Hungary, the Magyar chieftain Arpad, was exhibited around the walls of a tent in Budapest until its destruction during the Second World War. And second, of marginally more significance, Ogyalla had an

observatory. Built in 1871 on the estate of a rich landowner, Miklos Konkoly Thege, a gifted amateur astronomer, the observatory was the only site for gazing
at the stars for miles around. Soon after the turn of
the century a Heidelberg astronomer named an as-
teroid after the observatory at Ogyalla, but that didn't
stop the infant Czechoslovak government from
changing the village's name to Stare Dola when, at the
Peace of Trianon in 1919, the victorious allies took
such pleasure in carving up the remains of the
Austro-Hungarian Empire and Tomas Masaryk, the
architect and first president of the new state, obtained
what is now Slovakia for the Czechs.*

But seven good years before that dismemberment
took place, and almost two years before Europe can-
tered inanely into its last traditional war, Borbala
Czermanik walked and rode by cart down the dry
track from Ogyalla, onto the road to Komarno, along
the banks of the Danube as it curves its way east and
south from Vienna, to Budapest (where she had
thought of staying, but which she did not like), and so
still farther south. Through the waving, green to-
bacco fields below the southern shores of Lake Balaton, Hungary's inland sea—shallow and misty but to
Hungarians more beautiful than any ocean—past the
vineyards on the hills of Transdanubia, staying the
nights in the wretched homes of those landless and
starving peasants who were willing to accept her, she
crossed the fast-flowing River Drava (which now runs
along part of the Hungarian-Yugoslav frontier) until
finally, still within the empire, she came to the shores
of Illyria. There in the busy port of Fiume, now Rijeka, she found work as a maid to the town clerk, who
lived in a grand house in one of the town's more fashionable quarters.

* Ogyalla has been renamed again. It is now called Hurbanovo.

Stationed in Fiume at that time was the Forty-fourth Regiment of the Austro-Hungarian infantry, and fulfilling his national duty as a batman within its ranks was a young Hungarian peasant called Janos Kressinger. He came from Pusztaszemenes, a tiny village near Lake Balaton, past which Borbala had made her way south. One day in 1911 Janos and Borbala met in a café in Fiume; Janos took a fancy to this plain, plump, but rather likable and straightforward girl from Slovakia, and where Orsino and Viola found such poignant love so very long ago, they too slept together.

Borbala became pregnant. A wedding, declared Janos in alarm, was out of the question, and he thanked God that his posting in the town was about to expire anyway. His satchel on his back, he quickly tramped and hitched home to Pusztaszemenes, alone.

Borbala's boy was born in the general hospital of Fiume on May 25, 1912. The birth register, still in Rijeka today, records that she christened him Janos Jozsef; his surname is given as Czermanik and there is a line drawn through the space for his father's name.

After Janos's birth, Borbala, sacked by the town clerk for her shameful misconduct, found work in Fiume increasingly hard to come by and in 1914 with the shooting of the Archduke Franz Ferdinand a few hundred miles along the land, she decided that it was time for her and her infant son to seek out his father, her love. As the gun carriages were drawn up and the cavalry plumed all over Europe, Borbala began the long walk back north. But when she arrived at the village of Pusztaszemenes, which was just a row of single-story whitewashed thatched cottages on either side of the mud track running away from Lake Balaton, she found that Janos Kressinger had meanwhile married the girl next door. His bed was filled and his house was shut against her. Instead of leaving in despair, she decided to face him out and persuaded the village schoolmaster to give her work as a maid. Every day she walked past Kressinger's house and new wife with Janos in her arms until, in considerable embarrassment, her ex-lover agreed to give her a retainer if only she would leave the village.

Perhaps hoping that eventually Kressinger would tire of his wife, Borbala moved only twenty kilometers down the unmetalled lane to the village of Kapoly, a wretched little place, indistinguishable from thousands of others in a country where 68.5 percent of the population were peasants, only a third of whom could count on regular employment. One-fifth of all Hungary was at that time owned by three hundred noble families between them, whereas over one million peasants could all together muster only another tenth. Eight hundred thousand of these had not even a kitchen garden to call their own and so depended for work, food, and clothing entirely on the landlords or the rich peasants, the *Kulaks,* on whose destruction Stalin spent so much energy over 1929-31. An example faithfully followed by Rakosi in Hungary after the Communists came to power in 1948.

The villagers of Kapoly were divided almost equally into Protestants and Catholics, their two churches competing with each other at either end of the single street. It was an unequal battle in terms of material comfort, for most of the land around Kapoly was owned by the Benedictine Abbot of Tihany; it was therefore the Catholics who got first pick of such jobs as were available. There weren't many: few of the peasants had more than ninety days work a year—

mostly at harvest time when they had to labor twenty hours a day. Even though Borbala and Janos were registered as Catholics, she managed to work only infrequently as a day laborer on the land; by the age of four, Janos was supplementing their income and trying to meet the rent on their one-room hut by hiring himself out as swineherd, as shepherd boy, and as midget farmhand. He did not dislike the work. "It was my world and I knew every soul, every tree and every brook there," [1] he later said.* But to Borbala's thinking this world was not big enough for her son to grow up in. When the war ended in 1918 she decided that she and Janos must move to Budapest. Leaving him temporarily in the care of some friends called Balint, she traveled to the capital, some seventy miles away, found herself work as a concierge, came back to fetch her son, and together they took the train from the nearby market town of Kaposvar.

"I can't really express my amazement on coming out of the Southern Railway station and seeing Budapest. But it's understandable because for the first time I saw an electric lamp, a tram and the underground," [2] he said later. The underground is even more spectacular now. The first on the continent of Europe, it was built for the Great Exhibition of 1896 and still today the original *fin de siècle* wooden coaches draw passengers from East to West just a few feet under the town, from Lenin's new statue to Gerbeaud's café where the middle classes still eat cream

---

* This and other quotations about his childhood are taken from articles or interviews published by Kadar in official Hungarian newspapers after he came to power in 1956. They should therefore be read as the statements of a communist leader (and, at that time, an unpopular one) trying to appear as human and as sympathetic as possible. While I have not been able to discover that any of his recollections of his youth are deliberately falsified, they may well be romanticized. That does not make them any the less interesting as guides to his character.

cake in smart and ever bourgeois Vorosmarty Square. When Janos Czermanik arrived there, Budapest was no longer a gay and fashionable center, but a broken disoriented town, wrenched from its sibling Vienna and hardly recovering from other humiliations imposed upon it by the final defeat of the Hapsburgs in 1918 and the resultant Treaty of Trianon. Overnight a group of foreigners sitting in a Parisian suburb had arbitrarily (so it seemed to Hungarians) dissolved the great state which had existed ever since a thousand years before the famed Arpad had led his Magyar tribesmen over the Carpathians and into the middle Danube basin in search of new feeding grounds.

They had come west from the Urals, Arpad and his followers; some twenty thousand horsemen: handsome, strong, sharp-eyed and arrogant, their silk and brocade robes wrapped around them against the wind, gold swords by their sides, conquest in their minds. They recognized in the fertile plains and gentle hills of the basin a superb new homeland. But they were not content to settle there quietly, and to the more peaceful European shepherds they seemed just savages. These Magyars, so the frightened whisper went, their appetites are never satisfied; they eat not only unclean animals—foxes, wolves, and wild cats— they also drink human blood, crunch human bones in their strong teeth, and it is human flesh that they fling, half-gnawed, at their dogs.

Whatever the legend, it is certainly true that over the succeeding centuries the Magyars and then the Hungarian monarchs gradually and often cruelly extended their domain over what are now Slovakia, Ruthenia, Transylvania, parts of Austria, Croatia, and Slovenia. By 1914 Budapest's share of the sprawling Austro-Hungarian Empire comprised 282,876 square kilometers of Central European lands and within them 18,264,533 subjects of some dozen different races.

But by the time the English, the French, and the Americans had signed their papers in Trianon, Budapest was left with just less than 100,000 square kilometers and a mere 7,615,117 of its former subjects. The others had been transferred to those new or altered states, Austria, Poland, Czechoslovakia, Rumania, and Yugoslavia, to which, for the most part, they more properly and more happily belonged. More bitter still for Budapest, some 3,500,000 citizens whose mother tongue was Magyar were also lost to alien regimes. Still today the Trianon settlement arouses fury among Hungarians, as fiercely nationalistic a people as any to be found among the chauvinistic tribes of Central and Eastern Europe. And in the twenties and thirties that fury took the form of an angry determination to reverse what so many considered to be a totally iniquitous and unforgivable wrong done them by the French and English bourgeois. Little thought was given to the injustices suffered by the national minorities, like Borbala's own Slovaks, before Trianon forcibly freed them from the grasp of their tyrannical foster parent.

For at least the last sixty years the nationality question had been the most acute in Hungarian political life. After 1867 attempts were made to appease the various nationalities but they were to prove worthless largely because the Magyar authorities chose to disregard them. In 1867 5 percent of the population had the vote; by 1910 this had increased to only 8 percent—and nearly all were still upper- or middle-class Magyars. The working class and the non-Magyars were virtually unrepresented. To this structure of national life many Magyars hoped to return after the

First World War; it was the allies' impressing upon them that the days of empire were over that infuriated and disoriented them so. Out of that national inability to come to terms with the final destruction of Arpad's dream so very long ago grew Hungary's first flirtation with communism, the revolutionary government of Bela Kun.

Political organization had come slowly through the late 1800s to those starving Hungarian peasants who had walked off the fields and tried to find jobs in the new factories around the towns. Politics could, of course, develop only with unionism and although the government gradually allowed workers to associate together after 1860, they strictly forbade the new organizations to indulge in any political ambitions. So alongside each of the young, official union bodies developed a secret shadow organization known as the Free Union—it was this body which tried to arrange strike pay and strikes themselves. They were not, on the whole, very successful.

The first active Hungarian Communists were almost all soldiers in the Austro-Hungarian army who had been captured on the Russian front during the First World War, quickly indoctrinated by the Bolsheviks in the few months between the Revolution and the armistice, and then sent home to Budapest to lead the proletariat. Matyas Rakosi became a Communist thus. So did Ferenc Munnich, the man who led Janos Kadar to the Russians on the night of November 1, 1956; so did the mild little insurance clerk with a weasel face, named Bela Kun—one of the few men ever to have established a Bolshevik government outside of Russia.

In 1919 disgust with the way in which the Western powers were blithely carving up their country and with Western refusal to support even their legitimate national aspirations, led not a few despairing Hungarians to wonder whether they should not, in this last resort, turn to their traditional enemy, Russia, for help. Bela Kun encouraged them to see this as the only hope and, although he was in prison for agitation, the government, impotent itself, accepted his claim that only he, with Lenin behind him, could save Hungary's integrity. Such was the despair in Budapest that on March 21, 1919, he was installed in power at the head of the Hungarian Soviet Republic.

But his revolution was not to last long. It was, first of all, *too* revolutionary for the Hungarian people. He had promised to defend the country's territorial integrity but in fact he immediately sought to establish and extend the dictatorship of the proletariat. In Kapoly and in Pusztaszemenes and all over the country miserable peasants allowed themselves, for the first time, to hope: that he would break up the huge estates and distribute land to them. But despite his promises, he began to try and collectivize large parts of the agricultural system: there was to be no democratic distribution of land to individuals at all. Such policies were not easily imposed upon the indignant peasants. Not for nothing was Kun's government later known as the Red Terror.

But whatever the brutality of his commissars, it was almost equalled by the regime that followed him. The allies were not overeager to tolerate this new outpost of revolution so far to the west of Moscow and their armies were immediately thrown against Kun. He managed quickly and surprisingly to drive off the Czechoslovaks but then, as his support in the country waned, the Rumanians marched almost without opposition on Budapest. It fell to them on August 6, a day after Kun had resigned and fled to Vienna, from where he was sent to Moscow. Then, under the overall command of Admiral Miklos Horthy, the national army of the counterrevolution embarked upon a vengeful campaign against peasants, Jews, and Hungarian workers alike. It was known as the White Terror. These few short months of 1919 and early 1920 therefore saw all the most brutal traits of the Hungarian national character displayed in the service of both Right and Left. And the allies, thankful at the rout of the Left, were happy enough to allow the counterrevolution license in its revanchism and to see a weak and reactionary but beautifully dressed admiral proclaimed regent in a country which no longer had any access to the sea.

Borbala and her son were not Jews; they survived the White Terror. But the tips of a concierge were not enough for them to live on: as in Kapoly Janos had to supplement their income. Before he went to elementary school in Wesselenyi Street every morning he did a newspaper round, and as a result some of the social aspects of the town began to make as deep an impression upon him as its mechanical wonders had originally done.

While the aristocracy and the merchants relaxed and prospered in their apartments and palaces, thousands of people lived squashed ten to a room in the city. Less than 10 percent of the inhabitants had one room between two of them and as often as not a "room" for several meant little more than a hole in a wall. Up on the hills of Buda and down by the River Danube people squeezed against the sides of caves for warmth. Quite unable to find proper shelter, they dug themselves holes in the sand by the river and in the fields and woods around the city. One winter's night in 1905 the police, searching the municipal gardens, had found thirty-five people trying to sleep tied to the branches of trees, and things had not improved

much by 1919. Peasants still had to come to Budapest,
forced by starvation from the fields; and still, once in
Budapest, they were unable to find enough work to
enable them to live rather than just exist. By these
standards, Borbala and her son were not destitute. In
1926, Janos, aged fourteen, left school and became
apprenticed as a mechanic. But even after working
for a year he was still paid only four pengös a week
(the average worker's wage was twelve pengös). From
this he had to deduct health insurance and "the
remainder I had to give my mother if I didn't want us
all to drop dead of starvation." [3] He later bemoaned
the fact that with this income he had no hope of buying any Marxist literature, even had he had the inclination to walk to Vienna, the nearest town where the
subversive work was sold. [4]

A few years after their move to Budapest (exactly
when is not known), his father reneged on his promise to send them an allowance. When he was sixteen,
Janos found at home an old letter which his mother
had hidden carelessly. It read: "My dear Boriska, I
can't send you any more money because I have to
support my other children. But please keep our child
and try to educate him. Jozsef." This was the first time
that the boy discovered that he even had a father, for
his mother—perhaps because of the pain she felt—
had always blankly refused to discuss the subject with
him. Even now he was little the wiser, for the letter
bore no address, the signature no surname, and his
mother still refused to tell him who his father was or
where he lived. [5] It was only many years later that
Janos Czermanik discovered that his father had been
quite rich enough to support them had he wished,
for back in Pusztaszemenes Jozsef Kressinger was a
kulak, one of the class of rich peasants who were so

hated and despised by all good Communists every-where. The truth, had he learned it, could have served only to increase the "muddle" that he later said was then in his mind. "I didn't really know what I wanted. My mother's knowledge of the class struggle consisted in little more than repeating 'Son, the gentry are crooks! They are tormenting the poor, but they cannot be defeated because they are stronger.' " [6] He was pleased eventually to declare, somewhat smugly, that he "couldn't go along with that." [7] But at the time there was very little that he could or did do about it.

He was then, and still is today, both a keen football fan and an excellent chess player. "Almost every evening (my only free time) I either read or played chess sitting on the curb under the street lamp until midnight." In 1928, when his ambition was to become a chess master, he entered a chess competition organized by the Barbers' Assistants' Club in Havas Street, and won the prize, which, he later claimed, was a copy of Engels' *Anti-Dühring*. A strange and difficult reward for any young chess player but understandable if that section of the Barbers' Assistants' Union then sported left-wing convictions and was willing to defy the law banning left-wing books. It was, he declared, something of a turning point in his life.

> True, it was not class consciousness but my youthful illusions connected with chess which brought me to this workers' organisation, but it was well worth it. When I looked at the book I was surprised; the title itself seemed so strange: "Herr Eugen Dühring's Revolution in Science." I had even more trouble with the contents. I had previously read a variety of books, from trash like Mister Hercules, to Verne and Zola, but I had never

read a book like this. I was amazed after reading it for the first time—I understood the words and the individual sentences, but not the thing as a whole. At that time, needless to say, perhaps, I held my own intellectual powers in very high esteem.[8]

He became a prisoner of the book.

I read it over almost eight months, who knows how often? I became more and more absorbed in it. My friends tried to drag me away and tapped their foreheads, indicating that there was something wrong with me. I can't say that even then I fully understood the Anti-Dühring, the first Marxist book that ever fell into my hands, but from then on I considered life in a different way. It did not yet bind me finally to the ideal of Marxism, but it kindled in me the unquenchable thirst for scientific socialism.

That thirst was certainly not easy to quench in Hungary in the twenties and thirties. It was a defeated, disappointed, immobile society whose succession of authoritarian and incurious governments discouraged almost all attempts to reform the archaic pattern of feudal life that had persisted and ossified through centuries of mismanagement and exploitation. Now that Budapest was rid of its imperial responsibilities, the two decades after Trianon would have been the ideal moment to try and modernize Hungary, to make of that backward agricultural land a country perhaps a little more like the new Czechoslovakia which Tomas Masaryk was forging to the north. But under the right-wing regency of Miklos Horthy, one government after another did virtually nothing.

The 1920s and 1930s were, to be sure, a time of general stagnation all over Europe, but Hungary sank deep into the mud of nonprogress, faster and further

than all other European countries save Spain and
Portugal; those two decades simply preserved the social and economic backwardness of past centuries.
Over the years from 1910 to 1941 the agrarian population was reduced from only 55.8 percent to 50 percent of the total while the industrial population increased from only 19 percent to 23 percent. While
heavy industry was expanding over almost all
Europe, in Hungary it fell.[9]

Throughout the period the Communist party was
quite illegal (and practically nonexistent), but the zeal
with which the few Communists were pursued by the
police and the aggressiveness with which Party cells
were broken up fluctuated in inverse proportion to
the government's sense of security. And, like any repressive and reactionary administration, successive
governments, ever conscious of their lack of popular
support, were liable to severe crises of confidence
from which the Communists always suffered. The
years immediately following the overthrow of Bela
Kun were especially hard for the Hungarian Left and
many Communists left the country for the comparative quiet of Vienna; some even went to Masaryk's
new and liberal Prague.

In 1921 the regime extended its tolerance to the
least radical of the Hungarian Social Democratic parties in order to give itself the trappings of a working
democracy. The so-called Bethlen-Peyer Pact, signed
in December 1921 by the prime minister and the Social Democratic leader of the trades unions, accorded
the Socialists the right of assembly, freedom of the
press, restored their confiscated trade union property,
and released all internees except the Communists.
The Social Democrats for their part promised not
only to stop attacking the government but actually to
cooperate with it. In other words, say Communists

today, somewhat unfairly, they became the creatures
of the regime.

In 1924 the government temporarily relaxed its
control of left-wing opposition groups sufficiently to
allow the formation of a new political party under Istvan Vagi. Ostensibly this new Hungarian Socialist
Workers party was an offshoot of the Social Democratic Party: in fact it was controlled by the Communists who made the mistake of paying too little attention to the understandable jealousy of established
Social Democrats and to the suspicions of the regime.
The Party proved itself more than able to organize
strikes and demonstrations and was therefore soon
dissolved. Its death was hastened by the arrest of Zoltan Szanto, the secretary of the illegal Communist
party; the police discovered papers in his house which
proved conclusively that Vagi's party was merely a
front organization for the Communists.

In conditions of such uncertainty and persecution,
the Communists were unable to organize themselves
as a tight-knit group. The grand days of "democratic
centralism" had scarcely arrived. Cells remained totally detached from one another and none kept records of the rest. Still today there is no reliable estimate of the size of the Party in the late twenties or
thirties and in Budapest, Party historians discourage
speculation—largely because recruiting had been so
shamefully unsuccessful. It is very unlikely that there
were many more members in 1930 than the 12,000
the Party claimed in January 1945. This is explained
partly by communism's basic lack of appeal in a rural,
Catholic country where people traditionally hated the
Russians, partly by memories of Bela Kun's grim rule,
and partly by the fact that it was hard for any aspirant
Marxist to join the Party: the Party had to join him.
He could only enter a trade union organization, play

as radical and active a part in its work as times would allow, and hope to come to the notice of a clandestine Party member. So it was with Janos Czermanik.

The year 1930 saw the completion of the First Soviet Five Year Plan and, by contrast, so it seemed to left-wing workers of Central Europe, a deepening of the crisis of capitalism. In Hungary tentative strikes of peasants and workers succeeded one another, an anxious, uncertain mood developed in Budapest, intellectual life bubbled, and the banks blocked accounts. Then, on September 1, for the first time in eleven years, the Hungarian workers went on a massive nationwide strike and took to the streets. Czermanik was among them, though only by chance. The slump had prevented him from working his trade as a machinist and he had been employed for over a year in a carpet warehouse in Kluazal Street. That day he had no idea what was happening but he got himself into a fight with some soda-factory workers who were blacklegging the strike: he was knocked out.

"I returned to consciousness sitting on a bench in Karoly Korut. I ached all over, but still I had never felt better in my life than I did then. I had had a taste of fight: the hot wave of the fighting working class had carried me with it on the great fighting day of Budapest—on the 1st September 1930. I was not yet a communist, I was not yet a class conscious young worker, but I regretted not having known beforehand about this demonstration." [10]

Demonstrating didn't get him work and after he lost his job piling carpets he spent much of the next couple of years in and out of the labor exchange in Jozsef Street. These offices were then known by unemployed workers as "the spitter"; for there was nothing to do there but hang about for nonexistent jobs and spit one's disgust with the system and the lack of unemployment insurance on the floor. Nothing, that is, but to discuss politics and the spitter was frequently the scene of violent arguments between those Social Democrats who begged for patience and those crypto-Communists who wanted to fight, now. Although Janos Czermanik considered himself still unconscious of the class struggle, he claims to have been with the latter in spirit. "By now I had got rid of my childish dreams. I no longer wanted to be a football star or a chess master: I wanted simply to be an iron worker." [11]

A year after his first street fight, someone came up to him on the pavement and tapped him on the shoulder. It was an old friend from football days, Janos Fenekal, who had played in the same team when they were both kids at the Wesselenyi Street School. They each discovered that the other was unemployed and bitter about it. But Fenekal's bitterness had been more productive than Czermanik's: he had joined the youth section of the illegal Communist party. "It was a great surprise. I don't remember what was my concept of a communist at that time, but I was amazed that a young worker like me, with whom I had played football as a child, was a communist. My amazement turned to pleasure because I understood that, in that case, I, too, could become a communist." [12]

He did. A week later. By his own account—which has not been refuted—at teatime the next Thursday afternoon, he went to a meeting at 11 Paulay Ede Street, in the drab extended, working-class northern district of Budapest. He was enrolled in KIMSZ (the youth section of the illegal Communist party) and listened, overawed and excited, as the girl secretary and the two other members of the group described their revolutionary work. He was given the Party name Janos Barna—in those days it was quite usual to be known by one name at home and by another within the Party—and went home bursting with pride and his secret, crazy about the girl:

> Up to the time of this meeting, there were eight or ten people who were really close to my heart: my mother . . . two school mates, three friends from the neighbourhood, a former fellow apprentice, a workmate, and a girl I used to dream about. Suddenly they were now joined by these three KIMSZ members, whom I had not known the day before. . . . I considered them braver than the bravest boys I had ever met. The girl comrade seemed more lovely than the loveliest girl I had ever seen. In short, I would have gone through fire for them. They were communists and that was sufficient for my heart to open to them. I had become a communist, too.[13]

By now he saw the political system as one in which the franchise was totally weighted by means of property and educational qualifications against the workers and peasants, in which balloting in many parts of the countryside was open, and in which, in any case, the candidate was very often the local landowner, and woe betide any peasant who did not vote for him. In 1931 he and other crypto-Communists tried to nominate working-class (just working-class, not communist) candidates for election to Parliament. But they found that instead of the five thousand signatures normally required for nomination they needed at least twenty-five thousand for each candidate, because the police immediately declared most of the signatures invalid. Toward the end of the election campaign a working-class rally was broken up by the police, and the office of the Hungarian Socialist Workers party smashed. "Its candidates were taken to the police station where the Horthy detectives jeered

at them: 'How are the gentlemen from Parliament?' "
Thirty years later Kadar pointed out, with some relish
perhaps, that many of those who jeered had "come to
a sad end . . . But a few of the former candidates are
still living, enjoying the honours due to respected vet-
erans: some are even MPs at present." [14]

Electoral farce apart, 1931 was a bad year for the
Party. On September 13 a man named Matuska, who
may have been slightly deranged, blew up the
Vienna-Budapest Express as it rushed through Bia-
torbagy. Sixty-three people were killed. It was only
one of a number of trains he had already exploded,
says the Party today, but the Horthy police chose to
detect in it a vicious Communist plot and used it as an
excuse for imposing martial law on the country and
rounding up as many agitators, crypto-Communists,
fellow travelers, and tramps as they could find,
among them Janos Czermanik-Barna. Two of the
leaders of the illegal Party, Imre Sallai and Sandor
Furst, were hanged—the first such execution in ten
years.

One of the most prominent figures in the Party at
this time was in fact in prison. He was Matyas Rakosi,
who was to become undisputed overlord of the Party
from 1945 to 1956, give or take a few interruptions
after the death of his mentor Jozsef Stalin. Rakosi was
a political genius who became a rather evil man. Born
in 1892, the son of a country shopkeeper, he came to
resemble an alternately friendly and pugnacious
butcher himself. He was an excellent scholar and determined to become a banker, he even spent some
time in a London bank before serving with the Haps-
burg armies in the First World War. In 1915 he was
captured by the Russians and imprisoned. In 1917
the Bolsheviks took this clever, ambitious young capitalist to Moscow to make a clever, ambitious young

Communist out of him. They did very well; next year he was sent back to Budapest a dedicated Leninist, and he then became deputy commissioner for commerce in Bela Kun's government. After the defeat of the Kun regime, he fled to Austria, was imprisoned, and later escaped to Moscow for further and much more comprehensive instruction.

Together with another fat, but more jolly Communist—Zoltan Vas—he was sent home in 1924 to improve the Party's organization. They did not have time to achieve much. Arrested in 1925 with fifty-three other underground workers, Vas was given eight years imprisonment and, after an inspired and eloquent self-defense, Rakosi—eight and a half. In prison he successfully organized hunger strikes in protest against the conditions and maintained surreptitious contact with his comrades at large. At the end of his eight and a half year term he was retried and this time sentenced, despite an international outcry, to life imprisonment for "crimes" committed during the 1919 Revolution.

But by now, according to one account, he was no longer the prisoners' friend.[15] Indeed, he was the governor's clerk, a "trusty." Potential Communist leaders of that period seem to have had a surprising inclination, when imprisoned, to ingratiate themselves with their jailers. Antonin Novotny, leader of Czechoslovakia from 1953 till 1968, did exactly the same: in Mauthausen concentration camp he was also a trusty and as such earned himself the undying hatred of an insignificant Slovak Communist, Stefan Dubcek, whose son Alexander was one day, by default, to become Novotny's greatest enemy and cause his downfall.

As a clerk, Rakosi had unlimited access to the prison library and also, it appears, to the Hungarian and sometimes even the Austrian press. He put this privilege to good use and his second prison term was taken up with a prodigious exercise of self-improvement. He made of himself a man who could, when he wished, woo the cardinal with extensive and fulsome quotations from the Paternoster, and who could, as one critic put it, charm "second rate poets by reciting their poems, engineers by knowing their special problems." [16] All things to all men and most importantly, all Stalinist to Stalin.

Communist party politics strangely resemble a complicated game of snakes and ladders in which the tilt of the ladders is contantly shifting, and the tails of the snakes incessantly squirm. Whereas in a straightforward game you know very well while you wait your throw which fall of the dice will send you whistling merrily up a ladder to success and stardom and which will have you slithering inexorably down the back of a snake, in Party politics you can never be so confident. Throughout the thirties it was really safer to make no throw of the dice at all; hence Rakosi was very fortunate to be immune from all risk, safe inside a Hungarian prison. In 1936 Stalin really shook the ladders; many of them broke, sending their climbers gasping into the deepest snake pits of all, to which no ladders ever reached again.

After 1936 the Hungarian and other nonruling Communist parties were invited by Moscow to abandon sectarianism, the policy of separation from other working-class movements upon which the Kremlin had previously insisted. The change of policy was inevitably accompanied by a ruthless change of personnel: in the autumn of 1936 the Central Committee of the exiled Hungarian Communist party in Moscow was purged. It was now that Bela Kun, who had lived in tenuous exile since his brave, foolhardy, cruel, and (worst crime of all) unsuccessful revolution of 1919, was executed. Following his death, the home Party was purged on Moscow's instructions; the new elite, led by Ferenc Rosza and Zoltan Schonherz were advised that the quickest way of disposing finally of their disgraced rivals, the sectarians, was to denounce them to the secret police as Communists. They did so.

In an attempt to create a much broader-based working-class movement at home, Hungarian Communists were told that they were no longer to work only for the immediate establishment of socialism and that they were not now to oppose alliances with other political groups and functions of the Left, but instead were to try and create a broad left-wing coalition. They were, for example, no longer to sct up their own organizations within trades unions—rather than splitting the workers they were to aim at complete unity of the proletariat. Any political party not totally aligned to fascism was from now on to be regarded as an ally rather than as the automatic and most dangerous enemy of communism.

This policy of unity, not separation, was highly sensible but it came too late: the Party had wasted years of effort in its sectarian refusal to exploit the fierce patriotism and traditionalism of the Hungarian spirit, and this belated reform now had very little effect in terms of membership.

After attending illegal lectures by the popular working-class poet Jozsef Attila (before the new directives, of course), breaking up those of the Social Democrats, surreptitiously distributing Marxist pamphlets at factory gates and seeing two of his comrades—including the girl who was more lovely than all other lovely girls—arrested, Janos Barna was also caught by the Horthy police. "I believe this was when I stopped being a child and genuinely became a communist—when I first fell into the hands of the enemy of the class," he later claimed. Thirty years afterward he was delighted to boast publicly, "It is no longer interesting how they tried to break us at the police station with cajoling, threats and tortures, but the main thing is that they did not achieve their aim." [17] Perhaps one reason why this was "no longer interesting" was that by the mid-fifties he had supped in many jails under many regimes, and he now was forced to realize how relatively mild the "cajoling, threats and tortures" administered by the Horthy police had really been.

In 1936 he was ordered, in accordance with the new policy, to infiltrate the Social Democrats. He and his colleagues did quite well. By the end of the year they had several men in important Social Democratic jobs. Barna himself was elected to the committee of that party's organization in the Sixth District of Budapest.

Bela Kelen, who is now the ambitious, enthusiastic, and slightly bumptious editor of Budapest's evening paper, *Esti Hirlap,* was also a crypto-Communist in the late thirties; his nominal job was youth secretary of the Social Democrats in the center of Budapest. He remembers that the Social Democrats met only every Tuesday—for the rest of the week he and his Communist friends were able to make use of their premises. The Communists were certainly the most active members of the Social Democrats, keen on organizing cultural movements and dances (Fred Astaire was a great favorite) to attract new members. Indeed, it is probably true to say that before the Communists began their infiltration, the Social Democrats had done far too little to harness the radicalism of youth.

One evening in 1938 Kelen went to a Social Democrat meeting in the Sixth District of the city and, he says, saw a young man stand up from the floor and completely captivate the hall. "He presented workers' problems in a very witty and clever way, complaining, 'I pay my sickness insurance as a member of the National Health scheme, I pay for my medicines, but my salary is the same as three years ago, whilst prices have tripled. What am I to do?' This man held the floor against the official Social Democrat speaker. I didn't know who he was, but I thought him interesting—a man without pathos."

Pathetic (in the true sense of the word) or not, Janos Czermanik (Barna to his friends and comrades) was apparently a young man of some talent in the profession into which he had perhaps drifted, and up whose ladders he was now easing himself. He seems to have judged the movements of the snakes fairly effectively. He was arrested again in 1937 and spent almost three years in prison which helped him maneuver himself through the complex ideological twists necessary when Stalin, for his friendship with Hitler, permitted if not encouraged the Communists to join the fascist Arrow Cross Party and when, at the May 1939 election, they were commanded to vote for it.

Then came the Phony War when Stalin, allied to Hitler, ordered the Hungarian Communists to suspend all subversive activity against the Horthy regime, another ally of the Nazis. Stalin and Horthy became almost good friends; in November 1940 in payment for the return of a set of precious national banners which the Czarist armies had carried off to Moscow in 1849, Horthy freed Matyas Rakosi and Zoltan Vas after almost sixteen years in jail and sent them to Moscow while their comrades at large sat back and waited, ordered by Stalin to be indolent. So inactive were they that when a small group of peasant

Party members traveled to Budapest all the way from distant and mountainous Transylvania, they were told, as they searched for instructions, that Communists no longer had any quarrel with the Horthy regime. Confused and dispirited, they returned to their sheep, while Janos Czermanik-Barna, of whose reaction to the Hitler-Stalin Pact we know nothing, but who was now out of prison again, openly continued his work in the Social Democrats and stealthily rose the illegal Party's rungs. By the time Hitler invaded the Soviet Union and Hungarian Communists were allowed once more to organize against their right-wing government, he had clambered without noticeable élan, but with some steadfastness, close to the top of that ladder.

In 1942 the Party's two main leaders, Rosza and Schonherz, were caught and hanged. The leadership of the Party was taken over by a clever young intellectual who had fought in the Spanish Civil War and whose name was Laszlo Rajk. Rosza's place on the five-man Central Committee was filled by Janos Barna. His election, the most significant honor the Party had so far accorded him, warranted yet another change of name and it was as Janos Kadar (which means "barrelmaker" or "cooper") that he was promoted. This was the first time he had used the name and it was as Kadar that, a few months later, a warrant was issued for his arrest. He evaded it and in 1943 became leader of the Party for the first time when his friend Laszlo Rajk was captured by the secret police and imprisoned. For the rest of the war the two men ran the Party between them, the one taking over when the other was jailed.

The Party's record of resistance to the Nazis is not impressive. To begin with, of course, it was compelled, for the sake of the Hitler-Stalin Pact, to forget its distaste for fascism. But even after Hitler invaded the Soviet Union and the Germans changed overnight from "noble allies of the proletariat" to Nazi "hyenas" little was done by Communists in Budapest to frustrate the work of the Hungarian government, Hitler's ally. Party apologists in Budapest today are at great, if unconvincing, pains to explain away their poor performance during those years. The popularity of Hitler is their most usual excuse. Like it or not, Hitler really did have a lot of admirers in Hungary in the early forties. No, they say, this did not reflect the latent rightism in every Hungarian breast but rather the continuing national disgust at the Treaty of Trianon and consequent gratitude to Hitler for reversing some of its grosser injustices. After the Munich Agreement in 1938 Hungary was restored part of Slovakia, all the way from Cierna-nad-Tisou (where in 1968 Dubcek argued bitterly with Brezhnev) in the east, to Bratislava on the banks of the Danube. And when Hitler occupied Czechoslovakia in 1939 he even returned to Budapest most of the Carpatho-Ukraine. In the summer of 1940 the Magyars were able to embrace once more some of their kinsmen in Transylvania, who for the last twenty years had been subjected to cruel persecution by the Rumanian government. In 1941 they regained part of northern Yugoslavia, including the towns of Novi Sad and Subotica. All in all, the country's territory almost doubled in the space of three years. So how could the people feel anything but admiration and gratitude to Hitler? And how could the Party hope to explain that Hitler was in fact the greatest enemy that the people had ever had? As Dr. George Borsanyi, a smooth middle-aged historian of the

46

CRIME AND COMPROMISE

Party's Historical Institute says apologetically today, "Predicting catastrophe at such a time was not a very successful platform."

Things changed, of course, when the Germans actually occupied the country in 1944. But till then the Party had to satisfy itself with largely ineffective propaganda work. Bela Kelen, the editor of *Esti Hirlap,* compares its activities to those of the Russian Bolsheviks after the failure of the 1905 Revolution: "We published Lenin and Stalin under different titles, we painted slogans on the walls, and I remember bicycling through the city with bags of leaflets which we flung into the open doors of the trams. Otherwise we did our best to infiltrate the trade unions, which were legal till March '44, and generally to maintain links throughout the country. It was very difficult."

The links between the Moscow leaders of the Party and those, like Kadar and Rajk, who led the Party at home proved the most difficult of all to maintain. Usually comrades in Budapest were reduced only to listening to the overseas broadcasts of Radio Moscow and to trying to interpret them for the Hungarian situation. Such interpretation was often hard and not always successful. In 1943, at a moment when he was leader, Kadar decided that the Hungarian Communist party had to follow the example of the Communist International and dissolve itself. It was largely a question of semantics and the Party was immediately reformed as the "Peace Party," but the move caused some anger in Moscow and had to be reversed in 1944. It was a mistake for which Kadar was to suffer considerably later.

In April 1944 the Central Committee of the Peace Party decided that better contact should be established with the Moscow leadership. The easiest way seemed to be via Yugoslavia, enlisting the help of Tito's partisans. Kadar was chosen for the mission and, traveling under yet another name—Janos Liptak—set out with a Yugoslav guide. They reached the border, but while trying to cross the rushing River Drava, swollen with the spring thaw, they were caught by the police.

Despite the long-standing warrant for the arrest of Kadar, his identity was not discovered and he managed to convince the police that he was indeed just Janos Liptak, a deserter from the Hungarian army who was leaving the country because he hated the Germans. Even so, he was court-martialed and loaded onto a trainful of Jews who were en route to Mauthausen, the Austrian concentration camp.

They were offloaded at Komarno, in northern Hungary, and transferred to the town's prison. Bela Kelen says that he was then detailed by the Party leadership in Budapest to go to Komarno to bribe the prison governor, a man called Czsomka, to let Kadar (Liptak) escape. However, on the day that Kelen set off from Budapest on this mission, Kadar managed to effect his own escape from the prison.

More difficult was returning to Budapest, for the road was blocked every few kilometers by Hungarian and German soldiers. In order to disguise the length and purpose of his journey, Kadar took a large log, weighing some thirty kilos, on his shoulder. At every checkpoint he said that he was just carrying it home to the next village. Thus all the way to Budapest, where he made with his log for the house of Antal Babics, then a young doctor, now Hungary's leading urologist, whose home was a wartime haven for dozens of Jews and resistance workers. Kadar rang the bell and, before the door could be opened, collapsed on the steps from total exhaustion. He spent several weeks in Babics's cellar, holding his breath every time jackboots stamped across the pavement above, and recovering his strength.

Three

In March 1969 a quiet ceremony took place in an insignificant little road beside a theater in the center of Budapest. The street signs, *Pannonia Utca,* were removed and the street was renamed *Rajk Laszlo Utca.* The occasion represented a small but essential paragraph in the process of rewriting the history of the Hungarian Communist party. It was another, wholly incomplete, but nevertheless important step toward recognizing what really happened to Hungary during the late forties and early fifties. At the same time it could be and was seen as one more token promise by the Kadar regime that never again would the principles of "socialist legality" be so brazenly flouted as then.

So far as establishing historical truth was concerned, more crucial than the raising of the new street signs were an article and a letter published in the May and June issues of the literary magazine *Kortars* that year. The article was written by Aladar Mod, an old communist professor of Hungarian history, and the letter in reply was from Mrs. Julia Rajk, the widow of the man after whom Pannonia Street had been renamed. Both examined in more detail than had ever before been publicly possible in Hungary itself the details of the Rajk Affair of 1949; for the first time the motives and actions of some of the principal participants in the tragedy were scrutinized, and an attempt to apportion responsibility for the crime was begun.

Stalinism came to Hungary in the snow and the wind of the winter of 1944, as wild, sex-starved, undernourished, and impoverished Red Army soldiers poured through the hills into the middle Danube basin even more aggressively than had Arpad a thousand years before. That October they began to push the Germans back across the plains, or puszta, toward Budapest and by Christmas Eve they had reached the eastern outskirts of the gray and frozen capital itself.

But Budapest did not fall lightly to the Soviets. For the inhabitants of the town it was a terrible Christmas Day, a dreadful New Year's Eve, and a wretched January. It was not until February 13 that, after smashing their way from house to house, the Soviets finally reached the other side of the city, and the remains of the one hundred eighty thousand German garrison fell back farther toward Vienna. During those two months almost half the buildings of Budapest were damaged and an estimated one hundred thousand people died.

Ever since, the occupation of the Red Army has been hailed by Hungarian Communists as the "Liberation." And so it was. Despite their traditional distrust of the Russians, most Hungarians were delighted to see the Germans run. Over the next months, however, Hungarian peasants and workers could be forgiven for wondering what was the real difference between Fritz and Ivan, whether, indeed, the children of socialism and the disciples of fascism were not strikingly similar. The real distinction seemed to be that the Red Army soldiers were less disciplined than the Germans; to many people they seemed even more uncouth, even more fond of wristwatches and reluctant girls. It was certainly hard to see in them the dedicated vanguard of a great new world.

As the snows melted, the fogs lifted and the full damage to Budapest became visible for the first time, as the Germans were driven still farther westward and as Hungary therefore became an ever safer if not much more comfortable place, so back home in the baggage cars of the Red Army came all those Hungarian Communists who had spent the war in the shabby, but quite adequate Hotel Lux on Moscow's Gorky Street, where everyone knew whom Stalin favored at any given moment by the amount of food his wife had to cook in the communal kitchen. First to arrive in Budapest * was the fat and vulgar Zoltan Vas, who had spent sixteen years in the same prison cell as his leader, Matyas Rakosi, and whose job now was to get the starving population fed. With the maximum of bombast, coarse humor, and bullying, he did so and, for his manner as much as for his achievement, he was soon a popular figure throughout the country.

When life became a little easier, he was followed home by Matyas Rakosi himself, by Imre Nagy, the meek agriculturalist, by Mihaly Farkas, whose greedy, police mentality was already only too clear to those who feared him, by the economic overseer Erno Gero, and by all the rest whose war had been so easy.

They were welcomed joyously by those who had

---

* A provisional government had been established in the eastern town of Debrecen at the end of 1944.

fought at home, among them the nervous and unpolished young worker whom they knew now as Janos Kadar (he was a little overawed by these sophisticated "intellectual" Communists from Moscow) and, after their release from a German concentration camp, the emaciated Laszlo Rajk and his gaunt wife Julia.

Kadar decided that the days of Janos Czermanik, Janos Barna, and Janos Liptak were gone for good and that it was as Janos Kadar that he would be known to his comrades and to the world from now on. Lean and already balding, he was not a man of unbounded confidence in his own abilities; he seems, however, to have taken easily enough to the transition from a life of sabotage, subterfuge and illegality, dominated by fear of capture, to that of an associate —if not a leader—in an established and suddenly legitimate political organization dedicated to seizing total power.

One of his closest colleagues at that time told me in Budapest recently, "We all worked very well together to begin with. Rakosi had such a huge reputation amongst us that when he first came back we were just overjoyed. We were quite uncritical. And until at least the end of 1947 he appeared to be very pleased with us also; he was especially fond of Rajk and Kadar—as were they of him."

In fact we now know, from another of Rakosi's colleagues, Sandor Nogradi, who has published a book inside Hungary itself about those years, that Rakosi and his Moscow friends had decided well before their return to Budapest that they would not share any of the real power in the Party with "those ignorant home-based resistance fighters." And after they did get back they gradually made it very obvious to those who had spent their war fighting the Germans rather than plotting in Moscow that they were, as a result, politically inferior.[1] But that was unclear at the time. The orders of the men from Moscow, given them by Stalin, were to create a Communist-controlled state in Hungary within three years. It was a task to which all—home and exiled Party leaders alike—addressed themselves with zeal, and till 1948 unity in the leadership appears to have been total.

The Communists were still a tiny force (only twelve thousand) in 1945, and even with the Red Army stacked behind the Central Committee building they were too weak to take over Hungary at once. They needed to use the other political parties and therefore did not at first attempt to seize the major role in the postwar coalition. They tried to present themselves as more democratic than the Social Democrats, more patriotic than the Smallholders party or the National Peasant party, more representative of every Hungarian (whatever his politics) in every way, and they did all they could to allay fears that they sought either absolute power or so close a relationship with Moscow as would offend traditional Hungarian skepticism about Russian ambitions for the Danube. The Communists attempted to show themselves as the most reasonable of men all the time they conspired to destroy their rivals.

After 1945 the Party used the slogan "together with the Communists for the seizure of power" and over the next three years they and the Social Democrats did fight alongside each other on a number of issues. Kadar later, somewhat disingenuously, described their relationship:

> During that period I was the secretary of the Budapest Party organisation and presided at the weekly meetings of the district secretaries. I often told them: Communists, go ahead and argue with

the socialists whenever necessary, quarrel with them when you must . . . but do not overlook the fact that we have many allies in the Socialist Party, who agree with us on the nationalisation of the means of production. One day we shall all be members of the same Party; you must therefore quarrel with them in such a way that you will be able to patch it up.[2]

He was right. By 1948 the Social Democrats had been emasculated and incorporated by the Communists, and their main rival, the Smallholders party (which won 56 percent of the vote at the 1945 election), was totally destroyed. Rakosi later boasted about the way in which this had been achieved; "Salami tactics" he called the process. This involved "slicing the ground from beneath the feet of your enemies bit by bit until they fall. Salami, an expensive food, is not eaten all at once, but is cut one slice at a time as it is used."

"When we wanted something," he explained, "we carefully considered the opposition and began by requesting only a little—to make it difficult for the enemy to mobilise its forces. Later we increased our demands." Thus the Smallholders party was forced to expel individual members or ministers one by one, until "all reactionary elements were unmasked, removed and isolated."[3]

In order to weaken the opposition still further, the Communists kept the size of the army down to twelve thousand after 1945—although the peace treaty allowed Hungary seventy thousand men under arms. There were already enough problems dealing with other parties, explained Rakosi later; a strong army might have proved a far more dangerous enemy than the wretched politicians who had been so easy to bend, isolate, slice, and destroy. And, after all, what need had Hungary of its own troops with the Soviets deployed so dependably throughout the country? [4]

The Red Army, and its overawing presence in towns and villages all over Hungary, was in fact a bludgeon rather than a knife. But an even more effective instrument was the police force. At the beginning of 1945 Kadar was appointed deputy chief of police in Budapest. For the next five months he and the officers of the Soviet secret police, the NKVD—who had arrived in Hungary with the first Red Army soldiers as "advisers"—reorganized the force to the advantage of the Communists and the detriment of almost everyone else in the country. As soon as the Germans were driven out, the NKVD set about rounding up those antifascist resistance fighters who had not demonstrated their loyalty to Moscow. Some of the most courageous (and most prescient) of these men had fled to Austria; many of those who had not were murdered.

Not so the Nazi officers of the Arrow Cross. The NKVD was anxious not to waste the specialized skills that these men had so assiduously learned; in deference to the demands of the Social Democrats a few of the most brutal of the fascist secret policemen had to be executed or imprisoned, but many more were asked if they wouldn't like to reconsider their political views and keep their old jobs. Few said no.

Those who accepted didn't even have to move their desks. The new secret police force, the AVO,* moved straight into the Arrow Cross's old buildings on Andrassy Avenue, thus saving a lot of time, money, and effort—so much of the equipment they needed was already installed and in excellent working order. In

---

* AVO stands for Department for the Protection of the State. Its name was later changed to AVH, which stands for Authority for the Protection of the State.

theory the AVO was a state force; in fact it was from
the start the private army of the Communists. It was
the one organization, declared Rakosi, "in which our
Party demanded the leadership and tolerated neither
division nor respect of coalition proportions. . . . We
held this bureau in our hands since its first day of existence and saw to it that it remained a reliable sharp
weapon in the fight for a people's democracy." [5]

By 1948 the combined knives of the Red Army,
election rigging, parliamentary bullying, AVO murder, deceit, and many more tactics had slivered all opposition: the Communists, Rakosi beaming macabrely
triumphant at their head, were irresistible and now
surged forward to demonstrate the validity of Rakosi's belief that "after the victory of the Soviet Union
there is no need to prove that the principles of Bol-
shevism are fully applicable not only within the
borders of former Russia but also the world over." [6]
And without proof they began to apply them.

Turning a country like Hungary in 1949 into a
miniature carbon of the Soviet Union in the 1920s
was rather more complicated than Rakosi blithely
suggested and involved the dedicated application of
the principles of terror and compulsion. Over the
next five years the Communists showed a disdain for
the Hungarian people even more total than any
that the fascists had ever displayed, as they attempted to transform the agricultural Hungarian
economy into one in which industry played a major if
not the major role. In 1949, 56 percent of the people
still worked the country's fields. Rakosi boasted that
he would make of the peasant's endless puszta a land
of iron and steel and that to this glorious end any
means were appropriate. The same thing was happening wherever the Communists took power in Central and Eastern Europe. All over the backward and

largely agricultural area attempts were being made to ape the efforts of Stalin in the harsh and uncompromising Soviet twenties and thirties. This policy did have a certain economic logic, except in already heavily industrialized areas like Bohemia, but its main raison d'être was ideological. In Czechoslovakia, as in Hungary, the Party needed to break up the old established patterns of society, forcing upon the people not only industrialization but also a Soviet way of thought.

It needed to issue a challenge to the people, to throw down a steel gauntlet which, once lifted, could never again be laid aside. It needed an excuse for the creation of a continual state of emergency in the country; it had to conjure up a warlike atmosphere in which citizens would be convinced that, but for their own untiring labors and the even greater efforts of the Party, the future had no meaning.

The Party had to find and spread abroad a rationale for the brutal systems of control and punishment that it intended to introduce. This was provided, almost incredibly conveniently, by Tito's defection from the Stalinist camp in 1948. The subsequent freezing of the Cold War handed the new leaders the excuse they needed for turning their countries into industrial labor camps, ceaselessly smelting for battle.

Tito's "treachery" was also exploited by the Party leaders to weed out their own enemies and rivals: if Tito, the greatest antifascist fighter could suddenly reveal himself as a "Fascist agent," then how many more traitors must there not be lurking in the woodwork of other Parties? The order went out from Moscow that these men must be found and destroyed. They were; to the glee of Western diplomats, for the next five years, East European Communist parties deliberately fostered an atmosphere of terror and suspi-

cion and gave themselves over to an orgy of imprisonment and torture, fake trials and death as they tried
to cleanse themselves of all the impurities that Stalin
told them they conclealed. In Hungary the main "im-
purity" purged was the Party's wartime leader, Laszlo
Rajk.

It is probable, however, that Rajk would have been
destroyed even without the Titoist rationale, so jealous were the Moscow Communists of those who had
fought at home. Indeed, the process of his disgrace
began before Tito's defection. Of the men who had
returned from Moscow, after Matyas Rakosi the most
important were Erno Gero the economist, Joszef
Revai—who was concerned with culture—and Mihaly
Farkas—who became minister of defense. "Of the
four," recalls one of their Cabinet colleagues today,*
himself at the time as dedicated a Stalinist as the rest
of them, "Farkas was the worst. The others were
probably 'sincerely evil.' Farkas was just ambitious.
He wanted Rakosi's job and he was determined to destroy any man who might stand in his way."

According to this source it was Farkas who in-
stigated the campaign against Rajk—one man who
certainly might stand in his way to the leadership.
"You should not credit Stalin with all the details;
which of the leaders was arrested was unimportant to
him, so long as *some* were. It was Farkas, with Rakosi,
who decided on Rajk. He was the main threat to
them."

That is understandable, for Rajk, unlike Farkas,
was a leader of some quality. A tall, slender man with
a high forehead and prominent cheekbones, he was
remarkably good-looking and, as American journalists were fond of pointing out, resembled no one so

---

* In a private conversation in Budapest with the author.

much as the young Abraham Lincoln, who had been born just one hundred years before him. The son of a worker, he had been to university and had then fought in the International Brigade during the Spanish Civil War. He returned to Hungary in 1941 and became one of the leaders of the underground Communist party, playing a large part in the organization of the anti-Nazi resistance. One of his closest colleagues, with whom he shared the leadership, was Janos Kadar. Indeed, Kadar was in a sense Rajk's disciple: he felt great respect for this Marxist intellectual who had, in Spain, already demonstrated so courageously his loyalty to the international working-class movement. Furthermore, in 1943 Rajk's wife, Julia, had been arrested by the Gestapo and tortured for three days to make her reveal the whereabouts of Kadar and her husband. She had not done so.

Her husband was nonetheless captured and together they were taken to Sopronkohida, near the Austrian frontier. From there they were transferred to a concentration camp near Munich and did not manage to return to Budapest until May 1945 when, for his heroism in the war, Rajk was made minister of the interior.* In those days this was the most powerful post in the government for it gave control of the police and the AVO.

As Minister Rajk played a crucial part in the destruction of the "reactionary" parties, especially the powerful Smallholders party. He was considered slightly unbalanced by his enemies who used to murmur about his "fanaticism," his wild eyes, and his temper. Nevertheless, Rajk, unlike his colleagues from Moscow who immediately set about building themselves huge villas on the more fashionable hills of

---

* Julia Rajk became secretary-general of the Women's Union.

Buda, always retained a common touch. Perhaps for his looks, his war record, and his modesty (he lived in a small flat in the town center), he enjoyed considerable popularity for the first three years after the war. He was especially liked by the young left-wing intellectuals; indeed in his subsequent indictment he was accused, Socrates-like, of having tried to corrupt the country's youth. He would certainly have been the most popular choice as Party leader in the country at large.

At the same time, however, contemporary attempts by the Western press to portray him as a "national communist" in contrast to Rakosi, the "Muscovite quisling," were incorrect. They may even have been inspired by Western diplomats, eager to exacerbate tensions among the Communists, or by Rajk's comradely enemies, notably Farkas, as the first step in his destruction. In fact Rajk fully agreed with his colleagues about the pace of "revolution" in Hungary (Nagy was the only one who realized it was proceeding too fast), and no one could possibly accuse him of being less loyal to the teachings of Stalin than Rakosi himself. Perhaps the best way of assessing his character is to say that, had he lived, he would probably no longer have been a Stalinist in 1956: he might have been with Nagy and he would most likely have been with Kadar, but he would not still have been with Rakosi and Gero.

In December 1947 Rajk was accused of "anti-Party" behavior. The Party secretariat discounted the charges, but Rakosi proposed that he be dismissed from the Ministry of the Interior.

In August 1948 this took place. Rajk was demoted to Minister of Foreign Affairs. To begin with, Rakosi tried to represent the change of ministries as a promotion for Rajk. It was "explained" that communism had already been so firmly established in Hungary that it was no longer necessary to have a man of Rajk's quality as Minister of the Interior. Apparently Rakosi telephoned George Heltai, head of the Foreign Ministry's political department, just before Rajk's new appointment was announced. "Have you heard the great news?" he asked. "The Foreign Ministry has been a kindergarten long enough. Now you will have an adult to lead you."

Rajk made the move, with some apprehension, and in offices, police stations, and prisons throughout the country, his heavy-framed, stylized photograph was replaced by that of his successor, the new Minister of the Interior, his friend, Janos Kadar.

Five months later, in January 1949, Julia Rajk had a son. They called him Laszlo and they asked Janos Kadar to be the godfather at the child's Soviet-style name-giving ceremony. Whether they chose him because of their mutual friendship or whether it was more of an insurance policy that young Laszlo should be well provided for in case of mishap is not clear. Whatever the reason, Kadar accepted the honor, and in February the three old friends drank to the future in the smart villa in the Buda hills to which Rajk had been forced to move on taking up his new appointment because his old flat, he had been told, was quite unsuitable for diplomatic parties.

That April and May Rajk featured prominently in the elections, and was only fourth in the list of Party leaders.* During the campaign he made a triumphant tour of his constituency and, according to the ecstatic Party press, was greeted with a "rain of flowers" from cheering crowds.[7] On May 16 he received an ovation along with other Party leaders at an election "victory"

---

* After Rakosi, Gero, and Istvan Dobi.

rally. And then he disappeared. He was not at the opening of Parliament on June 8 and two days later the name of Gyula Kallai appeared as Foreign Minister on the new Cabinet list. None of this was explained until June 16 when *Szabad Nep*, the Party paper, baldly reported his expulsion from the Party as an imperialist spy and Trotskyite agent. Three days later the paper announced his arrest.

In fact Rajk had been arrested on May 30, twenty days before. There is a story that Janos Kadar abetted the arrest by playing chess with his friend until the arrival of the secret police, and then just sat back as Rajk was dragged, shouting, away. This allegation was first spread around after the 1956 Revolution and it is untrue. In fact Rajk and his wife were both arrested at their home. Their son Laszlo was taken off to a state orphanage: it is not known whether or not his godfather intervened to secure him reasonable treatment.

Rajk's trial began on September 16, 1949. He was accused not only of high treason and conspiracy but also of war and antisocial crimes. Allegedly he had worked in a "special" function for the Horthy police and the Gestapo.

He pleaded guilty and was hanged on October 15 in the courtyard of a prison in Budapest. His wife, Julia, was in a cell overlooking that courtyard; his execution was one of the fifty-one she was forced to witness that month. In 1956 she described it: "I heard the words 'Geza, the execution can be carried out . . .' and I heard the chair being taken away from beneath his feet. And in the great morning silence I heard the doctor confirm that he was dead." [8]

From the moment of his arrest almost no one, apart from his wife, had doubted that he was guilty. Practically without exception, his former friends and colleagues accepted the official dogma that he was a Titoist spy. Even those who knew him best repeated uncritically the lies that Rakosi told.

In his 1969 article, Aladar Mod, an old prewar friend and colleague of Rajk and a man whose outlook is in many ways similar to Kadar's, avowed that Rajk was someone whom he and his wife had trusted totally. Yet when Rajk was denounced Mod said, "Finally we arrived at the view that, though we could not regard him differently, as a man and a comrade, from what we knew him to be in the past, we nevertheless believed and rationalised the charge." To show his trust in the Party Mod then, quite voluntarily, wrote an article identifying himself totally with the indictment and denouncing his friend.

"Of course it was quite impossible that Rajk was a traitor," one of his former colleagues told this author in Budapest. "But it was even more impossible that Rakosi and Stalin should have fabricated the whole thing. In this situation we just had to believe what we were told. We knew that some of Lenin's colleagues, Bukharin and Zinoviev, had been traitors; why not ours as well? Our trust in the Soviet Union had been formed in the '30s; it was quite unqualified; that's why it was more difficult for us, the Party elite, to see the truth than for the man in the street."

But the man in the street, or at least the Party man in the street, also believed the charges. Why? Because, says Mod, "It was impossible to believe that there were in our Party leaders who, in serving an incorrect policy, would arrive at the point of liquidating politically and physically the best representatives of the Party and then actually do it."

Mod also places a large responsibility on Rajk himself because of his "confession" of all his "crimes."

Mod did not see the trial, nor any photograph of Rajk in the courtroom. Had he done so, he claims, "I should have realised that it was not the Rajk known to us who stood before the court, but his tortured shadow, an alien figure." As it was, listening to the radio, "I remember how that quiet objective voice staggered me. . . . One cannot disregard the fact that Rajk's confession played a decisive part in . . . (convincing) the masses of the people" of his guilt.

But in her reply to Mod's article, Julia Rajk pointed out, surely correctly, that he concentrated too much on Rajk himself and not on the socio-political circumstances which made the trial possible at all. "Thus you give—unwittingly—the impression that, because he accepted the charges at the trial, the defendant himself ought to be blamed for the fact that hundreds of thousands of honest people—a large part of the Hungarian public—believed the charges . . . I contest this statement."

She demonstrates the absurdity of Mod's self-defense when she reminds him that it was long before Rajk's "confession" that his guilt was generally accepted. "From the moment of his arrest in May until the beginning of September three months went by and it was only then that he publicly said 'Yes' in court. But the rope was already round his neck—as it was virtually immediately after the news of his arrest was made public. You should look through the June, July and August issues of Szabad Nep in 1949, in which thousands of institutions and factories condemned him and demanded his death." Even Mod's own article attacking him had appeared before the trial itself. "People judged him in advance and immediately."

Nevertheless she does agree with Mod that it is vital to try and discover what it was that made Laszlo Rajk say yes. It is therefore necessary to examine the 109 days he spent in prison between his arrest on May 30 and his trial on September 15, 1949.

The two of them complain that there is "insufficient source material" available to them on this period. But Mrs. Rajk nonetheless declares that he broke down only after "seven weeks of no small resistance" and she does not believe that he gave in just because he was tortured, arguing that he had earlier been tortured by the fascists to no effect. Mod points out that not only do we not know the physical ordeals Rajk had to suffer, but his "moral" ordeals are also unknown to us. "It can only be assumed that he might have been promised his life, and there might have been a time when he believed this, since for a short time one can hope for the impossible."

If, twenty years after the crime, Mod and Mrs. Rajk were able to complain that still so little had been revealed about just what had happened to Rajk in prison, just what it was that induced him to confess, it is from Rajk's friend Janos Kadar that an explanation must be sought.

In 1949 it was Rakosi who took credit for "unmasking the Rajk gang." He made long and elaborate speeches describing the sleepless nights he had spent trying to fit each tessera into the mosaic until finally he had realized the vast guilt of Laszlo Rajk and his "Titoist" accomplices. But realizing their guilt and then arresting them was not enough. Rakosi had to have Rajk's confession. For the confession of the accused is one of the essential ingredients in the vicious mix that has always made up Stalinist show trials. When he was first arrested Rajk naturally refused to confess. Torture was applied and as all important security matters were in the hands of soviet officers of the NKVD (it was General Bielkin who personally stage-managed the trial), it is certain that the torture was harsh. But Rajk still refused to admit that he had been a Gestapo agent or a Titoist, and denied every one of the other allegations made against him. His courageous obstinacy was a serious embarrassment to Rakosi. Stalin was demanding the trial and the trial demanded Rajk plead guilty. Although he called himself with pride "Stalin's first Hungarian disciple," Rakosi knew that he could retain this title only just so long as he performed the tasks that Stalin set him. There must be no delay; Rajk must be induced to confess. If torture could not do this, then perhaps persuasion would be more successful. So Rakosi apparently sent Rajk's best friend to see him in his prison cell.

"Dear Laci," said Kadar, "I come on behalf of Comrade Rakosi. He asked me to explain the situation to you. Of course we all know that you are innocent. But Comrade Rakosi believes that you will understand."

He reminded Rajk of the times he had risked his life in the International Brigade and in the anti-Nazi resistance. Now his life was not in any danger. Only his conscience.

He tried to persuade his friend to make a confession "for the sake of the Party" and promised him that if he did so he would not be killed, although "in order not to confuse the people" his execution would be announced. After a safe period he would be released and allowed to live with his wife and child, Kadar's godson, in exile, perhaps in the Ukraine or Crimea.

Kadar told Rajk that the Party had to simplify things if the people were to accept the truth. At the moment the people doubted; there was too much discussion. The people must be told that there was treason in the Party—that they could understand and appreciate. "The Party has chosen you for the role of traitor, you must sacrifice yourself to the Party. This is terrible, but after all you are an old militant and cannot refuse to help the Party."

It was only after this visit from his friend that Rajk, lying in his stagnant cell, decided to make the confession that his comrades demanded of him. Perhaps because he genuinely believed that this would secure his release. But more likely because he could seize Kadar's words as an excuse for submission and through them retain his self-respect, even while confessing, by at least pretending to himself that he really was aiding the Party he loved. In fact, such was his devotion to the Party and his concept of it, this was probably no pretense.

Like so many stories about Eastern European Party members, this one has never been confirmed officially; that is, Kadar himself has not admitted to it. And Julia Rajk will not now talk about it either. Nevertheless, it has been related by many independent sources and was published in November 1956 by a Polish paper (*Nowa Kultura*) [9]; it is difficult to believe it a fabrication. And in October 1956 Mrs. Rajk did give one interview to the Budapest correspondent of the Zagreb paper *Vjesnik*. After his talk with her, he wrote: "The tortures used to obtain a confession from Laszlo Rajk and those tried with him were not only physical. Only appeals to their consciences, by authoritative people they respected, broke these fighters and made them into mere instruments of dark plans." [10]

As for Kadar himself, following the jailers through the dark, damp corridors past photographs of himself on the walls, down to Laszlo Rajk's airless cell, perhaps he too really believed that his friend would be freed after a token confession. Or maybe he knew the truth, that Rajk would die anyway and felt that he therefore might as well confess "for the sake of the Party" for which they had both fought so hard. Given Kadar's primitive devotion to the Party in those days this is perhaps the most likely explanation. He may even have convinced himself that, were he in Rajk's position, he too would have confessed for the Party. It might seem unusual that after their long friendship he should have accepted the lies about Rajk and acted thus, but such was the atmosphere of the late forties and early fifties in Eastern Europe that his "betrayal" is understandable if not excusable. Probably even Rajk himself understood it.

In those days the Party was revered and obeyed with a religious fervor, invested with an abstract spiritual significance. Those were the days which tore men apart, which overnight forced friends for the undefined and undefinable "good of the cause" to betray themselves and each other. That was when the world was sharply divided and when in both East and West men convinced themselves that their wicked enemies would at any moment leap, fangs bared, upon them. It was thus the time when spies were thought to be breeding uncontrollably in the warmth of the Party's goodwill and in which, for the sake of the nation, for the sake of the proletariat, and for the safety of the Soviet Union, those spies must be sought out and unmasked as the mad dogs that they really were or anyway certainly ought to be. For Janos Kadar, as for all Stalinists, personal friendship came way behind loyalty to the Party. Whatever he himself believed about Rajk, the Party's opinion was the one that had to be respected, without question. And in those days the Party was effectively the Hungarian embodiment of Stalin's will.

One old Stalinist, who still lives in Budapest and in

great comfort, surrounded by bottles of various makes of whisky and dozens of brands of American cigarettes, says today that the "errors" of the fifties were not the fault of the men but of the system. This is too simple. True, the Stalinist system did have a certain inevitable destructive momentum of its own. At the same time, however, the politicians were not just creatures of the machine they had created. It was open at any moment for any one to rebel against it. Few did. Indeed their conviction of their own impotence and of historical inevitability, as expressed to me by one of the worst of them, is of interest:

> Kadar and I were both good men. Neither of us could have done anything against the system. That would just have meant imprisonment. I always say that if I did not do such dreadful things as Gabor Peter, the head of the secret police, then it's just because I was more concerned with economics than politics. If I had had Peter's job, I should have behaved in the same way. So would Kadar. We were not *really* responsible—Stalin, Beria and Khrushchev are the ones to blame. We revolutionaries believed that even Stalinism was a way to Socialism.

Less than a year after the death of his friend Laszlo Rajk, Janos Kadar, number four in the Party hierarchy, balder but also plumper than he had been before, his previously lean face filled out by the lushness of office, his hands a little pudgy with the work of moving execution papers, was himself arrested. Partly because he was, like Rajk, a "Home Communist" and partly because his personal diffidence was relatively popular in the country. In 1947, for example, he had addressed a group of furiously striking anticommunist workers in the ugly, black industrial town of Miskolc, calmed them down and induced them to return to work. He was thus a potential threat to Rakosi himself and to Mihaly Farkas who now saw him as the main obstacle to his succeeding Rakosi himself.

But he was also sacrificed simply because the logic of the system demanded it. The demon of political terror which he had helped to raise was not to be appeased by the sacrifice of Laszlo Rajk alone. There are no accurate counts of the thousands of Hungarians (communist and noncommunist) who perished in the purges after 1948, but at the time of Stalin's death in 1953 there were one hundred fifty thousand prisoners in the camps that they had been forced to build for themselves throughout the country. At least 1½ percent of the population had been dragged (often literally) from their homes on some trumped up charge or another. The Party still needed to maintain the atmosphere of emergency and panic in the country and the continual discovery of new "enemies," especially ones so highly placed as Kadar, was an important way of achieving this.

In June 1950 he had to resign from the Ministry of the Interior, as Rajk had resigned before him. Ostensibly this was to allow him to carry out "important Party work" and he was awarded the Gold Medal of Hungarian Labour and a check in recognition of his "good work in the interests of strengthening the Hungarian People's Democracy." That cannot have cheered him much; the whole scenario must have seemed frighteningly familiar. The following April he was, indeed, arrested.

According to a fellow prisoner, his arrest occurred when he was on his way back from a weekend in Siofok, a town on Lake Balaton, near where the road branches off to Kapoly, his old village. Just outside the town of Szekesfehervar, capital of the country several times before the sixteenth century, a black AVH car blocked the road and he was told that an antistate conspiracy had been discovered, that his life was threatened, and that the car had been sent to ensure his safe return to Budapest. He left his own car and was driven straight to prison.[11]

Seized at the same time were four colleagues, Ferenc Donath—an agriculturalist almost as mild as Imre Nagy himself; George Marosan—a rough baker who had been the Communists' main ally and spy in the Social Democrats; and Gyula Kallai and Geza Losconczy, two of the Party's leading intellectuals. They were all charged, predictably enough, with nationalism, espionage, and treason, and in Kadar's case "proof" was found in his mistaken dissolution of the Communist party during the war.

Like Rajk, Kadar refused at first to confess to any such crimes. This was an act of courage even more extraordinary than Rajk's for, unlike Rajk, who was the first prominent Hungarian Communist to be arrested, Kadar knew the relish with which Gabor Peter, the police chief, extracted confessions from his comrade prisoners. Just how much the Minister of the Interior knew of such delicate affairs was shown by the behavior of Kadar's successor at the ministry, Sandor Zold. On April 15, 1951, something that Rakosi said to him at a meeting of the Cabinet convinced him that he was about to become the third Minister of the Interior in a row to be arrested. Terrified by the brutality which certainly awaited him and the death which probably lurked unsmilingly behind it, he drove straight home, murdered his wife and children, and shot himself dead. In his self-justificatory apologia, Sandor Nogradi remarked, "This event shat-

tered a great many people but there was no one with
whom to discuss the tragedy; people were left alone
with their doubts."

Sandor Zold had reason. His predecessor, Kadar,
was suffering even more horribly in jail than had
Rajk. Years later he told a friend, "Prison under
Horthy and the Gestapo were bad enough, but they
were nothing compared to what one suffered in Rakosi's jails." [12] He was in the hands of Vladimir Farkas, son of his rival, Mihaly, and a remarkably sadistic
lieutenant-colonel in the AVH, reliable assistant to
Gabor Peter, the police chief. For Kadar to be
knocked unconscious by Farkas's blows was common
enough and he later related that on one occasion he
regained consciousness on the filthy slimy floor of his
cell to find Farkas standing above him, laughing, and
pissing into his bloody broken mouth. There are
other stories that his fingernails were torn out; they
are unconfirmed.

After the Revolution, the United Nations Committee on Hungary was informed, allegedly by an unidentified former minister of Imre Nagy, that Kadar
had been castrated in prison.[13] The story was rejected
for lack of evidence and is almost certainly untrue,
though a biography published in 1957 by the U.S.
Congress's Committee on Un-American Activities declared with predictable nastiness that while in prison
Kadar had "his manhood destroyed."

However, one of Kadar's old friends in Budapest
did tell the author recently, before the subject was
even mentioned, that when he once asked Kadar why
he had no children, Kadar had openly replied,
"When I was in prison I was so badly beaten in the
balls that although I can still fuck I am now sterile." *

* This is medically quite possible.

His balls so badly beaten or not, Kadar confessed. Unlike his fellow defendant, Geza Losconczy, he did not suffer a nervous breakdown. On December 11, 1951, he and his colleagues were all tried in the prison where Laszlo Rajk had been executed. George Marosan, one of some four thousand former Social Democrats imprisoned irrespective of whether or not they had been crypto-Communists, was sentenced to death. This was later commuted to life imprisonment and he was released in 1956 after the two British Labour leaders, Clement Attlee and Morgan Philipps, asked Molotov to intercede on behalf of imprisoned Hungarian Social Democrats. Losconczy and Kallai were also sentenced to death; this too was commuted, Ferenc Donath was given two years, and Kadar was lucky to receive only four. After the trial, they were all moved to the Conti Street Prison where Marosan, Kallai, and Losconczy spent two years in the condemned cells and Donath and Kadar in simple solitary confinement.

After the death of Stalin in 1953, Rakosi lost not only his master but also his main raison d'être. Within two months Khruschev and Malenkov, who were less committed to Stalin's teachings than Rakosi, insisted that Imre Nagy, a man whose moderation and belief in a "gradual" rather than a rushed communization of Hungary had been clear since 1946, be appointed prime minister. With his appointment began a restricted process of political rehabilitation and economic reform. For Julia Rajk, who had been arrested and separated from her child in 1950, and for Kadar too, this meant release. For him in July 1954, for her one year later.

Julia found, on her release in 1955, that she was no longer allowed to call herself by the hated name of the "counterrevolutionary Rajk": while she had been in her cell, remembering each morning that "great morning silence" in which she heard the doctor pronounce Laszlo's death, her name had been changed to Gyorki. She also discovered that her son had been placed in an orphanage and had been told that his name was Istvan Kovacs and that he had no parents. So limited was the de-Stalinization that Imre Nagy had been able to implement during his erratic New Course that Julia could get almost no official cooperation in finding either her son or a job. She even had difficulty in finding anywhere to live; it was several months before she was able to move into one windowless room in a dreary, dirty tenement block in one of the more unattractive of Budapest's suburbs. Eventually she managed to get a job (under her new name) first in a delicatessen, and then in a library.

It was not until after Khruschev's attack on Stalin in February 1956 that Julia was once more allowed to call herself Rajk, was readmitted to the Communist party, and had her son returned to her: he was left by the police in the street outside her sister's house. Even then it was long before she was able to persuade Laszlo that Istvan was not his first name, Kovacs not his last, and that his real name Rajk was not, however much other children taunted him, such a shameful one to bear. "For at least a year I was only an aunt to him," she later said.[14]

Kadar was more fortunate: according to one account Rakosi even invited him back into the leadership of the Party which had renounced him. Bela Szasz, a fellow prisoner, recalls that in 1954 they met in the waiting room of the Party sanatorium in Kutvolgy Street, Budapest. Pale, thin, his face blotchy and his cheeks sagging, his fingers trembling and bitten, wheezing and coughing, displaying all the symptoms of a man who has spent several years being tortured, forced to confess, tried, convicted, and then left to rot in a slimy cell, Kadar, sitting in his tatty dressing gown, explained to Szasz that he owed his release to Rakosi himself. Throughout his imprisonment he had written to the Party leader, he said, showing how unjust his treatment was, how he had always been surrounded by *agents provocateurs* in the Ministry of the Interior, how someone had lied about him, how. . . . But all his letters had been intercepted by Gabor Peter, and it was not until Peter's arrest that one letter finally reached Rakosi himself. Then, of course, he immediately responded and had Kadar released, and even gave him a prompt and charming interview, expressing amazement that Kadar had not written before, and even greater surprise and indignation on being told that Peter had waylaid all Kadar's memoranda. "Well, what would you like to do now, Comrade Kadar?" Rakosi had then allegedly asked, and Kadar had replied that he could do one of only two things: either he could return to manual work or he could resume his Party labors. To which, says Szasz, Rakosi reassuringly answered that manual work was out of the question, of course the Party needed him far too much.[15]

Szasz was understandably surprised at the gratitude that Kadar seemed to feel, surprised also that he believed Rakosi at all, and surprised that Kadar should actually want to return to the Party after all he had suffered at its hands. In fact, of course, Kadar owed Rakosi nothing, least of all his release from prison which the dictator must have authorized with as little enthusiasm as he allowed every other concession to the fashion of de-Stalinization.

It seems likely that even if Kadar did not yet understand the details of Rakosi's original plans to destroy all the Home Communists after 1945 and did not yet fully appreciate the intermittent thaw in the iceberg of Soviet power, his "gratitude" was rather more political than sincere. Most accounts suggest that he now utterly hated the man whom he had once so admired and who had nevertheless maltreated him.

But he certainly had no wish to return to a lathe and so accepted the post of leader of the Party in the Thirteenth District of Budapest, one of the city's main working-class areas whose dreary postwar tenements still tower over tumbling little prewar cottages and stretch along the tram lines up one bank of the Danube beyond the fashionable Margaret Island, where the rich and the once rich and the sick and the hypochondriacs take the sulphur waters. It was not a glamorous job, but it was influential enough and Kadar was pleased to have it, anxious to educate himself in the changes which had taken place in Hungary since his arrest and glad to avoid sharing power with Rakosi and Farkas.

But dislike the fat dictator though he almost certainly did, he was no fervent supporter of Rakosi's opponent, Imre Nagy. Kadar and Nagy had never been particularly close, either personally or politically. In the late forties when Kadar was a committed Stalinist he had viewed with intense suspicion Nagy's moderate, conciliatory views. He was now a Stalinist no longer and was apparently not pleased when Nagy fell from power at the beginning of 1955—but his displeasure was caused more by Rakosi's inevitably consequent reascent, than by Nagy's eclipse.[16]

Over the next months Kadar gradually built himself the reputation, especially among his comrades in the City Party's organization, of a man who was anti-Rakosiist and yet not closely aligned with Nagy and all the "wild" reformers and idealists around him. A man of the center, a man of balance, a man of moderation.

A useful politician, a man who could be trusted to trim gently to shifts in the wind without heeling too sharply one way or the other. A steadfast man, very reliable in these confused, confusing times. But not a supremely intelligent man. After Khrushchev had denounced Stalin at the Twentieth Congress of the Soviet Communist party in February 1956, Rakosi once more fell into disfavor. Yet he was not at once dismissed and at a Central Committee meeting in May, Kadar attempted to discomfort him further by insisting that, in the fashion of the times, all those responsible for the trial and execution of Laszlo Rajk should be brought to justice.

It was a foolhardy gesture. According to several witnesses, Rakosi then produced a tape recorder, switched it on, and the entire Central Committee heard Kadar speaking to Rajk in his prison cell and asking him to confess. His conversation, including the promise of freedom in exchange for confession, was played through to the end to a chamber which could probably quite properly be described as stunned. Kadar's own emotions at the production of this secret tape, of whose existence he had till now known nothing, can only be guessed.

Nevertheless, Rakosi's attempt to totally discredit Kadar as a proponent of reform misfired. For when the tape was over, one of the members, Eric Molnar, a brilliant historian, asked for it to be played again. It was wound back and this time the tape began "Dear Laci, I come on behalf of Comrade Rakosi," an introduction which Rakosi had been careful to omit on the first playing. By the end of the second recital, Rakosi's reputation had suffered even more than Kadar's.[17]

That Rakosi should have taken the trouble to record Kadar's conversation with Rajk is not that unlikely—it was a form of insurance that would automatically have suggested itself to his clever, jealous mind. But that he should have neglected to erase or remove Kadar's avowal that he came to Rajk on Rakosi's behalf might seem less plausible, and therefore cast doubt on the whole story of the playback to the committee. However, there were times during which to have dispatched a lieutenant on such a mission would actually have reflected credit on Rakosi and such are the convulsive twists of orthodoxy in Eastern Europe that he may well have wanted to keep this evidence in anticipation of a resurgence of Stalinist dogmatism. There is little reason to doubt the story, but even if fanciful, it illustrates effectively the paranoiac deceits with which Rakosi's system of government was characterized. It was to ensure that such methods should never again be allowed in their country that Hungarians arose in 1956.

Four

There are situations where one has to do something which is understood only by a few at the time. Yet it has to be done in the hope that they will understand one's motives later on.

J. Kadar on his sixtieth birthday, 1972

On the morning of Tuesday, October 30, 1956, shooting broke out in Republic Square, Budapest. Nothing unusual, since the people of Budapest had, for the last seven days, been fighting physically against both the Russians and their own political police force, the AVH. At the beginning of the Revolution, a small force of AVH men, many of them raw recruits, had been posted in Republic Square to guard the headquarters of the Greater Budapest Communist party. There, throughout the week, they remained, even though on October 29 the abolition of their hated organization had been officially announced.

By this time food, never plentiful under the Rakosi regime, was becoming scarcer than ever in the city, and that Tuesday morning several queues of townspeople, who had waited hours in front of a bread shop in Republic Square, were predictably enraged to see a truck draw up outside the Party building and unload provisions for the AVH men inside. Shouting their fury and shaking their fists, they milled around the building and tried to rush the door. Their spokesman was allowed or taken inside to see Imre Mezo, the leader of the City Communist party but, afraid that he was being held against his will, the crowd soon began to attack the building in earnest. Armed "freedom fighters" were called up and they started shooting into the windows. AVH men returned their fire.

That lunchtime, while the siege was at its fiercest, Janos Kadar was taking part in a crucial radio broadcast with Prime Minister Imre Nagy and Minister of State Zoltan Tildy. Nagy announced that "in the interests of further democratisation . . . the Cabinet has abolished the one Party system." He appealed to the Russians for a total troop withdrawal, and declared that Hungary would return to the post 1945 coalition system. Zoltan Tildy then promised that there would be free elections as soon as order was restored. Thus several of the main demands of the revolutionaries were conceded.

All that spring and summer those demands had grown more vociferous, especially among writers and intellectuals. Khrushchev's denunciation of Stalin had whetted an appetite that was not easily to be sated. In an attempt to satisfy it, Khrushchev had ordered the final dismissal of Rakosi in July. He was replaced, not, as the people wished, by Nagy, but by Erno Gero, his closest collaborator and a man who was just as unpopular in the country as him. At the same time Janos Kadar was fully rehabilitated and elevated to the Politburo. But in the weeks that followed, Gero's half-hearted attempts at reform had, if anything, helped convince many intellectuals that the system could not be changed from within but must be attacked from without.

One of the first incidents in the armed uprising was an assault on the National Radio building during the night of October 23–24. As a result Imre Nagy, whose appointment as prime minister the people had been demanding for weeks, finally got the job. But Gero remained as Party leader and at the same time, Russian troops were ordered to move from their camps some forty miles away into Budapest itself.

The arrival of the Soviet troops at this stage gave the revolutionaries a clearcut enemy; "Get the Russians out" was a much more effective rallying call than the long list of political reforms that had been demanded till then. These demands remained constant, however; they did not involve the end of communism but rather the right to follow, like Yugoslavia and now Poland, a specific Hungarian path to Marx's utopia. So far as millions of the Hungarian people were concerned, only Imre Nagy could lead them there, and not in the company of Stalinists like Gero.

After the AVH had massacred some six hundred demonstrators in Parliament Square on the afternoon of October 25, the Soviet Politburo, acting on the advice of Anastas Mikoyan and Mikhail Suslov, their two special envoys to Budapest, decided that Gero must indeed resign. He was removed from Budapest in a Soviet tank and is said to have been taken to the Devin Hotel, on the farther, Czechoslovak bank of the Danube in Bratislava. He was replaced as Party leader, again at the Russians' suggestion, by Janos Kadar.

The radio announced the changes just after midday on the twenty-fifth and at 3:12 P.M. the new First Secretary of the Hungarian Communist party came on the air to appeal for calm. He promised that the rebels would not be punished, but did point out that "anti-democratic and counter-revolutionary elements" had caused peaceful demonstrations to

degenerate into armed attacks. He guaranteed that
after order had been restored the government would
negotiate with the Russians "in the spirit of complete
equality," but said little more.

By the time he made his lunchtime broadcast five
days later on October 30 events seemed to have radi-
calized Janos Kadar. Soviet troops were still in the city
but Kadar now endorsed Nagy's promise to abolish
the Communist party's monopoly of power and to
hold free elections, declaring that he and his Party
Presidium "fully approve of all that was said by the
speakers before me." He admitted that the Communists would have to start completely afresh and try to
wipe the slate clean. "The ranks of the Party will
shake . . . but I am sure that no honest, sincere Communist will leave the Party. Those who joined for selfish personal reasons will be the ones to leave." Whatever misgivings he may have had about the
Communists' ability to survive annihilation let alone
maintain power in a free election, he did not express.

As he finished his sensational broadcast, the ammu-
nition of the AVH men in the besieged Party building in Republic Square was beginning to run out.
The "freedom fighters" were strategically placed all
around the building and closing in. After three hours
of pointless fighting, Imre Mezo gave the order to
surrender, and one by one men began to leave the
building, their hands above their heads. The crowd
showed no mercy. Two AVH colonels were strung up
to lampposts by their feet and beaten to death. As
other AVH men came out of the door they were
gunned down without hesitation. Imre Mezo was shot
in the chest as he carried out a white flag. He died in
pain in the hospital in Petofi Street on Thursday, November 1, two days later.

Thursday, November 1 was a tiring day for Kadar. Not only did he make his outburst before Yuri Andropov, the Soviet ambassador, later announce the formation, under his own leadership, of a totally new Communist party, praise the "glorious uprising" on Radio Free Kossuth and then defect to the Russians, he also found time to give his first ever interview to a Western journalist. It was to Bruno Tedeschi, the correspondent of *Il Giornale d'Italia*. His answers might cause Kadar some embarrassment in Hungary today.

Tedeschi: What type of Communism do you represent, Mr. Kadar?

Kadar: The new type, which emerged from the Revolution and which does not want to have anything in common with the Communism of the Rakosi-Hegedus-Gero group.

Tedeschi: This "new Communism," if it can be termed as such — is it of the Yugoslav or Polish type?

Kadar: Our Communism is Hungarian. It is a sort of "third line," with no connection to Titoism nor to Gomulka's Communism.

Tedeschi: How would you describe this "third line"?

Kadar: It is Marxism-Leninism applied to the particular requirements of our country, to our difficulties and to our national problems. It is not inspired either by the U.S.S.R. nor by other types of Communism, and I repeat that it is Hungarian National Communism. This "third line" originated from our Revolution during the course of which, as you know, numerous Communists fought at the side of students, workers, and the people.

Tedeschi: Will your Communism be developed along democratic lines, if they can be termed as such?

Kadar: That's a good question. There will be an opposition, and no dictatorship. This opposition will be heard because it will have the national interests of Hungary at heart and not those of international Communism.

Kadar ended the interview by telling Tedeschi that he thought Tito and Titoism *sehr gut* and even revealed that Hungary would accept Western economic aid if it was offered. "We need it; our country is in a state of economic breakdown." [1]

That night on Radio Kossuth he made his famous statement of support for the events of the last few days: "In their glorious uprising our people have shaken off the Rakosi regime. They have achieved freedom for the people and independence for the country. Without this there can be no socialism. We can safely say that the ideological and organisational leaders who prepared this uprising were recruited from among your ranks. Hungarian Communist writers, journalists, University students, the youth of the Petofi Circle, thousands and thousands of workers and peasants, and veteran fighters who had been imprisoned on false charges, fought in the front line against Rakosiite despotism and political hooliganism."

Referring to the formation of the new Communist party, which would compete in the promised free elections, he promised that it would "break away from the crimes of the past once and for all. It will defend the honour and independence of our country against anyone. . . . The Party counts on the support of every honest worker. . . . We expect everyone to join who, in the past, was deterred from service to socialism by the anti-national policy and criminal deeds of Rakosi and his followers."

Soon after he finished the broadcast he left the Parliament building. Within a few hours he had arrived at the Soviet Embassy along with Ferenc Munnich, the old Party militant and associate of Bela Kun who had more recently been Hungarian ambassador to Moscow. There are accounts from several sources about this all important journey—they differ in detail. According to one version, they drove together straight to the Soviet Embassy, but another account records that the chauffeur of the car next day told Geza Losconczy, now a minister in Nagy's government, that in a quiet, dark street Kadar and Munnich got out of the car and walked up and down the pavement, arguing passionately. Now and again they would stop and then resume their pacing. The chauffeur thought that Munnich was trying to convince Kadar of something. Finally he took Kadar by the arm and led him to another car parked along the street. It was from the Soviet Embassy. Munnich was said to have virtually pushed Kadar into the back seat and the car then sped away with them both inside.[2]

The United Nations report on the Hungarian Revolution stated that Kadar was seen in Parliament on the next day, November 2. This is almost certainly incorrect. Whatever the manner of his arrival at the Soviet Embassy, whether under pressure from Munnich or completely calmly of his own free will, he left it in an embassy car either later that night or early the following morning and was driven to a Soviet-controlled airfield outside Budapest. Where he was then flown

was for a long time a matter of some mystery,* and it
was not until three years later that Kadar himself revealed where he had gone.

After the Hungarian Party Congress of 1959,
Kadar accompanied Khrushchev back to the Soviet
Union. They stopped in Uzghorod in the Ukraine
and Kadar revealed that it was here that he had come
"three years ago when the Hungarian people had
been in great trouble"; when his new government had
asked for "brotherly help from the Soviet people, this
support was given and so the counter-revolution was
defeated." [3]

On Saturday, November 3, two days after Kadar's
defection, life in Budapest began to return to normal.
Over twenty-four hours had gone by since Nagy had
declared Hungary's neutrality and withdrawal from
the Warsaw Pact. The Russians had not reacted; indeed, they were still negotiating the removal of all
their troops from the country. Many people began to
hope that the worst was past and that the danger of a
full-scale invasion was over: shops reopened and, although it was the weekend, some of the city's factories
also began to resume production. Nagy published the
list of his new government ministers and, although he
had heard the day before of Kadar's disappearance,
Kadar's name was among them. Some say this is an
example of Nagy's naïveté, others of his generosity in
giving Kadar the benefit of the doubt. More probably
he was anxious to conceal the disappearances in order
to avoid giving the public yet another cause for concern. But it is quite possible that despite the chauffeur's story of Kadar, Munnich, and the Soviet Em-

---

* Some reports had him taken to Szolnok in East-Central Hungary,
others had him flying at once to Moscow, and others still to Uzghorod, just
over the Soviet border in the Carpatho-Ukraine.

bassy car, Nagy and his friends still did not realize or believe that Kadar was in the Soviet Union being rehearsed in his role for the Red Army assault on Budapest, planned for the following morning, Sunday, November 4.

It was Ferenc Munnich who introduced the new "Revolutionary Workers and Peasants Government" of Janos Kadar at dawn that next day. Broadcasting just a few hours before Parliament fell to the Soviet tanks and before Nagy and his colleagues fled to the sanctuary of the Yugoslav Embassy, he explained: "We were prompted to take this responsible step because we realised that within the Nagy Government, which became impotent under the pressure of reaction, we could do nothing against the counter-revolutionary danger." It was perhaps significant that as the first instance of this danger Munnich cited the murder of Imre Mezo as he stepped out of the Party building on Republic Square.

Approximately an hour later, Kadar himself came on the air. His address was later described in the official White Book, the "Counter-Revolutionary Conspiracy of Imre Nagy and his Accomplices" published by his own government as "the call which had been awaited from 23rd October onwards by the workers and other labouring people of Hungary."

Be that as it may, after an announcement of "Attention, Attention! Comrade Kadar speaking," he announced baldly that a new "Hungarian Revolutionary Worker-Peasant Government" had been formed.*

"The mass movement which started in our country on the 23rd October had the noble aim to remedy the

---

* According to Voice of America technicians, this broadcast was transmitted on 1187 kilocycles through the Balkan Radio Station of Radio Moscow.

anti-Party and anti-democratic crimes committed by
Rakosi and his associates and to defend national independence and sovereignty" he admitted, but:

> . . . since then our socialist achievements, our
> people's State, our worker peasant power, and the
> very existence of our country has been threatened
> by the weakness of the Imre Nagy Government
> and the increased influence of the counter-revolu-
> tionary elements who edged their way into the
> movement. This has prompted us, as Hungarian
> patriots, to form the Hungarian Revolutionary
> Worker-Peasant Government.
>
> Our nation is passing through difficult days.
> The power of the workers and peasants, and the
> sacred cause of socialism are in danger. . . . The
> counter-revolutionaries are becoming more and
> more impudent. They ruthlessly persecute the
> followers of democracy . . . We know that many
> questions are still awaiting a solution in our
> country and that we have to cope with many dif-
> ficulties. The life of the workers is still far from
> what it ought to be in a country building socialism.
> . . . The Rakosi and Gero clique has committed
> many grave mistakes and gravely violated legality.
> All this had rightly made the workers dissatisfied.

It was a fairly moderate speech, designed to appeal
to any such middle ground as might conceivably still
be left in Hungary.* His new program embodied
some of the original demands of the Revolution.
Quite apart from the promise of sovereignty, it also
foreswore any reprisals against those who had led the
uprising, and he ended his appeal with the words

* Kadar's government: Janos Kadar, Premier; Ferenc Munnich, Depu-
ty Premier and Minister of the Armed Forces and Public Security; George
Marosan, Minister of State; Imre Horvath, Foreign Minister; Istvan
Kossa, Minister of Finance; Antal Apro, Minister of Industry; Imre
Dogei, Minister of Agriculture; Sandor Ronai, Minister of Commerce.

"Workers, Hungarian brethren, Truth is on our side.
We will win." *
Kadar and his new friends returned to Budapest in

* Kadar's program, November 4, 1956, paraphrased:
1. To secure national independence and Hungary's sovereignty.
2. To protect the people's democratic and socialist system against all attack. To protect socialist achievements and the guarantee of progress along the road of building socialism.
3. To end fratricidal fighting and to restore internal order and peace. The government will not tolerate the persecution of workers under any pretext whatsoever for having taken part in the most recent events.
4. To establish close fraternal relations with every socialist country on the basis of complete equality and noninterference. The same principle is to govern their mutual economic relations and mutual assistance agreements.
5. Peaceful cooperation with every country, irrespective of its social order and form of government.
6. To raise quickly and substantially the standard of living, in particular that of the working class. More houses for the workers. Factories and institutes must be enabled to build apartments for their workers and employees.
7. The modification of the Five Year Plan, changing the methods of economic management, taking into consideration the capacity of the country, so that the population's standard of living may be raised as quickly as possible.
8. The elimination of bureaucracy and broad development of democracy in the interest of the workers.
9. On the broadest democratic basis, workers' management must be realized in factories and enterprises.
10. To develop agricultural production, abolish compulsory deliveries and grant assistance to individual farmers. The government to liquidate all illegalities in the sphere of the cooperatives and redivision of land.
11. To guarantee democratic elections in hitherto existing administrative bodies and the revolutionary council.
12. Support for retail trade and artisans.
13. The systematic development of Hungarian national culture in the spirit of our progressive traditions.
14. The Hungarian Revolutionary Worker-Peasant Government, acting in the interest of the people, working class and country, requested the Soviet Army command to help the nation smash the sinister forces of reaction and restore order and calm in the country.
15. After the restoration of peace and order, the Hungarian government will begin negotiations with the Soviet government and with the other participants in the Warsaw Treaty about the withdrawal of Soviet troops from Hungary.

a Soviet convoy on November 7, to a Budapest which was macabrely reminiscent of the city after the battle for liberation in 1945, a Budapest where eyeless buildings hung mournfully and emptily over burned-out tanks, cars, and buses which crazily littered the rubble-strewn streets, where the bodies of Hungarian and Soviet dead testified still to the bitter savagery of the fighting that had lasted the past three days. In their first occupation of Budapest in October, the Russians had shown some restraint; not yet certain of how to deal with the uprising, with no alternative government to that of Nagy, they had hesitated to crush the Hungarians totally. On this occasion they had returned with the sole purpose of razing all hopes and resistance, with, from their point of view, an excellent alternative government to impose as soon as the fighting had ended.

Although by November 7 the greatest part of active armed resistance had been crushed, pockets of revolt continued to hold out for weeks. Kadar was also faced with the almost total noncooperation of the Hungarian people and, until December, with a general strike in which the vast majority of Budapest workers took part. By the time he had finally· established order and managed to exact at least a grudging cooperation from the nation, he had broken almost every one of the promises he made on November 4, and to most Hungarians it seemed that the worst days of Rakosi's rule in the early fifties had returned with more than just vengeance.

But although his actions quite naturally engendered fierce hatred, strangely enough Hungarian contempt for Kadar never seemed to reach the same level as that felt by the Czechs for the political leaders who betrayed their country during the 1968 Soviet invasion of Czechoslovakia. It is very difficult to find anyone who even in the initial bitterness of 1956 described Kadar as the simple tool of the Russians. Few of those Hungarian writers who fled to the West and produced their own accounts of the Revolution were able to explain his personality, but almost without exception they considered his behavior more complex than mere opportunism. Perhaps this was because of all his colleagues, Kadar was almost the only one of who was not thought of as simply an arriviste. He was one of the few of the Party's leaders with a genuine working-class rather than petit-bourgeois background and was identified in the public eye as a simple, shy but sometimes quite jovial, rather unsophisticated militant. Both before and after his imprisonment he had shunned the trappings of Party power that his colleagues had so much enjoyed. He was not dismissed as only an ambitious, ruthless careerist; indeed with the young, he was even quite popular. Ever since August the student unions, delighted by attacks he had made on the AVH, had put in persistent requests that he be allowed to play a larger part in government.

To the Soviets he was, quite simply, the best choice to run the country. He was not too tainted with Stalinism (the Rajk story was not widely known) and yet he had never been close to Nagy and was uncorrupted by revisionism. Perhaps even more important, he was acceptable to Tito. Khrushchev was at this time anxious to improve inter-Party relations, and this amounted to little more than an improvement in Soviet-Yugoslav contacts. The purges, executions, and imprisonments of the Rakosi era had all been carried out in the name of anti-Titoism and so no one associated with them should now be selected to lead Hungary. Since 1951, at any rate, Kadar had not had the chance to make anti-Titoist pronouncements.

In a secret letter to Tito, Khrushchev wrote on November 9, 1956, of his satisfaction that "you have been in full agreement with our attitude toward comrade Janos Kadar as a distinguished personality with revolutionary authority in Hungary, capable of heading a new revolutionary government in these difficult times and conditions. . . . You were fully satisfied with the fact that in connection with the removal of Rakosi, the Central Committee of the Communist Party of the Soviet Union had, since the summer of this year, endeavoured that Comrade Kadar should become First Secretary of the Central Committee of the Hungarian Workers Party." [4]

In other words, Kadar's selection as Party leader had been agreed by Tito and Khrushchev (probably without Kadar's knowledge) in the summer, long before the Revolution.

There are some, not fully confirmed, accounts that several members of the Central Committee were indeed anxious that Kadar rather than Gero should succeed Rakosi in the summer of 1956, and that Kadar himself refused on the grounds that he had been too long out of touch with the realities of politics and was therefore unqualified for the job. This would be quite in keeping with his character, for up to 1956 he had always displayed a marked inferiority complex. Whether or not the story is true, it is certainly a tragedy that he was not given the post that summer: had the Hungarians then had a leader they could respect—and they already inclined to respect Kadar—the agony of the Revolution, its destruction, and the slow, slow process of reconstruction after it, might have been entirely avoided.

It is difficult to believe that Kadar took much joy in his betrayal of Nagy and the Revolution or that he saw that betrayal primarily as a brilliant chance of advancing his own career. He had other motives for leaving Nagy, more laudable than mere opportunism.

High among them was that Imre Mezo, who was shot in Republic Square on Tuesday, October 30, had been one of his closest friends ever since they had worked together after 1945 to build up the Party organization in Budapest; they had become even closer since Kadar began working in the Thirteenth District of the town. Kadar heard the news of the shooting after he had made his lunchtime radio speech supporting the restoration of the multi-Party system and free elections. He must have been horrified. Only two days before, Sunday the twenty-eighth, he had visited Mezo in that same building on Republic Square and the two old militants had spent several hours together discussing the achievements and the dangers of the uprising, assessing their hopes and measuring their fears.

Both agreed that many of the revolutionaries' demands were quite legitimate: neither wanted to see a return to the Stalinism of the early fifties and each recognized that many of the men responsible for those years would have to go. They left each other concerned about the future but hopeful that the Party would be able to seize this moment of public awareness for its own purposes, and that perhaps from now on—with the right leadership and policies—the Communists could, for the first time, gain the support of the people.

Imre Mezo died of his wounds two days after he was shot, on the day on which Kadar shouted at Andropov, on which he spoke of the "glorious uprising," and on which he later drove away with Ferenc Munnich. It may be—and some of his friends consider it likely—that it was in the first shock of the news of his friend's death that Kadar lost his temper with Andropov, equating, in his "semi-hysterical" state, the killing of Mezo with the first Soviet occupation of Budapest.

According to this scenario, it was only later that evening when his emotions began to subside that he fully realized how far the leaders of the Party and government had, under Nagy, allowed themselves to be pushed by the massive ground swell of popular demands. It was only now that he understood that the Revolution which he had originally endorsed as being anti-Rakosiist was becoming anti-Soviet and anticommunist as well.

A week before he would never have believed that the uprising would lead to Hungary's leaving the Warsaw Pact: even Imre Nagy had consistently declared himself to be unutterably opposed to neutrality. And yet here they were, he and Nagy, cabling their withdrawal to the United Nations and demanding recognition as a neutral state; here they were, in effect, announcing to the world their disaffection with the Soviet Union and their determination to end their hitherto "fraternal relations."

A week before he would never have dreamed that the character of the peoples' emotions was such that they would wantonly murder honest reformist Communists like Imre Mezo who genuinely sought to erase the abuses of Stalinism. Now he realized the full extent of the hatred which the soulless policies of Rakosi had for eight years nurtured in Hungarian hearts; now he understood that in any proper "free elections" the Communists would be laughed or thrown off the hustings and totally destroyed. Now he appreciated at last how important a factor was disgust with the Soviet Union and its imperialism in this uprising.

The contradictions in his behavior almost certainly

also reflect the hesitancy of the Soviets themselves. When the Chinese explained the roots of their disagreement with Moscow in the *Red Flag* and *The People's Daily* of September 5, 1963, they reproached the Soviet leadership for having dithered in the middle of the Hungarian "counterrevolution." It was only under the pressure of other parties, said the Chinese, that the Russians finally committed the Red Army to the destruction of the uprising. There is good reason to accept this analysis. Whatever the exact role played by the Chinese (and Mao would not have argued *against* intervention), that Khrushchev hesitated before finally deciding to crush the uprising does seem certain, and that Nagy's withdrawal from the Warsaw Pact precipitated his final decision appears most likely.

In 1963 Kadar told Andre Wurmser of *L'Humanité*, the French Communist party paper, something of his fears in November 1956 (or at least of his hindsight justifications for them). He recalled that in 1919 the enemies of Bela Kun's revolution had first of all hidden behind a socialist camouflage. 1919 and 1956 were similar, he said. In 1919 the right wing "overthrew the Republic of Councils and replaced it by a so-called Trade Union Government headed by a certain Peidl. The Peidl group was in power only six days. On the sixth day about fifteen counter-revolutionaries entered the Government building and declared, 'Now you get out.' And the ministers took their hats and coats and left." That, said Kadar, was the beginning of the Horthyite fascist terror to which Hungarians were subjected for twenty-five years. "I presume that Imre Nagy was destined to play a similar role. He too, would have been told after five or six days: 'Get up and get out.' And he would have taken his hat and coat and cleared out." [5]

It seems probable that (whenever they chose him and told him of their choice), Kadar's decision to side with the Russians was taken hurriedly in the early evening of November 1, after he had heard of Mezo's death and after he had realized just what withdrawal from the Warsaw Pact would mean: the end of communism in Hungary. His outburst with Andropov was genuine, but his speech in praise of the "glorious uprising" was made after he knew what he had to do. It was therefore a deception. But with the advantage of hindsight it is possible to see even in this speech a warning. His praise for events of the last week was not unconditional. The Uprising, he said, had "come to a crossroads."

> Either the Hungarian democratic parties will have enough strength to stabilize our achievements or we must face an open counter-revolution. The blood of Hungarian youth, soldiers, workers, and peasants was not shed to replace Rakosiite despotism with the reign of the counter-revolution. . . . A grave and alarming danger exists that foreign armed intervention may reduce our country to the tragic fate of Korea. Our anxiety for the future of our country leads us to do our utmost to avert this grave danger. We must eliminate the nests of counter-revolution and reaction. We must finally consolidate our democratic order and secure the conditions for normal productive work and life—peace, calm and order.

He concluded with "a request to overcome the danger of a menacing counter-revolution and intervention from abroad by consolidating the Government."

The original aims of the Revolution were contained in a sixteen-point resolution adopted by the students on October 22, 1956. This document circulated from hand to hand and was copied thousands of times during the next few days. It became something of a Bible to the movement, and it is useful to look at it today to see how far Kadar has, or has not, been true to the spirit of the Revolution even while crushing its form. The students insisted on the immediate withdrawal of all Soviet troops, the removal of all Stalinists from the Party, the election of new cadres, and the return of Imre Nagy to power. Matyas Rakosi and all other Communist leaders most seriously implicated in the crimes of the last years should be brought to trial. General elections with the participation of many parties should be held and workers must have the right to strike. Point six demanded a readjustment of relations with the Soviet Union and Yugoslavia on the basis of complete equality. The whole economy must be reorganized and rationalized and foreign trade figures should be published; Hungary must be allowed to use its uranium ore for its own benefit, not that of the Soviet Union. Workers' production norms should be made realistic, and private peasants treated properly.

All political and economic trials should be reexamined and their victims rehabilitated; all deportees to the Soviet Union must be returned at once. Freedom of expression, opinion, and the press must be unconditional, the huge Stalin statue in Budapest must be removed and replaced by a memorial to the 1848 Revolution. The old Kossuth national emblem should be restored and the Hungarian army should have new uniforms "more worthy of our national traditions." There should be national holidays on March 15 and October 6. It is in terms of how far he has met or ignored these demands that Kadar's "betrayal" of the Revolution and his subsequent government should be judged.

He promised to meet them at once, and he failed utterly—for several years after his brutal and seemingly unforgivable betrayal of the Revolution most Hungarians found little to choose between his policies and those of Rakosi. Nevertheless, he has worked fairly consistently since at least 1961 to ensure that some of the aspects of the Nagy program were fulfilled—certainly under another guise, but in spirit at least fulfilled. One of his colleagues recently explained him this way: "He realised on the 1st November that he must destroy the counter-revolution in order to save the Revolution." Another expressed it in exactly the opposite way: "Kadar now knows that he must meet the demands of the Revolution, if he is to contain counter-revolution in this country." Both statements are probably accurate assessments of his paradoxical attitudes in 1956 and ever since.

Five

I am fond of healthy humour. But there is no humour in public affairs. Of course, there are humorous events in political life, but they are in a different category.

J. Kadar
January 1, 1968

Zoltan Szep is blind. He is a lecturer in mathematics at Budapest University. He is not a Communist but in April 1971 he stood for Parliament and won the Budapest constituency of Obuda in a fight against the official, Communist party–sponsored candidate. His victory was, in a sense, symbolic of the degree of political reform that Kadar has allowed in Hungary since 1956.

In the general election of 1971, groups of citizens or, indeed, individual electors could actually nominate their own candidates for the first time since 1947. The man or woman of their choice could stand against the Party's official candidate, nominated by the Patriotic People's Front, the Communist-dominated electoral organization.

As a result, in 49 of the 352 parliamentary constituencies and in 3,016 of the 70,000 local council areas, voters had a choice between candidates at the elections. This does not mean that there was a genuine political opposition in these contested seats; even the unofficial candidates had to subscribe fully to the policies of the Patriotic People's Front (an estimated 60 percent of all candidates were Party members). But it did mean that in constituencies where voters had a personal dislike of their present representative, or where, whatever his ideological strengths, they considered him ineffective at pleading their case, they now had a chance to remove him. In fact eight sitting M.P.'s were defeated in the elections—one of them Tomas Major, an actor, almost certainly because of his arrogant, generally unpleasant character—and among the new M.P.'s was Zoltan Szep.

He thought some of his votes were out of sympathy for his blindness (he lost his sight as a child) but considered that his election and the new law itself completely rebutted "the accusations at home and abroad that Hungary is a dictatorship." Although he promised no great changes, his success was certainly greeted with great enthusiasm in Obuda, the oldest district of Budapest, where he lives in a small, modern two-room apartment with his young wife and baby. Throughout the country it was noticeable that the elections were followed with far more public interest in those seats which were contested. From the government's point of view, and from Kadar's—anxious as he is to encourage genuine interest in politics—the new law had worked well; by the time of the next parliamentary elections in 1975, he expects that over half the seats will be contested.

But to a journalist from the Italian Communist party paper, *L'Unità,* Kadar specifically denied in 1969 all Western speculation that the New Economic Mechanism (NEM), introduced the previous year, involved any political changes. "There is no plan for, and there will be no changes in the political structure, neither in the structure of the Party nor in realising the principles of democratic centralism," he asserted.[1] This is not true. To avoid Western praise (the chillingly damning praise of the bourgeois) such changes are indeed best skated over, but as Zoltan Szep's election shows, they are nonetheless taking place and represent, in toto, the most substantial degree of political reform to be attempted in any East European country since invasion froze to a premature death the joyful buds of Prague Spring in 1968.

The political structures of all societies are necessarily affected by any change in the economic foundations on which they are built and in a socialist system, where the Communist party is the only arbiter, guide, and director of the state and all its works, politics and economics are even less easily separated than elsewhere. Indeed, although the 1968 reforms in Hungary were deliberately entitled "economic," they are in fact just as much political. They are basically intended to improve the conditions of life of the Hungarian citizen and are designed to do this not only by increasing his consumptive power but also by allowing him a greater freedom in the way in which he makes his everyday decisions and conducts himself.

Nevertheless, Kadar has a point. The gross sum of all actual rebuilding of the political institutions in Hungary since he took power in 1956 is not large. The country is still ruled under the constitution with which, in 1949, Rakosi proudly established the dictatorship of the proletariat in Hungary. But, in theory, that document was democratic enough. It was modeled on the 1936 constitution of the Soviet Union which Stalin had described as the "most democratic in the world"—a boast which was laughable only because he disregarded it.

The 1949 Hungarian constitution also guaranteed,

on paper, freedom of the individual, of speech, of religion, and of conscience. It promised universal education, recognized the total equality of women, and it guaranteed the protection of national minorities. It was, on the whole, an excellent document, far more progressive and just than anything Hungarians had ever known under their previous rulers. The pity of it was that, so far as Rakosi was concerned, it was irrelevant; like Stalin he had his own theories about how a country should be governed.

Kadar has not abandoned and (apart from amendments introduced in the spring of 1972) has not much altered the 1949 constitution; his work since 1956 cannot be conveniently documented by a simple list of the legislation he has promoted and has had enacted. His achievement is much more subtle and complicated and can perhaps be best described as a change in the national mood, brought about by the gentler way he has fingered those instruments of government which Rakosi had handled so roughly, by the use he has made of those instruments which Rakosi ignored totally, and, perhaps most importantly, by the way in which he has completely discarded some of the bludgeons in whose indiscriminate power Rakosi most gloried. Since 1956 Kadar has pursued "legitimacy"—meaning the people's support for his government—and in his search has consistently tried to broaden the scope of what is known in Eastern Europe as "socialist democracy."

To Alexander Dubcek, socialist democracy was a hazy, muddled, idealistic dream of a Czechoslovak people freely and enthusiastically supporting a Communist party which it knew to be genuinely democratic and of whose good and incorruptible intentions it was convinced. That support should be won by the Party's demonstrating in its works that it was far the best guarantor of the people's interests. But while Dubcek had never really worked out what political rights Czechoslovak socialist democracy allowed to noncommunists, Kadar's ideas are—unsurprisingly—both less adventurous and more clearly defined.

To Kadar, socialist democracy means a social, political, and economic structure of society in which the Communist party is the monopoly power and in which there is absolutely no possibility of regression to any form of social democracy, let alone capitalism. It is, nevertheless, a society which is confident enough in itself to allow a certain measure of debate as to how best the aims of socialism should be achieved. It is, moreover, a society ruled by a collective will, not by the erratic and brutal methods of an omnipotent dictator, or a group of self-appointed oligarchs, and in which the individual can have confidence that his conditions of life, both material and "moral," are constantly improving—albeit within a strictly socialist framework. It is a society in which every citizen, Communist or not, should be able to live secure in the knowledge that there will never again be a return to the arbitrary terror of the early fifties; he should, by the activities of the Party, be convinced that not only are such aberrations not endemic to socialism (which many, with good reason, believed at the time) but that they were then just the unfortunate, if inevitable, products of the juxtaposition of such historical coincidences as the fight throughout Eastern and Central Europe to establish the dictatorship of the proletariat, the personalities of Stalin, Churchill, Rakosi, and Truman, the politics of Tito, and the creation of the North Atlantic Treaty Alliance.

After the Revolution Kadar realized that to win the support or at least the tacit acceptance of the sullen, embittered people, the Party could not afford to keep any section of society out of the community of Hungarian progress; all must be welcomed, for all could contribute to the building of a new, united Hungary. For Kadar, as for Dubcek, socialist democracy thus involves the creation of a society in which people have hope for the future not despite the continuing and supposedly everlasting supremacy of the Communist party, but rather just because of that supremacy. The Party should be seen by non-Party members as their protector, not as their secret and all too powerful policeman.

Before the end of 1961 Kadar had little chance of practicing this philosophy, so preoccupied was he with establishing order in a country whose economy had been badly disrupted and, more seriously, whose illusions had been shattered by the traumas of 1956, struggling as he was to maintain his own against the neo-Stalinists in his Party.

He came to power in 1956 with a ragbag coalition of a few anti-Rakosiists such as himself, Ferenc Munnich, and George Marosan, and other, more traditional Stalinists. In those early days of November and December 1956 he was in no position to choose his colleagues with care; he had to accept whoever deigned to betray the Revolution for the Soviet's and Kadar's cause. At the time he was grateful enough, but as soon as his government was more firmly established it became quite clear that there were almost irreconcilable differences between those of the new leaders who fervently sought a return of Rakosi's policies if not of Rakosi himself and those who, like Kadar, recognized that in the works and demonic genius of Rakosi lay the cause of the people's despair, and who hoped, therefore, to give Hungarians a socialism they could actually like rather than one they were compelled to loathe. If he was forced initially to renege on most of the liberal-sounding promises he made on seizing power in November 1956 (and he did renege fairly comprehensively) this may be not because he was lying all along but because in the next months and years his attempts to conciliate the Hungarian people were frustrated not only by his enemies (who are variously called by his supporters "dogmatists," "Rakosiists," or "Rakosiites," and "neo-Stalinists") within his Cabinet and Politburo but also by the exigencies of the communist world on which those enemies played.

It was not until the Twenty-second Soviet Party Congress in 1961, when Khrushchev's reformism triumphed, for the moment, over conservatism, that Kadar was really able to begin to work for the reconciliation and reconstruction of his country. In December of that year he was feeling secure enough (after Khrushchev's success) to proclaim his *Alliance Policy*. In a rather moving if slightly folksy speech of gently chiding good humor, he completely reversed Rakosi's snarling threat "Who is not with us is against us" into the promise that "Whoever is not against us is with us." Although Hungarians had already learned that his style of speaking was infinitely more sympathetic than Rakosi's arrogant, dogmatic boasts, it was, to most, a sensational invitation to come from the leader of the Party, a revolutionary policy which implied a role for the Communists very different from that they had previously played in Hungary, or anywhere else in Eastern Europe—except perhaps for a short time in Gomulka's Poland. Basically it involved winning over people by persuasion, not by coercion or corruption. This has remained Kadar's aim and, in a simplified sense, the basis of his philosophy of government ever since. Hungarians still constantly refer to the speech as the beginning of the times when things began to get better—the beginning of the end of Stalinism.

"Believe me," he said, in support of his policy of extending rather than narrowing the administration's power base, "we can be a hundred times more assured about the fate of the country if we know that hundreds of thousands or, I may safely say, millions of conscientious people are concerned with its fate than if only fifteen, five or perhaps even one single man were concerned with it."

He stumbled on: "Western political commentators say—because they keep needling us, and that is not really so bad, since we consider them unpaid fellow workers, paid by imperialism (laughter) to keep searching for the faults of Communists—well, they say now the following: This Kadar group is very cunning, they want to fool everybody. Because Rakosi used to say a long time ago: 'Whoever is not with us is against us,' Kadar now says: 'Whoever is not against us is with us.' (laughter) The Western political commentators are bringing up 'faults' like these nowadays. . . . We can safely acknowledge this. Indeed we do believe that whoever is not against the Hungarian people is with us . . . there are many hundreds of thousands who are not Marxists but who respect our Party and our Government for having created a legal order and a normal atmosphere in the country. They are with us." [2] In such rambling form was an invitation to alliance extended.

Kadar's continual expression of such anti-Stalinist concepts, and his attempt to realize them has been designed not only to win the support of the people, but also to browbeat his opponents in the Party. He has constantly had to tell Party members that not only must they no longer expect their membership to bestow on them any special privilege or grace, they must also forswear praise.

Many Party members have found it difficult to agree with him, and it was in their discontent that Kadar saw a continual threat to his leadership after his proclamation of the alliance policy. They had risen to power under the shadow of Rakosi, the example of Rakosi had been constantly before them as the ideal Communist and the methods of the early fifties were the only ones they knew.

They understood only a society in which the ordinary worker, peasant, or clerk did a job not because he was suited to it, not because he enjoyed it, not because it was well-paid, close to home, or in any other way convenient for him, but because that was the job on a piece of paper on which some Party official had happened, perhaps unconsciously, to print his name. They wanted no reforms which decentralized the administration and humanized the state. They thought that there was only one way to deal with nonCommunists and that only Communists understood it.

In private Kadar has inveighed incessantly against them; and, if any of them were more obdurate than usual, in public too. Thus, "In various posts, chiefly in the state and economic administration, there can still be found communist leaders who employ methods of work alien to the spirit of Party policy and the style of work of the Party. Such people are overbearing, order others about unnecessarily, stifle criticism, and even revenge themselves for it. An unswerving struggle must be waged against such symptoms inside the Party and in all other aspects of life as well." [3]

At the same time, however, he was anxious to establish in everyone's mind that he was still unutterably hostile to the "counterrevolutionaries" of October and November 1956. He was a de-Stalinizer, but he was no rightist.

> There are people among us who think now that Stalin's coffin has been removed from the mausoleum a new spring will arrive for the right. I have heard voices saying that one should rehabilitate in our country those who knocked down Stalin's statue. But this is my answer: If that statue were still in place, then we would adopt a resolution to remove it next December or January. But those who knocked this statue down . . . did not do it because Stalin committed errors but because they did not like Communism. We will thus never rehabilitate them.[4]

It was now, at the Eighth Congress in 1962, that Kadar buried the notion of the class struggle and thus promised a certain easing in the dictatorship which the proletariat was previously "forced" to apply in its government of the country. The directives for the congress, published in August 1962, declared, "The Party invites those members of society which previously did not sympathise with (the Party) and even opposed its objectives to join in helping to build socialism." At this congress he announced that the children of the middle classes would no longer be penalized for life.

A characteristic of Stalinism had been its total exaltation of all things proletarian, its blanket disdain for the rest. There was some justification for this sentiment; a large proportion of the Hungarian middle- and upper-middle classes had, like the Hungarian nobility, done little for its country before the war. Effete and arrogant, many of them were more concerned that their children should study the various gradations of address for peasants, women, servants, traders, ladies, and countesses that the language then

boasted than that they should ever learn to do anything constructive for a country badly in need of constructive work.

Nonetheless, the scorn and the cruelty with which
all who either did not join the Party or could not
prove themselves of the purest proletarian origin
were treated after 1948 was not only unmerited and
cruel but stupid. The Communists discriminated
against the bourgeois even more thoroughly than the
middle classes had previously persecuted and suppressed the workers. That factory owners should lose
their factories, that landowners should have to hand
over their land, that shop managers should have to
give up trading—all this was not only understandable
but necessary. What was less essential was that the
routed middle classes should be treated in the fifties
much as Hitler treated the Jews in the thirties. Few
were allowed to keep even one room in their homes—
these were divided into apartments and made over
sometimes for workers, more usually for Party officials. On often trumped up charges of sabotage,
thousands were exiled from the cities and set to building their own prison camps, thousands who were
luckier were not only dismissed from their jobs but
also denied the right to any other work for which they
were suitable. In the case of stockbrokers this was reasonable enough: to make a middle-aged, middle-class
doctor sweep the streets was less sensible.

Their treatment inevitably caused the remnants of
the middle classes to seal themselves off as tightly as
they could from the life that had come to their
country after 1948. "Let the communists make their
own mess of it" was their attitude as they sat through
the cold and coal-less winters of the early fifties, the
few pieces of antique furniture they had managed to
salvage looking strangely heavy and large in the tiny

flats they had eventually found. They sat gazing at old amateur paintings of their former homes, listening hopefully to the promises of liberation and to the hysterical abuse of their communist masters which, in those days, Radio Free Europe broadcast from Munich, and dreaming that things would change again. Well aware that their children were unlikely ever to be able to go to university, they comforted themselves with the pretense that no education at all was preferable to that given by "these stupid, brutal" Communists. This sort of polarization Kadar was determined to stop. In the future, he declared, the universities would be open to all, the quota system by which many places were reserved for children of the working classes was to be abolished. "I don't think the question of social origin calls for much discussion. Other things quite apart, at least now our teachers will be relieved of filing the pupils according to their origins . . . they will have more energy left to help the worker and peasant youth in their studies." [5] Things have not turned out quite as simply as he hoped, but the intention was good.

Equality of opportunity for the bourgeoisie and the promotion of non-Party experts was hard for Party apparatchiks to stomach. The complaints that came in to the Central Committee from Party organizations all over the country in the early sixties seemed never-ending. It was an "internal difficulty" that Kadar tried to keep out of the public eye: nevertheless the references he made throughout the period to the resistance that new "experts" were encountering, to the difficulties that Party officials were making for them, to the importance of accepting their word and their guidance despite their noncommunism are surprisingly numerous. In February 1965 he quite literally lost his temper with those of his comrades who refused to accept his advice. He addressed Parliament on the economy and his speech was broadcast live. He admitted that people were justified in some of the complaints that they made. But, and now he began to shout, the country's achievements were just as obvious and should be recognized. "We have laid the foundations of a socialist society so firmly that no one will ever be able to destroy them!" Quite apart from that, the economic policy was basically good. "Why did he say that?" he asked rhetorically. "Because it is good!" he shouted once more. "It's the implementation that is bad. Where? Everywhere—at the bottom, in the middle and at the top. Even at the ministerial level it's bad." [6] In many ministries it still is.*

Outside of limited Party reform, it is the new electoral laws under which Zoltan Szep came to Parliament in 1971 that have gained most attention in Hungary itself—not that the Parliament to which they

---

* Kadar and his colleagues have become increasingly concerned in recent years by the composition of and recruitment to the Party. The old Party of Rakosi had disintegrated totally in the face of the Revolution. At the beginning of October, 1956, there had been 900,000 members; by December Kadar's new Party had only 96,000. But he was unable to keep out all the old Stalinists; by 1961 the Party had grown again to 500,000 and few of these new members were joining for the first time. Of all Hungarians 6.5 percent are now in the Party—it has approximately 660,000 members altogether. But what concerns Kadar greatly is the background of those members. Not only is the Party getting older and older as fewer and fewer young people can be induced to join it: the proportion of manual workers in it is also falling—by 4.5 percent between 1966 and 1970. Manual workers now make up only about 38 percent of total membership and, according to the Party's theoretical paper, they and peasants have to be "prodded" into joining. In one sense this is a tribute to Kadar's success in making Party membership no longer an essential prerequisite to success: now that the Party is no longer the only means to advancement (though it is still the surest) many ordinary people would rather be without the tedious discipline that membership involves.

came has much authority. Its activities are limited by
the fact that it meets only three or four times a year
for sessions of two or three days.

Nevertheless, since 1967 there has been an attempt
to return to it some of those legislative functions
which had been purloined over the years by the presidential council, the Party, and the government and
also, in theory at least, to extend its control over the
activities of the state. In the last six years M.P.'s have
actually played a part in shaping, or at least discussing, the annual budget; previously they simply
rubber-stamped it post facto. They have also helped
draft several of the laws which form a vital part of the
New Economic Mechanism: the labor code, the land
law, and the agricultural producer's cooperative law.
But, because of the continued infrequency with which
the whole House assembles, all such improvements
have been confined to the work of the parliamentary
committees, which meet far more often.

Some commentators have argued that the limits on
political democratization in Hungary today are somewhat irrelevant. What matters is the extent of workers' control of industry, democracy within the country's work places.

In fact shop-floor democracy is hardly more extensive in Hungary than it is in any bourgeois society;
top management is appointed by the relevant ministry, lower management by top management, and the
trade unions are allowed no part in the process. In
the cooperative farms, on the other hand, the peasants not only elect their leaders, they also dismiss
them. Official trade union spokesmen understandably find some difficulty in justifying this discrepancy
between the rights of workers and those of peasants.
Nevertheless, Kadar has never considered possible,
indeed he has specifically rejected, any reform which

would involve the creation of the sort of workers' councils which allow Yugoslav workers real authority over their enterprises.[7] The unions have just two weapons against management. They can, in theory, organize a work stoppage (this term is preferred to the term "strike") when and only if labor conditions in their enterprise are intolerable and management has refused to improve them. They are also now entitled to veto any wage settlement or management action which, in the definition of the Labor Code of 1967, "infringes the regulations relating to employment, or which offends against socialist morality." Although it can be exercised solely at the enterprise level, and not higher, this veto can be used not only to attack measures which affect the whole enterprise but also in cases in which an individual worker's interests are threatened.

There is no direct record of how many times the veto has actually been applied, but it seems almost certain that it has been used less frequently than one might have expected, since it was originally heralded as a major breakthrough in industrial relations. After the veto was introduced, the unions were asked privately by the government to exercise their new right only with "great responsibility" when all else had been tried and had failed. They obeyed and, as a result, have sometimes been accused by the press of "excessive timidity" in their recourse to the weapon. At the same time, however, a public veto has often been unnecessary: usually, the first step of a "silent veto," just registering their disapproval with management, is enough to have the management back down. No manager likes to face the unpleasant publicity which a public veto inevitably involves, and will almost always try to appease the unions rather than compel them to take their case outside the factory. In this sense the very existence of the veto provides some control upon mismanagement.

The trade unions are also supposed to have the right to "evaluate" the performance of managers and to advise the ministries on the promotion or dismissal of management personnel. Again this is a right of which they have made disappointingly little use. But in July 1970 they did use Radio Budapest to attack the way in which a minister had dismissed two factory managers.[8] However, the cause of their complaint suggested that it was the self-esteem of union leaders, not the problems of workers, that really worried them.

The radio program was called "What do you think about the decision of the Minister?" and in it Jozsef Bondor, minister of public construction and urban development, was violently attacked for ignoring union rights when he had summarily dismissed two top-ranking managers of the Cement and Lime Works the previous month. No one disputed that the managers' work was totally unsatisfactory or that they should have been sacked. Bondor's explanation that "we need cement not self-criticism" was accepted, even approved. What angered the union was that the minister had not consulted it before this decision was announced.

Worse still, the union representative had actually been humiliated by the minister because he was present when the managers were carpeted, yet had no previous inkling as to what would happen. This, said union officials on the radio, was a major violation of the internal democracy of the enterprise and of the rights of the unions.

It was an outspoken attack on the minister, but nothing came of it and at the next session of the assembly, the union leader, Sandor Gaspar, made no mention of the matter. Incomplete as democratic procedures are in the state and legislative processes of the country, nonexistent as they are in the factories and other public enterprises, the people's guarantee that life will continue to improve necessarily lies not in their own participation in any electoral process but in the leadership of the Party and, most specifically, in Kadar himself. At the Tenth Party Congress in 1970 Bela Bisku, Kadar's number two, declared, "it would be wrong to consider the strengthening of Party democracy as only an internal problem of the Party. In fact, of course, it is the most vital step toward democracy throughout the country." Even so, inner-Party democracy is still far from complete: there has been nothing even remotely like the decentralization of party procedures that Dubcek attempted in 1968. The personality of the leader, imposed from above, is still all-important to the character of the Party.

Kadar has not sought arbitrary personalized power of the sort that was so essential to Rakosi but has allowed the development of collegial leadership. Indeed, the very fact that during the early years of his rule he was so subject to pressures from his Stalinist enemies is a testimony to the comparative openness of his government; no such situation could have developed when Rakosi was supreme—until, that is, Khrushchev showed him in 1953 that a man who could rightly claim to be "Stalin's first disciple" would get little change out of him, Nikita Khrushchev. The most important of all the changes that this involves is in the part played by the police and the courts in the pursuit of political ends.

Six

Feeling well, like a human being, does not begin
with having a large portion of casserole steak put
on one's table. What is decisive is that one is not
humiliated by anyone and can live and work as
one pleases.

J. Kadar
March 19, 1967

His years in prison did not turn Kadar completely
away from the use of political trials and imprisonment as instruments of government. After the Revolution, some twenty thousand freedom fighters were
arrested and at least two thousand of them are
thought to have been executed, quite apart from the
unknown number (perhaps fifty thousand) whom the
Soviets deported to the U.S.S.R.

Nonetheless, he has never used imprisonment and
terror as political weapons in the same personal or indiscriminate way as did Rakosi. In 1961 he declared,
"Seven or eight years ago everyone in Hungary was
suspected and spied upon. One chose a man by
chance and told him 'You are suspect; you are flirting
with the imperialists!' At first the man was afraid.
Then he spent his days trembling. The former leaders of the Party pushed men towards our enemies to
such a degree that at the end certain of them in fact
did find themselves in enemy ranks. Nevertheless we

do not wish to persecute the officials who were sectarians or revisionists in the past." [1]

As Ferenc Fejto, a brilliant exile journalist, points out, this speech gives the impression "not of a man who is just talking but of one who evokes his own experiences, who has stupidly, uselessly suffered and does not want atrocious things to be revived." [2]

In July 1956 General Mihaly Farkas, Rakosi's minister of defense, who had conspired to have Kadar imprisoned, was expelled from the Party for "breaches of socialist legality" and on April 25, 1957, the press announced that he had been sentenced to sixteen years imprisonment. On December 28, 1956, Radio Kossuth had published the fact that his son had been jailed but made no mention of the sentence. There are unconfirmed reports that they were both treated unusually well in the Gyujto jail in Budapest, sharing a comfortable cell equipped with radio and telephone and allowed to receive both letters and visits from their family. Whether that is true or not, they were definitely not tortured and they were both amnestied in 1960 and given jobs in Budapest publishing firms. The father, Mihaly, died on December 5, 1965; his son still has his own job. His only problem is that his colleagues refuse to have him in the office; he therefore draws a salary and sits at home doing nothing. By any standards, and certainly by those of Eastern Europe, the punishment accorded both of them was remarkably mild. It is a tribute to Kadar's disinterest in the concept of revenge.

Thanks largely to Kadar, the term "socialist legality" no longer has a completely mocking, hollow ring about it today. But it is still subject to political restraints. The judicial system is that established in 1949; it has never been completely overhauled and there is still no habeas corpus. Most changes in the way in which justice is administered have been political rather than statutory. Since Kadar considers that "antagonistic class relationships" no longer exist in Hungary, the political police are now encouraged to perform a more limited role than that which they played in the fifties "to impose the dictatorship of the proletariat." But they still exist; they have simply been placed under closer Party supervision than before—a change which offers no *guarantee* of their continued observance of the law.

Nevertheless, a partial reform of the criminal code in 1961 did abolish some of the more unattractive aspects of previous laws. From now on it was no longer a legal duty to report the crime of a relation to the police, and anyone caught trying to escape across the border illegally would be charged only with an offense "againt the good order of state administration" not with a "crime against state security." Torture was officially banned and anyone who used it to extract information could be sent to prison for up to five years. There was a full-scale purge of those policemen and officials in the Ministry of the Interior who had previously practiced or condoned it, the system of internal exile without trial was abolished, and as a result the number of forced labor camps was reduced.[3]

Despite these important reforms, Kadar was less than truthful when he used the occasion of U Thant's visit to Hungary in 1963 to declare enthusiastically, "No-one is actually imprisoned today because of political offences." [4] Perhaps he was carried away by pleasure at the Secretary-General's visit which he saw as a seal of international approval upon his government, for at that time there were still many political prisoners in Hungary. So there are today, as even the official statistics demonstrate; almost every year the figures are greeted with self-congratulatory articles and speeches praising the "low" incidence of political crimes and trials.

In fact, ever since 1956 the number of convictions on "political" offenses has acted as a barometer of the political climate in Hungary. Kadar has used the arrest of such "criminals"—who are usually guilty only of abuse of the Soviet Union or of the Party—as a means of appeasing his more dogmatist rivals within the leadership. At any time when he feels more threatened from the Left, he allows the police greater freedom of arrest. It is in this sense that it is meaningless to speak of socialist legality in absolute terms; it is still a political matter.

In 1963 almost all those imprisoned after the Revolution were amnestied, and that year, according to the Procurator General, only 0.3 percent of all those brought to trial were charged with antistate activities. At the end of 1964, however, the authorities suddenly began to take a stricter line and the number of arrests increased.

There is every reason to believe that this new harshness was directly related to the fall of Khrushchev, after which Kadar's own position became, for a time, somewhat tenuous. His Stalinist enemies in the Party made one more attempt to unseat him; two years later he declared that they had eagerly awaited a new leadership which would pursue "a genuine militant stronghand policy." [5] But once more he outmaneuvered them and stole their clothes; opportunistically, he simply allowed the police and courts to act more strictly than in recent years against those who were foolish enough to express their disaffection with the regime.

As a result, in February 1966 the International Commission of Jurists was moved to report on the growing number of trials for antistate activity in Hungary. It concluded: "It is alarming that the Hungarian authorities seem to revert once again to holding in camera trials in which the articles of the Criminal Code are interpreted according to the directives of a 'firm line' of Party policy, a procedure which, from the experience of the past, has always had to be 'corrected' and denounced later as a violation of socialist legality." [6]

As if in response to such criticism, later that year the deputy chief public prosecutor, Karoly Csendes, warned in the Party paper *Nepszabadsag* that there were still attempts to interfere with the process of justice. "We cannot yet say that the law is fully observed. True, there are no framed trials and none can be staged; nevertheless, attempts at exerting influence still sometimes occur when the leader of a local state body or an enterprise leader tries to interfere in the judging of a case." He also stated that such instances, while incomparable with the violations of the fifties, nevertheless harmed the socialist cause and should be stamped upon. [7]

Over recent years, the proportion of "political" crimes has remained fairly constant at about 0.5 percent of the annual total, but the actual number of such offenses fell between 1967 and 1970 from 180 to 55 a year. This reduction could mean two things. First that the police are now less active than they were in the mid-sixties, which is healthy, and second that ordinary people are now more careful about what they say and do in public, which is not.

The Ministry of Justice publishes no detailed breakdown of the figures and the Hungarian press is probably justified in its claim that most political prisoners are short-term offenders serving a few weeks for drunk and disorderly abuse of the state or the

Party or the Soviet Union. Nevertheless, in June 1971 Amnesty International adopted fifty Hungarians as "prisoners of conscience" and there are estimates that about one-third of all political prisoners are religious offenders: it is still not infrequent to read of the arrest of village priests on subversion charges. Many of the others who are arrested for incitement are apparently under twenty-five and some of them belong to left-wing groups. In other words, they are probably student Trotskyites (before 1969 they tended to be more Maoist) who have somehow registered their protest against what they regard as the petit bourgeois values of Kadarization.[8]

Much of police and court procedure has been reviewed since 1968, and in 1972 there was another liberalizing reform of the penal code.* The chief prosecutor, the president of the Supreme Court, and the minister of justice now have to submit regular reports to Parliament, and in April 1968 the chief prosecutor himself admitted to the House that the police sometimes did not make enough efforts to establish a man's innocence before declaring him guilty. Probably the most interesting development was the review of the entire work of the Ministry of the Interior, undertaken by the November 1969 plenum of the Central Committee.

It was on this occasion that Andras Benkii, then minister of the interior, declared that in the future those who were guilty of ideological errors should be dealt with not by the police but by the educative influ-

---

* There is still capital punishment for murder, but in 1971 a new decree abolished the death penalty for crimes against "social property." It had never been enforced by Kadar and was thought a meaningless deterrent. To replace it, life imprisonment, meaning imprisonment for life, was introduced. Till then this had been considered incompatible with the principle of socialist education and "life" could never mean more than twenty years.

ence of Marxist-Leninist ideology itself. This could, of course, sound rather sinister; did he mean the use of mental asylums and other "educative" processes? It seems not: he meant simply that persuasion and example were far more effective at winning loyalty to socialism than was coercion. He intended to complain that there were still some people in authority who constantly demanded that his ministry should act as Ministry of Thought or Truth and who expected it to intervene in all political, cultural, and even economic problems. Well, it would not do so.

He would see to it that his staff was retrained to tell the difference between "pardonable ideological political errors and outright political crimes." He asked that the new rights and duties of the Ministry of the Interior be laid down by decree. In the future the ministry would have the strictest regard for socialist legality and would do its best to dispel the unfortunate image which still lingered from the fifties in the minds of many citizens.[9]

Old fears, however, do die hard and some people still worry that they are or might become the objects of surveillance. One does not discuss politics loudly in a café; if one listens to the BBC or to Radio Free Europe at home, it is with the volume turned down so that the neighbors cannot hear through the thin walls of the cheap flats that the Party put up in the fifties, and people are still careful about what they write in letters to friends abroad. Hungarians still feel that they live in a police state, and so, of course, they do. But *Nepszabadsag*, the Party paper, not infrequently has little parables to persuade them how times have really changed. In one, for example, it told the story of the director of an enterprise who had a disagreement with the head of a department. Instead of bringing the matter to the attention of the Party, he "began to jot down notes" about every conceivable aspect of his subordinate's personal and official life. To this end he was "unfortunately" helped by many informants in the factory. But when the Party organization heard of this disgraceful action, the director and his colleague were both summoned and the director was forced "to rip up this 'black' dossier with his own hands, in the presence of all concerned." *Nepszabadsag* declared that "anyone who is even superficially familiar with the policy of our Party knows very well that no one can compile such a dossier, whether black, white or whatever, on anyone. We condemn this vile form of 'data collection.' . . . Anyone may look at his own cadre file in the personnel department. There is nothing in it which has been entered on the basis of secrets, rumours or reports." [10]

There was some overall justification for Kadar's claim, at the Tenth Party Congress in 1970, that "the oppressive power of the State is gradually decreasing." But it is too gradual for some and it is not by any means an irreversible process. The roots of Stalinism may have been buried deep in Hungary, but they have not been burned out. Perhaps the limits to the process of de-Stalinization are best shown by an examination of what has happened to Laszlo Rajk since 1956.

Khrushchev's secret speech in February 1956 compelled Rakosi to review the Rajk case and in March he declared stiltedly and with, one can imagine, some trepidation: "It has been found that the Rajk trial originated in a provocation. That is why the Supreme Court, on the basis of a Party resolution of June 1955, has pronounced the rehabilitation of Laszlo Rajk and other comrades."

But he could not dare to take the blame on himself, and hoping that his earlier boasts to have unmasked the Rajk gang single-handed would be conveniently forgotten, he announced that the truth about the Rajk trial had come to light "after exposing the activities of the imperialist agent, Beria, and those of the Gabor Peter gang in Hungary." [11]

Rakosi's attempt to squirm out of responsibility for staging the charade was not well received. Throughout the early, passionate summer of 1956, demands were made by writers, journalists, and even Party militants that the full truth about the affair should be revealed. In June Julia Rajk, whose spirit had not been broken by her six years in prison, publicly demanded the unqualified rehabilitation and reburial of her husband. Her plea was taken up by the Party press. Hurriedly the Party tried to locate Rajk's remains and they were eventually found by one of the men who had buried them, in a sandy forest near the baroque castle of Godollo, outside Budapest. They could be identified only with the help of his old dentist.

On October 6 Rajk was reburied, with the honor that millions of Hungarians believed he deserved, in the Kerepes cemetery, burial ground of Hungarian heroes since 1840. At least one hundred fifty thousand people (some say it was twice as many as that) stood there in total silence. Not a policeman was to be seen; there was not a single incident.

In many ways the funeral resembled the quiet dignity in which Jan Palach, student martyr, was buried in Prague thirteen years later. Occasions of that sort long retain their political power and significance in Eastern Europe. Just as Palach's death reunited, for a short time, the Czechoslovak people against their

Soviet occupiers, so did Rajk's funeral set a mood of
national unity and determination which was to break
into Revolution just seventeen days later. One Communist journalist was moved to recall that way back in
the mid-1920s Rajk had written, with uncanny fore-
boding: "The storm silences. This is the storm of the
people, the storm in which I became a martyr without
name. But my bones remained alive and my people
greet me from the pillars made of marble."
But for several years after the Revolution, little or
nothing more was said publicly about Rajk. While
Kadar struggled against both the intrigues of the Stalinists within the Party and the hatred of the people
without, the Rajk affair was conveniently shelved.
Mrs. Rajk and her son, after all, were deported to
Rumania after the Revolution along with Imre Nagy,
and there was no one else with either the inclination
or the authority to continue to press an investigation
into the affair. Rumors that Julia Rajk had been executed, however, were quite untrue, and she and Kadar's godson returned to Budapest in October 1958.
In 1962, when Kadar was pursuing more vigorously his policy of appeasing the people, the
Central Committee passed a resolution on the illegal
trials of the fifties. This made no mention of Rajk by
name, but it declared *inter alia:*

> Rakosi, to secure his personal power, invented
> the slanders that the leaders and members of the
> workers' movement who lived here in Hungary
> before the liberation were agents of the Horthyist
> political police, and those who fought in the
> brother parties of the capitalist countries or in the
> Spanish civil war became agents of the imperialist
> intelligence organisation, again for the purpose of
> securing his personal power. In claiming this, he

slandered the entire Hungarian revolutionary workers' movement and created an atmosphere of general suspicion in the Party.[12]

Rakosi and Gero were now expelled from the Party, homage was paid to Rajk by *Nepszabadsag* on the fifty-fifth anniversary of his birth in 1964, and his heroic record was recalled. At the same time a street and a school in Leningrad were renamed after Bela Kun, till now still in official disgrace. In 1966, after two years in which the pace of liberalization, such as it was, slowed to a halt, Sandor Nogradi was allowed to publish his book on the Rakosi regime.

Although Nogradi's apologia for his own crimes was inept and dishonest, the book went further than anything before it in answering the questions that the Revolution had been designed, but had failed, to settle, once and for all. Then in 1969, after the re-naming of Pannonia Street for Laszlo Rajk, came the attempt by Aladar Mod and Julia Rajk to establish the truth a little more clearly, to explain slightly more fully the Stalinist mentality.

Neither article nor letter is conclusive. Neither can explain why Rajk chose to confess—perhaps that will never be fully revealed, and certainly it is no fault of either writer that those days in the prison cell are still unexamined. But both also fail to give a really adequate explanation of how it was that the monstrous deception should have been so uncritically accepted by almost everyone. Julia Rajk is quite correct to say that Rajk's confession itself is not reason enough: "Could it have been unquestioning faith?" she asks. "To some extent, but it is inadequate for an explanation. Was it due to the deception of the Party membership and the unsuspecting and honest mass of the people? These, too, played a role. Or was it the increasing atmosphere of terror? That, too, had an effect on many people."

Perhaps another clue to the problem is provided unconsciously by Mod when he admits that if any Hungarians disbelieved the accusations then they were Social Democrats and other non-Marxists. He quotes from a study by Ferenc Fejto, a prewar friend and comrade of Rajk whom Mod himself calls "the most outstanding intellectual in the field of literary history and philosophy." After 1932 Fejto, unlike Rajk, rejected Marxism and turned to social democracy. In 1949 he wrote, in the West, a study of the Rajk trial, in which he dismissed it as an obvious charade. Mod read this study in 1956; it was, he says, "one of the most bitter experiences of my life. . . . I had to face the fact that, on the basis of the material published in the papers on the trial, and of Rajk's communism and his character, Fejto saw clearly even then that the whole trial was a fake."

Consequently Mod was forced to ask himself, who was right—Fejto, Rajk, or he himself? As a communist, it is a question he does not really dare to answer properly: "Undoubtedly Fejto gave a correct judgment on the trial itself, but this by no means proves the correctness of his political attitude as a whole."

But this is an argument that he is unable to support intellectually. In 1969 Mod was finally forced to admit the corruption of Stalin (which Fejto had seen as early as the mid-thirties) and the dogmatic errors of prewar Hungarian communism. Nevertheless, Mod claimed, "I have no doubt whatsoever that we were right from the point of view of realistic historical progress." And why? Because the Communist movement became "ideologically and practically the leading force in democratic and independent Hungary, while Rajk, as a fighter of the Communist movement, became a constituent part of the establishment of the new Hungary and of the transformation of the country into a socialist nation. On the other hand Fejto—as a sceptical critic of the Soviet and Hungarian people's democratic line—has acquired only the position of a free critic of the Soviet Union and Communism."

The weakness of these arguments, which are much the same as Kadar himself employs, are obvious enough. Fejto did not wish for any part in the building of the sort of world that Hungary became after 1945—indeed he made his disgust with Stalin very clear by leaving his country. Nor can Mod see, or admit, that the prewar Hungarian Communist party itself had been a total failure, that in 1945 it had less support among its people than almost any other Central European Communist party, and that it would never have been able to transform Hungary into a socialist nation without the threatening support of the Soviet Union.

In fact when Mod says that he has "no doubt whatsoever" as to the historical correctness of their cause, he is simply expressing an article of faith. It was faith, not reason, that caused the mass (even joyous?) acceptance of the Rajk trial by Party members. It was faith that sent Kadar to corrupt his friend. Mod and his comrades believed the lies then because they had been taught never to question their leadership. And still today, after such de-Stalinization as has taken place, he is reduced to declaring that Fejto's intellectual honesty has prevented him from "taking part in any respect in the forming of a new world." There is no reason to believe that Mr. Fejto, who is now a distinguished journalist in Paris, has ever regretted that particular failure on his part.

The 1969 article by Aladar Mod and the reply to it by Julia Rajk are together the fullest explanation that the Hungarian people have yet been given of the Rajk tragedy. Today Kadar himself rarely if ever mentions his old friend. Julia Rajk, who lives comfortably with her student son, Laszlo, in a prewar tenement just behind the street renamed after her husband, wants to write a book about him but is constrained by both lack of information and by the exigencies of the present political situation in Hungary. For Kadar has allowed no such examination of the political trials as that which Dubcek commissioned in Czechoslovakia in 1968.

But that study—the *Piller Report*—was suppressed after the invasion. For very obvious reasons. It is the most comprehensive indictment of Stalinism ever to come out of Eastern Europe. It is a harrowing and horrifying account of how the Russians stage-managed the whole saga of the trials; it is a study which names all those, Soviet and Czechoslovak, who played a part in the police or judiciary at that time and condemns roundly the political leaders who either endorsed or actively aided the tragedy.

Such a report was possible for the Czechoslovak Communist party to make before the Soviet-led invasion only because Dubcek's Czechoslovakia was truly revolutionary (counterrevolutionary in Soviet terms). In the belief that socialist society could become really humane and acceptable to its peoples only by the total transformation of all its institutions and the comprehensive confession of all its sins, Dubcek tried to make a complete break with the Party's past—first in terms of methods and then later in terms also of personnel.

Nothing like that has happened in Hungary. True, the Communist party that Kadar built after the Revolution was new and many of the old Rakosiites were barred from it. But reform has been Kadar's aim, not revolution. And reform by the Soviet grace. Because of Soviet participation then and Soviet sensibilities now, to publish the truth about the Rajk trial would be both politically and diplomatically unthinkable in Hungary today, whether or not Kadar visited Rajk alone in his cell.

The Rajk case and its only partial explanation are not public issues in Hungary today. Nor are the crimes of Stalinism in general. Whether this indifference is bred of political apathy or of contentment is harder to say.

Fewer Hungarians than at any time since the war now seem to believe that their neighbor may be a police informer and fewer still are concerned lest their friends or relations might betray them. They are, however, concerned lest this should change. Because the knives which Rakosi used to slice his salami hang still on the Party wall, a little rusty perhaps, but just in need of some sharpening, because many of their leaders, and especially Kadar himself, are men compromised by their involvement in the trials, because the quality of Hungarian life still depends so completely on the requirements of the Kremlin, precisely because Kadar (unlike Dubcek) has chosen reform not revolution and because reform (unlike revolution) is reversible, many Hungarians are unconfident for the future. Arrests are still made on political grounds. That is to say, people are arrested not only for political or so-called political offenses, but also for offenses which may at one moment be deemed political, at other moments not, depending on the mood, security, or whatever of the government. This makes life a little unpredictable, and there is, unfortunately, no reason to suppose that the number of arrests will not continue to fluctuate according to the fortunes of East European and Soviet politics.

People's uncertainty will remain. Laszlo Rajk's hope to be greeted from pillars of marble has not yet been fulfilled: in Hungary the pillars of justice are still cardboard. It may be true, as Julia Rajk declares, that the fact that her husband played his compulsory role out to the end and why he did so is no longer of importance. What is important is that twenty-four years later the man who was Minister of the Interior at the time of Rajk's death and who apparently coached him in that role (or at the very least played a strange, unspecified supporting part in the charade) is ruler of Hungary and a Hungary through which the roots of Stalinism still twist. What is important is that, should the Kremlin require it, Kadar could, for the sake of the Party in the 1970s, demand of others what, for the sake of the Party in 1949, he demanded of his friend Laszlo Rajk.

Seven

Janos Kressinger, Kadar's father, was one of the rich peasants whose social influence in the countryside propped up the semifeudal economy of Hungary which Admiral Miklos Horthy inherited in 1919 and did so little over the next twenty years to change.

The semifeudal pattern of Hungarian society did not end in 1945 with the defeat of the Nazis and the destruction of the Horthy state. It was perpetuated by Stalinism. That, at any rate, is the opinion of one of the most brilliant of contemporary Hungarian economists, Tibor Liska.

The *enfant terrible* of his profession, Liska, energetic, jovial, and original, finds that whatever his colleagues say to him in private, they are not always prepared to agree in public with his more colorful assertions. But the equation of feudalism and Stalinism is still one that he insists on making, arguing that "the essential point of feudal ownership is that economic power is not a commodity to be exchanged according to the free choice of people with equal rights, but a grace bestowed from above that can be obtained only by humble and loyal service to the distributors." And that, he maintains, is just as true of the small class of petty officials who dominated economic life in the fifties as it was of the small class of aristocrats and landlords who dominated it in the twenties and thirties, as they had for centuries past.

Liska's theories are based on the belief that all politicians, socialist or bourgeois, overemphasize the political aspects of democracy at the expense of its vital economic content. His original study of a Stalinist economy and the need to reform, or rather, to replace it, was written in 1960 but it was considered too heretical to be published until 1963. Even then his ideas were utterly revisionist. Now the opinions he then expressed have become commonplace in Hungary and the most orthodox economists will admit, privately, that an effect and perhaps even an aim of the Stalinist economy was to exploit the worker and deny him all economic and hence political power. But today Liska himself is once more being regarded askance as a crazy revisionist, as he now rushes ahead with new schemes for making all citizens of a socialist country genuine shareholders in the national wealth by issuing them bonds in a nationwide stock exchange.

Following the feudal analogy through, the New Economic Mechanism is designed to transfer economic power from the bureaucracy into the hands, if not of the people, at least of the managers; away from clerks to technocrats. It is based on the belief that total central planning is not, after all, the best way of achieving favorable economic results, that political dogmas conceived in Budapest are not always good criteria against which to judge the quality and quantity of the output of a show factory in the town of Miskolc. It assumes that the manager of an enterprise knows best what and how his enterprise should produce and, in many cases, the price the market can stand for his product. It constitutes an almost complete rejection of the economic philosophy of Stalinism.

In 1963 the economist Gyorgy Ranki was allowed to publish a book which for the first time in Hungary analyzed the economic and hence the political distortions of the Rakosi era from a Marxist but also a non-Party point of view. He described how the initial policy of a gradual transition to socialism was abandoned after 1948 and replaced by "war hysteria, by the mechanical application of Soviet economic practices, and by the theory of the unconditional sharpening of the class struggle." At the same time as terror and repression caused the people to lose more and more faith in the Party (they had had little enough to start with), so the principles of centralization and bureaucracy became aims in themselves. Worse still, rises in living standards were deliberately suppressed in order to hasten the day when Hungary would truly be a miniature U.S.S.R.[1] Never has the rule of the industrial-military complex been more powerful than in Eastern Europe at the turn of the fifties.

Industrialization itself provided the logic for setting up a huge and sprawling Party apparat which now stretched its demanding tentacles into every crevice of the nation's life. For forced industrialization could be achieved only by compulsory directives issued from above, according to the unquestionable dogma of an all-embracing national plan. And that could be done only by host upon host of officials, a great new bureaucracy which would, in time (and which did, in fact, very soon), generate its own life force, spawn its own raison d'être and reproduce itself ad infinitum. It worked for a time, but the process carried within itself the promise of its own inevitable destruction. The machine certainly provided the logic for its own existence and created a false impression of *perpetuum mobile,* but still today it is the clogging, immobile apparat which constitutes the main block to efficiency and to reform in Eastern Europe.

Whatever the merits of attempting the revolutionary transformation of the economy, few Hungarian economists today consider that the means sel cted in the late forties and the early fifties to achieve it were correct. Economic policy was totally corrupted by false ideological commitments. First of all, the process of industrialization was far too rushed; it was quite absurd to think that it could be carried out in the course of one five year plan. But this is what it was intended to do. For as Erno Gero, then the country's economic overlord, declared in 1950, "The main task of the Five Year Plan is to provide for laying the foundations of socialism in every field of the Hungarian economy, both in the towns and villages, in essence to ensure the victory of the socialist economic order in the whole of the Hungarian national economy." [2]

A child of the petit bourgeois (he did not change his family name, Zinger, till 1945), Gero was an eager follower of Bela Kun in 1919. When the Revolution was crushed he sensibly exiled himself and began to study the more elementary principles of Bolshevik economic theory. Traveling from Vienna to Prague to Moscow, he developed a reputation among his fellow socialist exiles as an immensely hard worker, who gave the most studious if somewhat uninspired application to detail.

During Stalin's great purges he was sent from Moscow to Spain to watch carefully over the communist contingents in the International Brigade and to audit the men who, even here, were to be sacrificed to Stalin's fantastic whims. He must have done the job well enough, for he was not purged himself and was able to spend the war in the Hotel Lux with Matyas Rakosi, Imre Nagy, Mihaly Farkas, and the other Moscow-based Hungarian Communists, working out the plans for the eventual transformation of their country.

On his return home in 1945 he worked very hard (far harder than many of his colleagues) and was not flamboyant. He was reasonable looking; with iron gray cropped hair, dark eyebrows, and a bland, open face—he resembled a rather superior hairdresser in a very superior men's salon. Throughout 1945 and 1946 he tried assiduously and finally successfully to control Hungary's raging inflation and to find the money for the rebuilding of Budapest. It was not until after 1948, when he became the country's economic czar, that his limitations as an economist became a little more obvious. Such successes as he had had before were due only to industry, not to imagination, intelligence, or understanding, and now industry alone was no longer enough.

Still, his methods did work for a time—at a cost. Collectivization drove the peasants off the land into factories hastily built in and around nonexistent towns.* Little money was spent on the infrastructure and as a result living conditions there were execrable, but the economy grew—by a staggering 13.8 percent per annum in the first half of the fifties. With it went a policy of full employment, which all the socialist countries pursue and which means in effect overemployment, which in turn too often involves the un-

---

* In 1950 only 19 percent of the labor force was employed in industry; by 1967 it was 32 percent—for the first time more than in agriculture.

dervaluing and therefore the exploitation of labor. This itself demands a neglect of technological progress—with a cheap and available labor force, who needs technological development? So limitless was the supply of cheap labor in those early years as the peasants first rushed and then were dragged off the fields that almost half of all industrial workers were employed not on the main production line but in secondary activities, such as carrying materials from one part of their factory to another. Conveyor belts were of course quite unnecessary luxuries.[3]

As a result, the quantity of Hungarian industrial production grew enormously fast but because of the stagnation of technology its quality did not. As the economic historian Ivan Berend declared: "The great production volume appears sometimes in the form of little useable and fast deteriorating products." [4] Productivity rose scarcely at all in the early fifties—it was just the huge input of new labor that made for the rise in production. Although Hungary was, in 1970, seventh in the world table for industrial employment per thousand inhabitants, it was only twenty-second with regard to per capita value added. This is partly explained by the inefficiency of investment policy in the fifties; there was sometimes a gap of two to three years between the making and completion of an investment decision—by the time the new plant was constructed it was often technically obsolescent.

In any case the investment program of the country was almost totally unrelated to its needs. And no wonder, for in 1951 the leadership formally advised that "investments are at all times to be governed by political considerations; economic index numbers may play only a secondary role." [5] With all the contradictions that such economic management involved, the government found that its more ambitious programs could be fulfilled only if the needs and demands of the people themselves were completely disregarded. Improvement of living conditions and rises in the standard of living were practically taken off the agenda altogether; repeated threats that "we are consuming our future" served as the excuse for ever cutting back the percentage of consumption and raising that of investment in the National Plan. For years after 1950 there was absolutely no increase in real income per head; indeed its constant fall was obvious to all those workers and their wives who tried unsuccessfully to buy the goods—coal, tea, butter, sugar, fruit—that they needed. Rarely were they to be had.[6]

This exploitation of the working classes and, by extension, of all others lies at the root of the social problems of Hungary and of many other Eastern European countries today. Stalinist economics merely transformed them from labor-intensive agricultural-industrial societies into labor-intensive industrial-agricultural societies in which the illusion of progress was sustained by the pace of industrialization. But by the end of the fifties, because of relaxation in the speed of Sovietization, the industrial market was no longer growing as fast as it had; new markets had to be found.

For societies such as Hungary there is a choice of only two such markets today. To counter the slowdown of industrial development either the military side of the military-industrial complex can be expanded, or the consumer can be wooed and bought. Either the state can continue to feed the economy and maintain full employment from a deficit budget, concentrating on the creation of further military defenses to shore up the system from otherwise increasingly unlikely attack, or it can allow the economy to develop its own free market momentum in which the demands of the consumer are gradually allowed a greater role in the share and hence the direction of society. Because of the need to appease the people (rather than because of the process of détente, which itself follows from the need for that appeasement), the Hungarian government has, like most of its allies, chosen butter not guns. In Hungary's case the choice inevitably follows from the 1956 Revolution, but it was not until 1964 that Kadar was actually able to begin to sketch the changes and it was only in 1968 that they were introduced.

Ever since the death of Stalin, attempts had been made to rebuild the Hungarian economic system. They always failed because of the limits that political conditions put upon their architects. True, Imre Nagy's New Course of 1953 was characterized first by efforts at economic rather than political reform, but its most prominent feature was chaos: in 1953, the economic plan was modified 225 times—as good a testimony as any to the indecisiveness and inability of that well-intentioned regime to forswear consistently the methods of its predecessor.

Similarly, the first reform initiatives of the Kadar government were in economics. In December 1956 Kadar set up a commission of some two hundred economists under the guidance of Istvan Varga, once a member of the Smallholders party, to advise on the "revision of the economic mechanism." The commission reported twelve months later and that report consisted of a cautious but fairly detailed indictment of almost the entire structure of the Hungarian economy as it had developed over the past eleven years. It recommended considerable decentralization and far greater reliance on indirect methods of economic control and administration than ever before. Although Kadar was at first anxious to accept its pro-

posals, by mid-1958 the international situation had
changed so much for the worse and the pressures
upon him from his dogmatic colleagues had so intensified that the report had to be labeled "revisionist"
and shelved.[7]

The years from 1958 to 1964 were characterized by
the same uncertainties and fluctuations in the economy as in every other area of Hungarian life. There
were partial attempts at establishing a more rational
price system in 1959, but they dealt only with producer and not retail prices. Nineteen sixty and 1961
saw the recollectivization of agriculture, at first with
a degree of brutality reminiscent of the first collectivization in 1949. Investment decision-making, the
fixing of wages, the structure of production, and
the pattern of retail prices—all these crucial regula-
tors remained in the hands of the central bureaucracy. The idea of the market was still a dangerous
heresy.

Partial economic reform failed totally to galvanize
the Hungarian economy simply and obviously because the old framework was not demolished: the
new components just did not fit into it properly.
True, enterprises were no longer told from whom
they should buy their materials and precisely to
whom they must deliver their finished products, but
they were still offered no incentives to seek out new
and better markets, no encouragement even to improve the quality of their goods. The concept of socialist competition was still only a concept. Quality
norms were certainly introduced, but they had little
effect because managers and workers continued to be
rewarded on a quantitative basis. And even that incentive was limited: wages and bonuses did not rise in
direct proportion to production over the norm, but
always much more slowly.

Frequent cartoons and jokes in the press testified to the stagnation of the economy, the lack of interesting work and the incompetence of management. Three workers playing cards at a building site: "As soon as the reforms start operating we'll finish the game." A television crew in a factory causes enormous industry on the part of the workers: "Why is everyone working so hard?" "Because they think they're going to be on the box." Two men stand in the door of an office where all the clerks are asleep: "It's not that people are indolent here, it's just that they've been forbidden to do their private work during office hours." A factory director out shooting with new colleagues misses a rabbit: "The new director's not a very good shot, is he?" "Well, he's only had the job three weeks."

It was in 1964 that Rezso Nyers, Kadar's principal adviser on economic affairs, began to suggest publicly the possibility, indeed the necessity, of a total overhaul of the economic system, arguing that such was now the pace of technological development in the West that even just to maintain its present place in the world economy Hungary had to redesign its system of controls. That December the Central Committee authorized a new commission, similar to the Varga Commission, to consider where total reform was necessary. The following November the main recommendations of its report were accepted in principle and Nyers was instructed by the Central Committee to work out the directives of the new economic concepts. They were formally approved in May 1965.

One of the most intelligent and reliable of Kadar's colleagues, Nyers was born of working-class parents in Budapest in 1923. He became a printer and worked in the Social Democratic party till its enforced merger with the Communists in 1948. After a variety of minor Party and administrative posts in the early fifties (he escaped being purged or imprisoned), he joined Kadar as soon as the latter set up his Revolutionary Worker-Peasant Government on November 4, 1956, and was made chairman of the new Commission of Public Supply. This body replaced the Ministry of Food, which he had run before the Revolution. Minister of Finance between 1960 and 1962, he has since become the Party's main economic adviser. He is a technocrat through and through, straightforward, serious, honest, and intelligent.

To Nyers, as to Kadar, economic reform is really political. It is a device to encourage the economy to function more efficiently and thereby alleviate public discontent. Since 1963 he has argued that there are four main interrelated problems on which the Party should concentrate its attention: how to increase national income faster, how to improve the balance of payments with the West, how to raise the standard of living, and how to produce better enterprise management.

One of the bases of Nyers' economic philosophy is that none of the laws of a socialist economy is eternal and that to live and remain effective Marxist thought must never be allowed to ossify into dogma. What was suitable for the Hungarian economy in the early fifties (forced industrialization at that pace certainly was not) is almost inevitably unsuitable in the mid-sixties or early seventies. Like Tibor Liska, he believes that it was a disaster to "raise administrative pricing to the rank of a socialist theory" when it was never more than a perhaps unavoidable mistake. He believes it high time that socialist societies dropped the claim to omniscient infallibility.

His reform, the New Economic Mechanism, came into operation on January 1, 1968. Its principal distinguishing feature is, as Nyers says, that it gives "the

market an active role, on the basis of socialist ownership of the means of production." To those skeptics
who considered any marriage of socialist ownership
and market forces unholy or impossible, Nyers replied that the capitalist and the Marxist use of the
market are quite different. Most importantly, he declared in 1968, labor could never become a commodity in Hungary. Unfortunately he was to be proved
wrong; so successful was the encouragement of market forces and so short the supply of labor that by the
end of 1970 Hungarian labor had indeed become a
commodity.

This is partly because, in manufacturing industry at
least, labor is still grossly undervalued in Hungary
today. The more adventurous of Hungarian economists argue that the "consumerization" of the economy will be incomplete until all men and women are
paid their worth. But this is difficult for the Hungarian regime to achieve. If it increases wages, it increases
buying power, but as industry is not yet fully geared
to the consumer market, this has an immediate infla-
tionary effect in which the only solution is to rush to
imports. The other way of raising the price of labor is
not to increase wages but to reduce working hours.
This is happening all over Eastern Europe at the moment and only partly for humanistic reasons; it is certainly good politics to give the workers Saturday off,
but it is primarily a device to raise the cost of labor
without increasing its buying power.

The regime's present theory is that it is the market
which should regulate the supply and demand of individual products, while the plan should just determine the basic patterns of the economy such as the
relation of consumption to investment. Nyers maintains that "it is not only the plan that influences the
market by regulating it in accordance with the na-

tional objectives—the market, the opinions of society, of the consumers, also influence the national plan." [8] In other words, no longer is the concept of a national plan sacrosanct and no longer should the plan fix obligatory individual targets and index figures.

This change alone is the beginning of a fairly radical political as well as economic adventure; if the output of an individual enterprise is not to be centrally planned, then the managers themselves are responsible for fixing that output. But this involves not only allowing managers far greater access to information but also a new price structure; it is meaningless to have managers decide on the amount of goods they should produce if they cannot also fix the price at which they should sell them. To do this, the reform has created a complicated four-tier price system, ranging from completely free prices set by management, through those which can move within limits fixed by the state and those for which the state fixes only a maximum, no minimum price, finally to those, such as basic foods, which the state still controls totally. The system of subsidies is being gradually abolished.

Enterprises are now supposed to make at least 7.5 percent profit on both fixed and working capital every year. Of this, 4 percent goes to the state and about 2 percent is for reinvestment. The rest—1.5 percent—is for distribution among employees. Snags have arisen in the system of profit sharing because the managers get a higher proportion of it than the workers. But Nyers defends this apparently unsocialist inequity on the grounds that profit is "the most comprehensive expression of efficiency." [9]

If a factory goes bankrupt, the workers are now, in theory, automatically employed elsewhere, the management sacked, and the capital sold off. This has rarely in fact happened, for although the regime declares itself in principle against lame ducks because they "are always a factor that holds back development" the state is ready to subsidize any lame duck enterprise whose work is "socially useful"—a broad enough generalization to avoid most closures. The shoes produced by the Minosegi (Quality) Shoe Factory were well-known by all Hungarians to be of an appallingly low standard and even the Russians, who are not usually choosers, wouldn't buy them. Before the reform, the enterprise was nevertheless able to survive and prosper: its profits in 1968 were ninety million forint. But when, in a new response to public demand, better shoes came on the market after 1968 its sales fell drastically. By 1970 profits had dropped to nine million forint. However, rather than close the enterprise down, men from the ministry came and restructured the whole output so that now the Quality Shoe Works produces only women's shoes.

On September 20, 1971, Radio Budapest reported that the Veszprem Bakony Works had gone bankrupt. The news caused something of a stir, for this was an enterprise which was exporting to the Soviet Union parts for the Soviet Fiat 124 (known as the Zhiguli and widely considered less reliable than its Italian counterpart)—windscreen wiper blades, motors, ignition switches, distributors, and mirrors all went East from Budapest under an agreement signed in 1968 and greeted at the time with much thumping of the Hungarian chest. The paper *Magyar Nemzet* declared, "The fact that Soviet industrial leaders have chosen us as their partners in a co-operation venture considered to be the greatest business deal of the century means that they recognise and appreciate Hungary's precision engineering industry." [10]

Alas for such appreciation. By mid-1971 the factory had received 253 demands for payment of outstanding bills and it was clear that the Russians had in fact given Bakony the contract not because of any recognition of traditional Hungarian skill but because the factory had quoted a disastrously unrealistic price. By the summer of 1971 each part supplied to the Soviet Union represented a 31 percent loss to the factory, not the 16 percent profit it had hoped for. Hardly the greatest business deal of the century.

But although the factory was declared nominally bankrupt, its liquidation was a solution that the Hungarian government could hardly afford politically —grist to the mill of those Soviet economists already oversuspicious of their revisionist comrades in Budapest. It was preferable that Bakony should become an import-export agency—import the requisite parts from Fiat in Italy and then reexport them to the Soviet Union—and that the factory be given extensive loans over the next four years.

Radio Budapest considered that the blame for the fiasco should be shared by the factory's management and by the Ministry of Metallurgy and Machine Industry. What were the repercussions in the ministry is not recorded; the management was partly replaced, but it was clear that Bakony would never be able to make a profit out of the Soviet contract, however efficiently it was run. It seems probable that the enterprise had originally been urged to tender a low bid by the ministry simply for the prestige of the five year deal. But that happened as far back as 1968, at the outset of the reform, and Hungarian economists are now quick to assure that such political pressure would never be applied today; nowadays, they say, any contract, Soviet or otherwise, is considered purely according to profit criteria.

Although the Soviet-enforced abandonment of the Czech economic reforms, which were very similar to and were planned to supplement those of Nyers, harmed the Hungarian economy, for the first two years after its implementation in January 1968 the reform was, on the whole, a startling success. The standard of living immediately improved in Hungary. Queues for washing machines, televisions, record players shortened and began to disappear. Food shops, clothes shops, and hardware shops all suddenly seemed to be more fully stocked and to be stocked with much more attractively packaged goods: everyone was pleased. The Party paper was also able to declare, in some triumph at the beginning of 1970, that since January 1968 sales had grown at least as fast, if not faster than production, the balance of payments with both East and West was favorable for the first time, and agricultural production had begun to grow quicker than industry, also for the first time. Everyone seemed to have more money and more to spend it on.

Since the beginning of 1970 the NEM has developed problems, and in October 1971 Prime Minister Fock read, sotto voce, something of a riot act to the Hungarian people, showing them how, in certain ways, the reform had gone out of hand. But it is safe to say that none of the problems so far encountered are of fundamental economic importance. Imports were certainly rising far too fast and a great many bad investment decisions had been taken by managers quite unused to making such decisions for themselves, but there was nothing drastically wrong with the basic functioning of the reform. More important were the side effects that the reform had had; the new emphasis on the forces of the free market has moral and ideological implications far more significant to a socialist society than the efficient running of a shoe or car parts factory, than the number of radios on the shelves of the shops. It has not only changed the aspirations of millions of people, it is also fundamentally altering many aspects of the nation's cultural life.

Eight

Just after he joined the Communist Youth movement in 1931, Janos Barna was taken surreptitiously to the office of the Metal Workers Union. There he heard an illegal lecture, illegal because no police permit for a meeting had been obtained, on "The Culture of the Proletariat." The talk, an excellent one, was delivered by Jozsef Attila, a man whom Kadar later described as "a good comrade, a militant communist, a great man and a great poet." It was an encounter which Kadar repeated as often as he was able and to which he has constantly referred. Perhaps that is partly because Attila, (before the war he was always known by his distinctive first name alone) * is one of the few poets he has ever known well and, in a country where poets have throughout history played an immensely impor-

---

* The poet's first name is Attila, his surname Jozsef. In Hungarian, however, the surname is always spoken and written first. So beloved is Attila that his name, Jozsef Attila, has become a concept in his country. He is never known as Jozsef alone though people do often refer to him as just Attila.

tant political role, he was anxious to capitalize on that first encounter. But to ascribe all his interest to political pragmatism is unfair: he has always felt a great personal sympathy with Jozsef Attila (a tragic figure whose early life so eerily resembled his own) and for his melancholy poetry. This sympathy was already shared by thousands of working-class Hungarians in the 1930s and is passionately felt by almost all the nation today. For, throughout his short life, Jozsef Attila was a committed socialist, his verse inspired by an intimate knowledge of working-class and peasant poverty which convinced him that the beastly misery of Hungarian life between the wars could be alleviated only by radical political change, by revolution. Just before the end of his life in 1937 he became interested in Freud and he recognized the dangers of fascism far more perceptively than his comrades. He criticized Stalin and was expelled from the Hungarian Communist party. Later Kadar said. somewhat disingenuously, of the rupture: "We were angry with him and it hurt us—yet our devotion to him was growing with the years. . . . Our differences of opinion remain the private affair of a big family and he was ours as he was, with his great qualities and some mistakes, right to his death and beyond his death, for ever." [1]

What he should have said was that so burning was Attila's zeal, so devoted a spokesman of the working class was he, and so loved in return by the ordinary people, that after they came to power in 1948, the Communists had to try and ignore his "mistakes." He was published even in the fifties.* To have banned him would have been politically unthinkable.

---

* One of his early poems "Pure of Heart" became especially popular. Because of its nihilist philosophy, Jozsef Attila had been forbidden to teach after its publication in 1925.

How far Attila would have accepted the regime that the Russians imposed upon Hungary after the war is, however, open to question. For throughout the history of the Magyars, as of all small peoples whose languages and literature are an important part of their fight to survive, writers have been the leaders and prophets of the nation. And those who have come to be regarded as the greatest writers and especially the greatest poets have invariably been the most fervent nationalists, and have struggled against foreign domination. This is a tradition which stretches, almost unbroken, back to the Renaissance writer-soldier, Balint Balassi, who was Hungary's first great lyricist, whose verse—shot through with the restless imagery of a wandering soldier—mingles ardent love for women and for liberty, and who was finally killed by the Turks, fighting for at least the second of those two passions.

Just as Jozsef Attila had become the spokesman of working-class discontent in the 1930s, so in the late forties and early fifties Hungarian writers expected once more to play their historically progressive role.

No father, no mother
No country, no God
Not a cradle, nor a shroud in the world,
Not a lover, not a kiss.

For three whole days I haven't eaten
Not a lot, not even a little, but nothing.
I'll sell you my twenty years,
My might and all my goods.

But who will buy?
Only the Devil will.
Pure of heart,
I'll steal, I'll kill.

They shall come and I shall hang
In hallowed ground they lay me down
Where the grass sprouts and feeds
On my proud and splendid heart.

Jozsef Attila had been the first individual working-class poet, and now a group of working-class and peasant writers emerged for the first time, as was appropriate to the formation of a socialist state. But they found that whereas the new regime praised as revolutionaries all the aristocratic poets of history who had struggled against oppression and injustice, so now those working-class writers who protested were branded "Titoist agents, fascist reactionaries and spies." All at once beliefs and concepts which had supposedly inspired Hungarian writers for centuries could no longer even be held, let alone voiced. Preliminary censorship and Party control stifled all.

In any society which seeks to restrict the freedom of debate, a class of so-called intellectuals tends to emerge. These people—writers, journalists, broadcasters, scientists, teachers, musicians, and even technicians—can be classed together in a far more legitimate way than they could, for example, in England. They all knew each other, and as a group they play a far more important political role than they do in any "bourgeois democracy."

Marxist-Leninist terminology itself in fact enshrines those who would elsewhere be known by their individual professions as the class of the "intelligentsia." It is the alliance of the workers, the peasants, and the intelligentsia that, in theory, constitutes the unity of a socialist society—thus it is for such an alliance, again in theory, that a regime aspiring to socialism necessarily strives.

So far as scientists and the members of the "technical intelligentsia" are concerned, unity with the workers and peasants often consists of little more than carrying out whatever is their professional duty in the most effective possible way. For writers and other artists, however, such unity is sometimes rather more difficult to define and almost always much more difficult to achieve. Under Stalin it had to be expressed through the medium of "socialist realism." This meant, for poets, verses in praise of the tractor, the herd of cows, and the cowherder himself, the metalworkers' drill, and the solid coal face. For the painter, it meant committing all these things and more to canvas. For the novelist it involved a "moral" romance set in the pastoral surroundings of a collective farm.

It was the gradual understanding that the "eternal truth" of Stalinism was in fact a lie and that the conditions of the workers and peasants were by no means so idyllic as they were compelled to declare that led the writers into revolt. Despite the restrictions of censorship, they played an indispensable—perhaps even the crucial—role in fanning the embers of disillusion until they burst into flaming protest in 1956.

For this, of course, they had to be punished when those flames were finally doused. In 1957 Kadar closed down both the Writers Union and the Union of Journalists. Many of the more liberal papers were abolished and some writers were imprisoned.

Kadar's own feelings toward the writers at that time were at best ambiguous. In the early months of 1956 he had told a group of journalists, "You imagine that you are an important, influential force in society. You are not: the working class is the only such force and you are like flies sitting on the yoke. It's the oxen, not you, who are pulling the cart, whatever you may think." In 1957, however, after the uprising had shown him that he had underestimated the power of flies to irritate the working classes and others, he told a recalcitrant group at the Writers Union, "It's said that a people gets the government it deserves. Well, you writers deserve a far more repressive government than this."

But, mindful of the traditional respect in which they were held, Kadar was anxious not to alienate the writers unnecessarily and consequently eschewed a policy of total repression. Preliminary censorship was not reintroduced, a remarkably outspoken and wide-ranging new monthly paper, *Kortars,* was established and in 1958 and 1959, respectively, the Journalists' and Writers' unions were allowed to reorganize. But these tentative gestures of good will from a regime whose leader was being constantly urged by his dogmatic colleagues to stiffen his resolve against the "scribblers of counterrevolutionary tracts" and who was not himself certain just how much he should or could concede them were not enough to win the support of many writers.

In fact his dealings with the writers during the first four years after the Revolution were subject to just the same inconsistency as every other aspect of Kadar's policies, thanks to the twists in Soviet-Yugoslav and Soviet-Chinese relations and hence in Khrushchev's ideological stance—which in turn affected the balance of power within his own administration. After the Moscow Conference of November 1957 (when Soviet-Yugoslav relations again deteriorated) and when revisionism was once more proclaimed the main enemy, a new antiintellectual campaign was launched in Hungary. It was now that those writers who had been detained since the Revolution were finally tried and sentenced, their philosophies denounced. "We do not consider the groups formed by the so-called 'populist' writers to be a stylistic literary trend. We know they are political groups which, in one way or another, stand in the way of progress.

(They are) . . . opposed to the leading role of the working class; such a viewpoint cannot be reconciled with the construction of a socialist society." [2]

Then again the paradox in all Kadar's policies showed itself. Even at the height of this antipopulist campaign the regime still allowed writers a latitude of expression that would have been inconceivable under Rakosi. For example, Peter Veres, a peasant and an excellent writer, could attack collectivization in the Party paper *Nepszabadsag* and in 1959 another writer could claim that "not a single peasant would have joined a co-operative of his own free will, without being won over and organised" and could go on to describe many of the details of that organization. [3]

But Kadar always realized that such concessions to the writers were not the best way of winning their allegiance. He was shrewd enough to understand that he would find it much easier to gain the support of the intellectuals once he had won that of the people. Far simpler thus than the other way around. For, as he himself says, where can the intellectuals go if not with the people? "I am deeply convinced that they will follow the masses, because their ties with the people and their honesty prompt them to take this direction." [4] And he has been proved largely right.

The man in charge of the nation's cultural affairs today is George Aczel, a cheerful, lean fellow with a thick black mustache, who is informal enough to have been mistaken, on occasion, for a taxi driver. A close friend of Kadar, he was, like Kadar, a prewar member of the illegal Party and was imprisoned in the Stalinist purges. He came into the administration in 1957 as deputy minister of culture and has dealt with cultural affairs ever since. He is now secretary to the Central Committee with full responsibility for cultural matters. He is generally liked by most intellectuals and is regarded as both straightforward and intelligent. Whether or not he was born with an understanding of the arts, he has managed to cultivate a strong sympathy for the work of artists and has consistently seemed anxious to enrich the country's cultural life.

It is difficult to compare the roles of culture in the fifties and early sixties with the early seventies if only because, as Aczel himself has pointed out, "Specialists in Party and cultural history still owe us a detailed scholarly study of the cultural policies of the last 20 years." [5] Nevertheless, he has his own very definite views on that period and admits that the roles of the Party and of culture were distorted by such factors as "the doctrine of the constant sharpening of the class struggle, the principle that the enemy must first be sought within the Party . . . the lack of confidence in the masses, which at the same time was connected with the 'prescribed' slogan that the masses were rapidly 'becoming filled' with socialist consciousness." [6] That's quite unlike his predecessor, Jozsef Revai, who had declared back in 1954, "After the year of change [1948] it was absolutely correct to use administrative means to sweep out the bourgeois dirt of the ideological front." [7]

Aczel is adept at trying to demonstrate how the Party has followed a correct and balanced "anti-revisionist and anti-dogmatist" line in cultural policy. He claims that while rejecting any glorification of "bourgeois decadence," it has also dismissed the dogmatic view "which narrowed down literary and cultural traditions close to the working class. It has rejected all merely formal glorification of Soviet culture and art, in this way ensuring and increasing the prestige and influence of their real values." [8] In fact, the main threat to the quality of artistic and intellectual creation in Hungary comes now not from dogmatic politicians but from the economic reform (N.E.M.). In 1968, before the reform was introduced, the state was supporting cultural bodies (other than educational concerns) to the tune of about 430 million forint a year (about $14 million).[9] But in an effort not totally unlike that of the conservative government in Britain after 1970, Kadar's regime tried in 1968 to make cultural institutions self-supporting by snatching away this crutch.*

According to George Lukacs, Hungary's grand old Marxist philosopher, NEM's emphasis on profit making has drastically cheapened cultural life. Contradicting Aczel's optimistic theories on the effect of mass participation in culture, he and others complain that to survive today, cultural enterprises must pander to the lowest common denominator in artistic tastes.[10] Before his death in 1971 Lukacs constantly maintained that the profitability criteria of the NEM should never have been applied to culture, arguing that, unlike many other social products, cultural matters have value but are priceless. And this was as true, he thought, of films as of books.

Since Hungarian poets are no longer able, thanks as much to the universal decline of poetry as a medium of propaganda as to the exigencies of the censorship system, to fulfill their traditional role as revolutionary heralds and political commentators, that

---

* Financial responsibility for many institutions was transferred from the Ministry of Culture to local councils and enterprises. Most controversial of all was the introduction of a cultural fund to subsidize all schemes that were "artistically and culturally" correct and a cultural levy to penalize those that were not. Neither fund nor levy has in fact been very effective either in encouraging or discouraging the sorts of work they are supposed to deal with. But they have raised no less a storm of protest for that; many intellectuals see the scheme as a return to the bad old days when the Party had total control over artistic creations.

part is now played by young Hungarian film makers.
Hungarian film making has a long and honorable
history, but usually it has been made by Hungarians
in exile. In 1904 the first cinema in New York, the
Crystal Hall, was opened by a Hungarian—Adolf
Zukor, who also founded Paramount. Directors like
Alexander Korda, Pasternak, Benedek, and Michael
Curtiz have all played an important part in West
European and American film making, but until 1956
almost no good film was ever made in Hungary itself.
After the war the film industry was nationalized and
the Communists, mindful of Lenin's advice to Luna-
charsky that the film was the most important propaganda art form, used it for just that. In the thaw of
prerevolutionary 1956, one film, *Merry-Go-Round,* excited acclaim at the Cannes Film Festival, but its
scriptwriter, Imre Sarkadi, committed suicide after
the Revolution, and most of his colleagues did the
same—in at least a professional sense. So much so
that in 1962 the writer Peter Veres was able to complain in an open letter to the minister of education
that "our films are worse than everyone elses', more
crass and tasteless. Rather let us produce nothing.
. . . Let us leave the mill empty rather than feed it
smutty wheat for it will destroy the flour and damage
the reputation of the mill as well." [11] But Veres need
not have worried. The early sixties produced as rich a
crop of films in Hungary as they did elsewhere in
Eastern Europe. Taking their inspiration from the
Polish film by Andrej Wadja, *Ashes and Diamonds,* a
new generation of directors who had been brought
up and trained in socialism and who knew no other
societies began to portray and even to examine those
societies in their work. In Prague one of the best of
the new directors was Milos Forman, whose *Blonde in
Love* gave a haunting glimpse of the more melancholy

aspects of growing up in Czechoslovakia in the mediocre years of the 1950s and early 1960s. Throughout the mid-sixties, no East European studios were as prolific as those of Budapest. In 1959 there were only about ten active directors in the country. By 1966 there were forty. The best known of Hungary's current directors is Miklos Jancso whose films include *The Round Up, Silence and Cry, Red and White*. His international reputation is so much greater than those of his friends and fellow directors as to cause a little understandable and, on the whole, justifiable jealousy among the others. Jancso is certainly brilliant, but he is not without peers. Men like Istvan Szabo, Andras Kovacs, Ferenc Kosa (*Ten Thousand Suns* and *Judgment*), Peter Basco—all regularly produce films which are both compellingly beautiful and often disturbingly powerful—so much so as to cause some dismay among the Party orthodox.

For both Jansco and the others tend to seize on incidents—revolts, massacres, insurrections, and battles—in Hungarian history or mythology and to display them in quite uncompromising revolutionary terms. Often their films have heroes who stand up against and are destroyed by authority. The power of the state is frequently shown as being opposed to that of the people. It is this praise of insurrection that today's leaders find disconcerting. No matter that they too have learned their history from the same books as Jansco, Kosa, and the others. No matter that the heroes of the films are always revolutionaries—this, indeed, is just what worries the authorities: so conservative are Hungarian officials that they consider it far better that the people be shown films about cowboys than freedom fighters.

Because the overall standard of all their works is so high and because everyone knows that the young film makers are regarded with not a little suspicion by the government, it is they rather than the writers who are today the brightest stars of Budapest's tiny, slightly inturned but immensely stimulating intellectual galaxy. Some of them do not hesitate to bask in this position: "we have inherited the revolutionary mantle worn before by Balassi, Kossuth, Ady, and Attila" they say, "and we wear it very well." Too well for the regime.

Until 1971 any director who wanted to make a film had to present the scenario to one of four state studios who could give him the money to do so. If one turned him down, whether for political or commercial reasons (even if the reasons were political they were always called commercial anyway), he could still apply to the other three in turn. More often than not one of them would approve his idea. In 1971, however, the system was changed and the four studios were reduced to two. The official explanation was, as usual, that a rationalization had to be made in order to save money,* but many of the avant garde directors denounced this as a fraud; the reorganization was in fact, they complained over their wine in the corner of the Intercontinental Hotel's garish bar where, for some unknown reason, they enjoy congregating on a Sunday morning, an attack upon themselves.

The government, they declared privately, was resentful of the progressive role that they had played over the last nine years. They complained that the Party did not like the spirit of camaraderie that had

* Sales of cinema tickets certainly did fall catastrophically during the sixties as more and more families bought a television set. One hundred and forty million seats were sold in 1960—only eighty-five million in 1968 so that by the end of the decade the box office was covering only 30 percent of the industry's costs.

developed among film makers—who certainly do inhabit a very small, in-crowd world: Jancso even uses his friends, not professional actors, to star in many of his works. Their greatest fear was that with only two studios to choose from it would in the future be much harder to get finances for a politically adventurous film; whereas it was quite possible for one in four studios to reject a film and for another in the four to accept it, it would be almost impossible for the two studios to contradict each other thus.

Arbitrary actions like this, small though they may be, demonstrate the insecurity in which all Hungarian artists and intellectuals live. The relationship which they now pursue with their government is delicate, subject always to relatively major changes as the result of really quite minor shifts in government policy. Like every other aspect of life in Hungary, peace and quiet for film makers, painters, poets, and writers to follow their crafts obtains only when all's well in the Communist world. In 1969, the film director Peter Bacso was given the permission and the money to make a film about the Rajk trial. But by the time it was completed the studio directors decided that they could not take the responsibility of allowing it to be released; it was too politically sensitive for the moment. Three years later it still had not been seen by the public.

It is, of course, true that there are commercial grounds for restricting the number of avant garde films made in Hungary: within the country, they do not recoup their costs of production. But these are usually offset by sales in the West, and a more cogent argument against the production of intellectual films is a political one: because so few Hungarian workers and peasants enjoy them or even watch them, their manufacture cannot be justified in a socialist country.

It is rather sad, but the situation is, at present, that Budapest intellectuals make films about Hungarian peasants for other Budapest intellectuals.

Of some twenty films produced by the industry a year, usually eight are "avant garde." The others are pure entertainment and they are the ones watched in their cold, gloomy cinemas by villagers. In their own defense, the film makers point out that the same is true of the West: there are two cultures everywhere. But the issue which concerns the government, and especially George Aczel, is that ideally this *should* not be so in a socialist society.

Trying to resolve this problem, Aczel talks of the achievements of the "new intellectuals." An "intellectual" (*ertelmisegi*) is, by his definition, anyone in an occupation that usually requires a university education: a *new* intellectual "is one whose world outlook is new, that is socialist."

A characteristic of the new intellectuals, he maintains, is their eagerness for ever closer links with the people. This is not to suggest a division of the people into culture-bearers and culture-receivers, for there is no question of "elevating" the masses. Far from it. "The people act on the socialist, humanist, technical and scientific intellectuals . . . and the work of these intellectuals acts upon the people." [12]

In truth this does not happen, and so Aczel quotes Brecht: "The people cannot be replaced. You can serve only the real people and not some kind of imaginary ideal." As a model for such artists he cites the composers Bela Bartok and Zoltan Kodaly "who in the creative period of their lives did not consider it a senseless waste to wander round Hungarian villages and towns . . . to teach the masses to love music." He points out, with considerable justification, that it is due to such devotion that provincial concert halls are full today.[13] But, sadly enough, it is also true that in the early and mid-sixties many young film makers attempted to follow the example of the composers and toured the country showing and explaining their films, discontinuing the practice only because of the disappointing lack of response from the peasants.

Hungarian intellectuals still have not really worked out in their own minds whether the people should be given what they, the intellectuals, think they seem to want—trashy novels and cowboy films—or whether they (the intellectuals) should try and educate them by their work. The New Economic Mechanism makes it much less easier to do the latter. Before NEM Budapest intellectuals were able to be somewhat more elitist than they are now; confident in the belief that their films and other works were artistically honest, politically progressive, and educationally valuable, they were untroubled by any commercial consideration. Now publishers and film distributors are loathe to buy scripts which they know they cannot sell. This is perhaps the main explanation of why the Hungarian film industry has not since 1967 really produced such a dazzling surplus of brilliant works as it did in previous years of the decade.

Intellectuals—painters and sculptors and musicians, as well as writers and film makers—sum up the change that NEM has made in their lives by complaining that before they had to struggle only against political restrictions, now they have to fight also against financial barriers. That's why they think their life is even more difficult than in the West where artists usually have only commercial battles to fight.

In fact almost the only cultural or semicultural activity which has not been much altered by the introduction of the economic reform is journalism. The role of the press in Hungary today is much the same as it has been ever since 1956. As Kadar refused to reinstitute preliminary censorship after he came to power, what appears in a newspaper is the responsibility of its editor. Hopefully it is clear from some of the articles already quoted that an editor can often get away with expressing quite stringent criticism of various aspects of government policy or Hungarian society. But censorship can be retroactive: if a paper publishes something of which the Party disapproves, that disapproval may be expressed by the Party cell in the paper passing a resolution condemning the article in question. More serious offenses are dealt with by appropriately more influential Party bodies, but discipline is very rarely needed, for both you and your editor know very well the limits of comment and develop an acute sense of just what, at any moment, you simply cannot hope to get away with. Of course, self-censorship is not peculiar to Hungary or indeed to those regimes which exert direct control over the press; it is practiced by all journalists everywhere according to the editorial policies of their paper, the libel laws, or any of a host of other factors.

The Hungarian situation itself was explained in 1970 to a mass communications' seminar in Yugoslavia by Pal Ipper, once a brilliant Radio Budapest correspondent in New York and now the radio's chief commentator at home.[14]

He said that he did not believe there was such a thing as absolute objectivity and freedom of the press: "All newspapers in the world and all radio and TV stations are dependent on somebody or something, whether it is a government or a group of interests." This much is hardly in dispute. But Mr. Ipper went on to declare that "the press should not be used against the general interest of the nation's development simply for the sake of informing the public." It is here that many Western journalists would part company with him and argue that, except perhaps in very exceptional circumstances, the press's prime duty of informing the public cannot, by definition, be "against the general interest of the nation's development."

In Mr. Ipper's view, the press must impart information "only up to a certain point, because it is in the nation's interest to refrain from hurting certain feelings abroad and to help the possibilities of further development." To prove his case he cited the example of Czechoslovakia: "When a nation's interests are jeopardised, then the press should shut up. My conviction is that if the Czechoslovak press could have kept its mouth closed, or at least a little more closed, then August 1968 would not have happened." Given Soviet hatred of the freedom of the Czech press that may well be true, but Mr. Ipper's generalization from one particular case to the universal thesis that when a nation's interests are threatened its press should "shut up" is not as easy to accept.

Hurting feelings abroad, as he so charmingly puts it, means, of course, criticizing the Soviet Union, its friends, and its policies. That you just cannot do as a Hungarian journalist. It was all right to attack Dubcek over his runaway reformism (actually Hungarian journalists were largely sympathetic and the press was very restrained), and it is permitted to criticize the pro-Chinese foreign policy of the Rumanian government. Of course there's nothing wrong with analyzing Albania and, if you want to, you can take a gentle knock at Tito—many journalists just don't want to. But during the invasion of Czechoslovakia you were not able to report the very real dismay which thousands of Hungarians and you yourself felt about the events in which your country had taken part. The best you could do was to admit that "not everyone immediately understands the need for this action."

It is at such moments that millions of Hungarians turn automatically to the news broadcasts of Radio Free Europe (RFE) in Munich: in 1968, for example, no other station provided so comprehensive or reliable a survey of the Czechoslovak events. Despite its irresponsible promise of Western aid and its broadcast instructions on how to make Molotov cocktails in 1956, the station still has a vast and loyal audience in Hungary today. It was RFE, not Radio Budapest, which informed Hungarians that a small group of Hungarian intellectuals, mostly linked to George Lukacs, had signed a protest against Hungary's participation in the invasion, while attending a socialist conference on the Yugoslav island of Korcula.

On March 10 of the following year the director general of the national news agency, MTI, did his best to explain away some of the restrictions imposed upon news coverage in the country. About the coverage of the Czechoslovak crisis, he said, "It's true that after August 21 we reported little. For 48 hours our news service was, shall we say, paralyzed, mostly for technological reasons. We lost contact with our Prague correspondent. It is true we had enough material from Western news agencies but most of this was provocative and contradictory. We could not assume the responsibility of misinforming the Hungarian public." [15]

Home affairs are less sensitive. In October 1971 *Magyar Nemzet,* the Patriotic People's Front Daily, published a cartoon entitled "The Farsighted Building Manager," which showed a businessman being fitted for a convict's uniform. The meaning was obvious and two days later the paper published an angry letter from the minister of construction and urban development, Joszef Bondor, who wrote that the cartoon implied that "building managers are criminals and the more provident among them have already ordered their prison garb from the tailor." He complained that the cartoon was grossly offensive and liable to mislead public opinion and demanded that the editor publish a retraction, condemning this "unfounded slander." In response all the paper did was to note, "By publishing this letter we have complied with the comrade minister's demand for a correction. Naturally, neither the cartoonist nor the paper intended to generalise."

In February 1971 the trade union paper, *Nepszava,* attacked a minister for giving allegedly misleading information in answer to a question in Parliament. An M.P.— anxious, perhaps, to secure reelection under the new laws—had complained about workers' conditions and pay in the printing industry, and the deputy minister for light industry, Laszlo Foldes, then denied that there was really very much wrong. His reply reached the union officials who were incensed enough to declare in *Nepszava* that it "contains statements and omissions which could lead the reader to draw false conclusions." The paper then went on to prove, in a manner which any Western journalist might well applaud, how the minister had cooked the figures and how the printworkers' situation was far worse than he pretended.[16]

In September 1968 the television started a program which was, in East European terms, unprecedented. Called "Forum," it featured a studio panel of journalists, ministers, and other experts who answered questions sent in by telephone from viewers. True, the questions are not asked live on the air, but are filtered through an editor; nevertheless the program has proved a great success and many of the questions actually put to ministers have been pertinent. The program was originally meant to deal only with foreign affairs (in the most cautious sort of way) but proved such a popular format that it has been extended to cover questions of domestic policy also. As a step toward audience participation in television and toward increasing the contacts between government and people it was important and, significantly enough, one of Edward Gierek's first acts when he succeeded Gomulka in December 1970 was to set up exactly the same sort of program in Poland.

Not to be outdone by the television, in February 1971, Radio Kossuth launched a ninety-minute Saturday afternoon program on domestic and foreign current affairs of the past week. A sophisticated blend of music, comedy, news, and views, it is the creation of Pal Ipper, who doubtless got the idea from his time as a correspondent in New York. The program goes out live and Ipper is at pains to stress both its topicality and its originality: the editors, he says, are all very open minded people who do much as they like. Anything can be discussed on the air, even "scandalous" subjects, so long as the motives are good. The public response to the program seems to have justified Ipper's enthusiasm: "168 Hours" is known and listened to as one of the frankest political forums in the country.

Of the newspapers, the only one that really rivals the work done by "Forum" and "168 Hours" and, indeed, other programs, is *Valosag,* an independent socio-literary journal—editorially a sort of cross between *Encounter, The New York Review of Books,* and the *London Sunday Times.* It has only a small circulation, almost exclusively within Budapest, but M. Sukosd and E. Vitanay, its brilliant young editors, can be relied on to produce the most controversial article of the month, often some sociological survey which shows that Hungary is not the workers' paradise that the government claims it to be. These examples notwithstanding, much of the most important news is not reported in the Hungarian media. Although reading the Hungarian press and listening to its radio or television is immensely rewarding and although they seem to tell fewer and fewer deliberate lies, they often do not tell quite the whole truth either. People have learned to make up for their shortcomings. As in all East European capitals, there is an extraordinarily effective underground information service in Budapest. Real news—that Kadar has had a row with Brezhnev, that the Russians are about to put more pressure on Rumania, that the Cabinet minister did not in fact resign for health reasons but was sacked for corruption, that Kadar canceled his last Monday's engagements not because, as officially stated, he had a cold but because he had in fact had a heart attack—news such as this all passes by word of mouth.

"Perhaps now Kadar's prison ordeal is really beginning to tell on him? . . . Yes, of course he's only sixty, but he has never looked well, and if you'd been kicked about by Farkas and then left to rot alone in a dripping cell for three years, not to mention the strain of 1956 and for years after, wouldn't you be having heart attacks by the age of sixty? Well, who will replace him? . . ´. Not Aczel, he only knows about culture, nothing else . . . Nyers is too radical, the Russians would never allow a reforming economist to run the place. . . . It would have to be some idiot like Bisku—someone the Russians can trust because he's so obedient and so stupid. . . . Well, it hasn't happened yet; let's hope he just gets better again: he has before. . . . You know the row about the Zhiguli—

the Russian Fiat which falls to pieces three times faster than any other car in the world? . . . Did you hear Brezhnev's latest attack on consumer values? Yes, well, it now seems . . ."

Nine

Andras Hegedus is small, rotund, and bald. He wears a beret and a goatee beard and looks like a caricature of an unsuccessful *fin de siècle* Impressionist as he sits on the banks of the Danube sipping thick Hungarian coffee from thick Hungarian tumblers in the high-ceilinged, paneled Gresham café (which, perhaps for its anonymous, unpretentious, and utilitarian decor, is so popular among Budapest intellectuals), worrying about the future of Hungarian society.

Hegedus is no painter. From April 1955 to October 1956 he was first Rakosi's and then Gero's young but apparently hard-core Stalinist prime minister and as such was dismissed by Imre Nagy and given no job in Kadar's subsequent Revolutionary Worker-Peasant Government.

Unlike many of Rakosi's lieutenants, however, Hegedus was not a stupid man. His political career prematurely (and, he would now say, happily) destroyed by the disgrace of Stalinism, he retired to academic life and began to study sociology. The analysis of the society which he had helped to build led him to realize many of its most startling defects and in the early sixties his political views shifted completely: he became a revisionist extraordinary, convinced that only the most radical reordering of national and political priorities could enable socialism to develop into a sane, humane, and effective system of government. Many of his opinions were quite heretical and his expression of them did not endear him to the more cautious Kadar.

Since then, however, Kadar has been forced to listen to some of the proposals put forward by Hegedus and other sociologists. Insofar as he is himself now attempting to reform Hungary's socialist system, so he and the Party need to rely more than ever on the work of sociologists for diagnosis if not for cures.

Before the war Hungarian sociologists were a tiny breed, their time spent in making unheard and unheeded protests against the plight of the landless peasant in the decaying society over which Admiral Horthy squatted. Indeed, the science of sociology was then almost exclusively identified with a study of agricultural problems; this was the time of the "Village Explorers movement," when men like Ferenc Erdei, a brilliant academician of peasant origin who died in 1971, described minutely and with great sympathy the dissolution of traditional peasant mores.

This role of sociologist as documenter and critic had to be abandoned abruptly after the war; the Communists were concerned neither with criticism nor with truthful portraits of contemporary society but only with the transformation of semifeudal agricultural Hungary into a socialist industrialized state. In the pursuit of the Soviet ideal, discrepancies between Hungary in 1945 and the Soviet Union in 1917 were just ignored; as one Hungarian sociologist recently put it mildly, "certain policies had to be carried out without regard to their dysfunctional consequences." In these circumstances sociological examination of the prevailing conditions was, with few exceptions, forbidden: the social sciences had only a "justificatory" function. On orders from the apparat sociologists were set to defending the objective necessity and essential correctness of those political decisions which had had and were having distorting effects upon society. There were no real sociologists, just social philosophers.

Things changed immediately after the Revolution and the Kadar regime began to use sociologists to study those very distortions which, under Rakosi, they had been compelled to praise: since the introduction of the NEM, sociologists are needed and are being used more than ever before. This is not altogether surprising, for the NEM has caused and is causing greater changes in the pattern of Hungarian society than anything since 1948. These changes need to be understood and Party policy and attitudes developed accordingly. "Political management can only be effective, and its standards improved, if we have reliable information on the opinions, aspirations and general and specific situation of the social strata of a given area," declared *Partelet,* the Party's doctrinal journal in 1969.

In effect the government is now trying to use sociologists as any other technocrats. This is a function which some reject utterly. For Hungarian sociologists are embroiled in the same arguments as their Western counterparts: Do they pursue knowledge for itself, or do they do so only within the context of a specific social or moral theory?

The sociologist as technocrat par excellence is Dr.

Kalman Kulcsar, since 1968 the director of the Sociological Research Institute in Budapest. Sympathetic enough to meet, he has done little important original work. "Manipulation," he was once heard to say, "is not a word." His view on the sociologist's role is very straightforward. In bourgeois countries, he claims, sociologists have come to believe wrongly that theirs is the science which forms society and solves its problems. But Marxist sociology seeks only to serve its society, not to guide it. It does this by discovering the problems of society and then simply supplying the authorities with a body of information to enable them to make their future political decisions more rational. Sociologists should not try to show the government what are the alternative political decisions.

However, despite the somewhat narrow limits Kulcsar sets upon sociology in theory, in practice he allows the members of the institute to do pretty much as they please. Since many of them were appointed by his predecessor, Andras Hegedus,* their work is not always of the kind which Kulcsar approves.

In the dispute as to whether sociology should serve the state or itself there is little doubt where Hegedus stands. He has constantly and vigorously denounced any attempt to make the science serve the interests of any institution. He has adopted, but adapted, the Marxist theory of class struggle; to him, conflicts between strata of society are not only inevitable but also necessary and healthy provided that they can be expressed through institutional channels. The trade un-

* Like so many other aspects of intellectual life in Hungary, sociology was disrupted by the backlash of the invasion of Czechoslovakia in 1968. Kadar was determined that the same thing should not happen in Budapest as took place in Prague. Among those who protested the invasion was Hegedus. He was duly reprimanded by the secretariat of the Cental Committee and by the beginning of 1969 his job had been given to the more reliable Kulcsar.

ions, for example, should be the true defenders of the workers, not a transmission belt for the Party's orders. When he first expressed this idea in the mid-sixties, it was an almost unforgivable heresy. Now, of course, Kadar has paid lip service to it under the NEM. But Hegedus himself has gone on further, and in an unexpected direction. For his heresies he and two like thinking philosophers were expelled from the Party in 1973—a demonstration of insecurity and ideological belt-tightening caused, in part, by Moscow's insistence that its friendship with Nixon should in no way lead to any relaxation of controls on speech either in the Soviet Union itself or within its empire.

From being an orthodox East European revisionist who wanted to see the introduction of market principles into the economy and a lessening of Party control, he has now become one of the most dedicated critics of the NEM and thus finds himself once more allied (though for very different reasons) with his old Stalinist friends who have remained unchanged since the 1950s. But the company is not all bad: he has found men like George Lukacs there with him too.

Other Hungarian sociologists, particularly young men like Ivan Szelenyi and George Konrad, disagree. They feel that sociology in Eastern Europe, and particularly in Hungary, needs to be secularized and rid of its clichés. Perhaps Leszek Kolakowski, late of Warsaw, now of All Souls, is their closest model. These men not only reject the dogma of contemporary Hungary, they also question its aims. They refuse to accept that Hungary is necessarily departing from "socialist" standards.

Thus they reject Hegedus's criticisms of the NEM for the way in which it introduces an allegedly "petit-bourgeois" spirit into social choices. Was the appalling underinvestment in the infrastructure—housing, roads, and schools—in the fifties anymore "humanistic"? they ask. Whatever the answer to that question, Hegedus's complaints are well worth examining.

Even before the introduction of the NEM, fears were expressed in Hungary as to the "moral decline" of the people. Of course, such fears have been voiced for decades. But in the four years since the reform has operated they have become much more widely asserted, as the new economic stimulants have genuinely begun to change the whole basis of Hungarian society. It is an old debate in Eastern Europe—Khrushchev used to call it the question of "goulash socialism"—and it centers on whether the first duty of a socialist state is to satisfy its citizens' material needs or whether their moral and ideological well-being should be its prime concern. As Hungarians get richer, so the debate becomes more ferocious; first "refrigerator socialism" took the place of "goulash socialism" as the subject of dispute, and now that every fourth family has a refrigerator and every other one a television (in 1960 there were virtually no refrigerators and only ten thousand TVs in the country), the dispute is over "car" or even "weekend-cottage" socialism. Since the NEM has encouraged people to think more than ever in terms of profit margins and incentives, a new and, for the government, somewhat alarming phenomenon has appeared. The Party calls it "moneygrubbing."

The moneygrubber is in a sense the "New Hungarian Man." No longer the loyal, stupid, dogmatic Party bureaucrat, he is the technician. The fixer. The man who makes it materially. The expert. The product and producer of a consumer society. The little fellow working for himself. The petit bourgeois.

In 1966, when moneygrubbing was known but was certainly not so widespread as it is alleged to be today,

Nepszabadsag, the Party paper, defended the concept of material wealth and pleasures: "Are all those who have cars, summer bungalows, fully mechanised households, money-grubbing and dishonest people? Haven't we in fact always fought, and aren't we still fighting so that as many people as possible should have everything they need for a comfortable quiet life? To call it petit bourgeois to increase your assets is to attack just that socialist principle which is most important to us—to each according to his work."

The paper agreed, however, that when the planned NEM was brought into action "value relations will play a larger role in governing the economy, individual income will increasingly depend on individual achievement, competition amongst companies will increase. And all this will reinforce petit bourgeois selfishness, and the money-grubbing urge." [1] So it apparently has.

On April 13, 1967, Radio Budapest carried a program on the petite bourgeoisie which included interviews with various workers: a woman declared, "I love money and if I bought a dress for $25 or even a fur coat, that wouldn't mean I'm petit bourgeois." Another worker observed, somewhat more shrewdly, that "those who write articles against petit bourgeois attitudes and who speak against them are to be seen climbing into their cars, banging the doors, and marching into their country cottages . . . not bothering at all about the worries that the workers often have." The radio commentator was forced to conclude, a trifle lamely, that "it is not easy to define just what is petit bourgeois, but it is most important to get rid of it."

Kadar summed up the dilemma between profiteering and poverty when he told the Tenth Congress, "Socialism serves man; our aim is that people should

live a better and more cultured life and that their circumstances should improve. We refuse every kind of
sham modesty and asceticism. But we shall not reconcile ourselves to the spreading of the spirit of crass
materialism which is contrary to the morality of our
society and to the ideals of socialism." He did not
suggest just how that should be done.

Hungarians today have far more possessions—
radios, tape recorders, TVs, motorcycles, even cars—
than ever before. As their demand for consumer
goods is met, so their demand for consumer services
increases. This is true not just for such services provided by the hairdresser, the waitress, the nightclub
singer; they already existed and their role changes
only in that they become accessible to many more
people as society is consumerized. Affluence also
breeds its own new servants, car mechanics, television
repairers, part-time builders, house painters, elec-
tricians: their importance and numbers grow in direct
proportion to the sale of consumer durables.

The service sector is now regarded as a crucial com-
ponent of the economic reform, not just an indicator
of the rise in living standards. Numerous tax concessions and the easier granting of licenses raised the
number of private artisans and retailers in the first
two years of the reform. But the petit bourgeois still
account for only 2 percent of the population, a fact
which Nyers uses to justify his public confidence that
the influence they have upon society can only be neg-
ligible. Indeed, he thinks, so harmless are they that
further measures should be taken to increase their
number, and he points out that whereas in more developed countries between 20 to 30 percent of the
work force is engaged in the service sector, in
Hungary it is only about 17 percent—far too little.[2]
His enthusiasm stems, of course, from the belief that

the provision of efficient services plays a large part in securing public contentment. Buying off the people.* The last few years have also seen a growth in what is, sometimes at least, one of the most private services of all—prostitution. This was an industry which was officially closed down and outlawed by Rakosi in 1951—before that there were several well-known brothels in Budapest and free-lance prostitutes could register with the police. The trade continued, unsurprisingly, but only recently, with the expansion of tourism and hotel building, has it become easily noticeable once more, and nowadays lovely girls and not-so-lovely ladies are to be seen drinking inquiring coffees in all Budapest's best and worst restaurants and cafés.

Cafés always have been and still are an integral part of Budapest social life. Today in many of them and certainly in the worst of them, gypsy music seems compulsory after dark: every night the sad old violinists shriek their tunes over the goulash and the wine as a busty sequined lady of indeterminate middle age pours herself loudly down a microphone. Bold on their wine, other ladies, sometimes attractive but usually not, thrust themselves forward and ask for a dance or a beer or a wine or a cognac or a taxi ride home.

In 1964 four women were given up to four years' imprisonment for prostitution. It was said that they had not been punished more severely because of "mitigating circumstances": to wit, their clients had included "high-ranking officials." It could be that their pimp was a high-class rogue called Lajos Onodi.

---

* It is virtually impossible to translate forint values into sterling or dollars—so many and varied are the different exchange rates. All translations here are very approximate and are based on the tourist rate of 1972: about $1=30 forint.

For the following year Hungary had its own Profumo Affair when Lajos Onodi, who was brother-in-law of Ferenc Nezval, Minister of Justice, and who had been head of Budapest's giant Catering Enterprise since 1951, was arrested. He had for years been running an orgy service for prominent party officials and foreign diplomats; lurid (largely true) stories about the Egyptian chargé d'affaires licking clean the chocolate-coated bodies of naked girls delighted the gossips of Budapest. Although the scandal was played down as much as possible, everyone in the capital knew exactly what had happened; news travels fast on the unofficial grapevines. The affair excited a mass of oblique comment and criticism in the Party and local press, and was seen by many, and especially by the dogmatists, as another shocking symptom of Hungary's moral decline since the pure days of Stalinism.

Hungarian prostitutes prefer Western men, and sometimes they rationalize this discrimination by arguing that their work is of not inconsiderable help in easing Hungary's foreign exchange shortage. One girl was quoted by a Budapest paper in 1969 as saying, "We bring grist to the mill of the state. If anybody counted up all the hard currency the Western tourists and businessmen spent on us, some of our great and wise guardians of morality would be struck dumb. If the customer pays in dollars, we exchange them; if he pays in forints, that's only because he's already changed his dollars; the money remains here either way." [3] This is not just an isolated example of prostitution being linked with the tourist trade; the connection seems to be quite widely assumed.

In August 1971, *Dunantuli Naplo,* the local paper in the beautiful southern university town of Pecs where the wine is strong and the girls are certainly very charming, reported that the annual invasion of sex-mad Italians had begun. Italian men, wrote Denes Foldessy, were restrained from promiscuity at home by the "hard bonds" of public opinion. But in Hungary "there are beautiful affectionate girls who just love Fiat cars." According to one hundred prostitutes interviewed by Radio Budapest, it's not only the Italians' cars and life that they appreciate. Italians, they claimed, were far more efficient lovers than other Westerners. Also according to the radio, many Italians believe that "Hungarian girls are the cheapest in Europe" and will sleep with a Westerner just for a pair of tights to wear, afterward.[4]

For many Hungarian girls, prostitution is, in more senses than one, moonlighting and at the Tenth Congress in 1970 Kadar declared that "socialism cannot be built on secondary employment." Nevertheless, 7 percent of all working Hungarians have a second job and the number is growing all the time.*

Through 1969 employment officially increased 10 percent, but moonlighting grew by over 50 percent, and whereas normal wages had increased on average by only 16 percent since 1967, moonlighting had become a third more profitable than before.[5]

Until now most moonlighters have been skilled technicians or men with professional qualifications. In a survey conducted in 1970 all those professional people questioned said they needed the extra money because their basic salaries did not allow them the style of life to which they thought they should be accustomed. A doctor wanted to buy a car, a teacher

---

* In 1967 moonlighting earned Hungarians about $80 million (2,300 million forint) and since the NEM was introduced, this figure has increased considerably, though the average income from moonlighting is still only $17 (500 forint) a month, about a quarter of the average main income.

needed new clothes, and an engineer declared that "one has to study languages, to buy books and periodicals and to travel. My work puts me in a group whose members live on a higher financial level and they expect me to keep up with them." [6] Teachers, relatively speaking, are as badly paid in Hungary as they are in Western Europe.

Despite the fact that moonlighting is, on the whole, a symptom of economic advance, the Hungarian authorities see in it considerable danger and believe that "a person who holds two or more jobs conserves his working energy and capacity and takes his ideas and pleasure in his work elsewhere." Another, equally dangerous, result is "lack of leisure, rest, and time which could be spent on cultural pursuits, not to mention overtiredness." [7]

Their concern is shown by a joke heard in Budapest in 1970. It told of an aunt, visiting Hungary from the West, asking her nephew, "Why does everyone have two jobs here?" "Well," he replies, "in the second one people earn the money they do not get in the first one." "But surely that's very tiring?" she responds. "Not at all, they rest in their main jobs," exclaims the nephew.

On February 25, 1971, the Central People's Control Committee submitted a report on the problems of moonlighting to the Council of Ministers. According to Radio Budapest, "The survey stated that this form of employment has many advantages. However, despite the regulations, there have existed for years a large number of instances which are both legally and morally objectionable. The Council of Ministers accepted the report and (decided) to revise the statutory provisions governing secondary jobs."

The sort of abuse they were bemoaning includes the case of the man who moonlighted as an architect and in the daytime approved his own plans in his full-time capacity as building manager of an enterprise; one planning institute did not seek tenders for a job but allowed its workers to do it in their spare time for extra pay; and in the town of Gyor a resourceful engineer accepted a monthly fee of around $68 for looking at the Savaria cinema for a few minutes every month just to check that it hadn't fallen down. Despite his strenuous efforts, however, the Vas County Council refused to relicense the building.

Later in 1971 the penal code was altered to punish the new forms of economic crime that the NEM had inspired. New legal interpretations were provided for the offenses of charging excessive prices, depriving customers, marketing inferior industrial products and bribery. For, as the minister of justice admitted, "It has been very difficult to bring prosecutions for bribery, 'greasing' (*Kenes*)· or 'You scratch my back and I'll scratch yours' (*Kez Kezet Mos*), not only because of the problems of detection but also because . . . the law has till now only punished the recipients of favours." From now on the briber himself will also be punished, and it will also be criminal to incur irresponsible debts.[8] Probably the only lasting solution was best expressed, surprisingly enough, by the Party's theoretical journal: "One reason for the appearance of seriously mistaken attitudes is that the development of factory democracy has not been tied closely enough to the development of the reform." [9] Despite such understanding, the Party has, as we have seen, been reluctant to increase worker participation in factory management in any way.

Perhaps a symptom, not of the economic reform, for it existed long before that, but of the changing tastes of a richening Hungary is Luxus. Luxus is an expensive clothing department store in Vorosmarty

Square, the poshest area of Budapest. Opposite it is Vaci Street, a short, narrow road parallel to the Danube, which boasts the most expensive shops in the city; with books, linen, jewelry, glass, furniture, antiques—it looks much iike Bond Street and it is always very crowded. Across the square from Luxus is Vorosmarty's café (still known to many by the name of its prewar proprietor, Gerbeaud) which, with its small marble tables, gilt chairs, long mirrors, velvet drapes, and middle-aged middle-class female customers appears, and is, more bourgeois than almost any café in Europe. Many of the women who sip coffee and devour cream-filled pastries and chocolate puddings in Gerbeaud's are dressed in Luxus; it's a long, long way from the drab and shapeless conformity of the fifties when all the clothes seemed to be made of gray cardboard and were far too large, if they were not too small. In 1969 each Hungarian spent an average of $72 (2,163 forint)—one month's wages—on clothes, but the women who shop at Luxus spend much more. The shop imports half its stock from the West and the rest it copies from Paris. A sweater there sells for $36; the monthly wage of a waitress is only the equivalent of $48: she will never buy it. In 1970 the minister of internal trade, answering questions on television, was caught off his guard when asked why such disparities were allowed. He could give no answer, but the next day all the sweaters were sold within hours.

Some of them were bought by the wives of Party officials, but it was not only (nor even principally) bureaucrats' wives who rushed to the shop next morning. For another by-product of the New Economic Mechanism is that Party officials are no longer the richest people in Hungary. Back in the fifties and the early sixties the best-dressed, best-shod, and "bestcarred" families were always those of the officials and the wives of many apparatchiks and Party leaders— who found their economic power as exhilarating as their husbands found their political influence. This still happens. One of my interpreters, a girl of almost unbelievable prissiness, spent a long time denouncing to me the evils of Western society. She said that she had seen it all, for her father had been a trade counselor at the Hungarian Embassy in London; she hated capitalism, she said. Then she had to hurry home to pack, for next day she was going on holiday with her family to Italy and they were traveling in the white Mercedes her father had bought in the West—"We have a Mercedes because it's the best car there is."

Today Party officials are still the [New Class] certainly—just as they were in the fifties—but they are not now the only *nouveaux riches*. That particular section of society is now mainly made up of the moonlighters, the private repairmen, the concierges who hum their knitting machines all day and all night in their free basement flats, coming out only to receive the equivalent of ten cents every time they unlock the door of the lift, and who make at least $15 a day providing sweaters for sale in the little private shops that are jammed into one side of Tanacs Street behind Luxus. These are some of the new millionaires who ride the Ford Capris and the Renault 16's; not the cheaper and unreliable Soviet-built Fiats and Moskvitchs or the East German Trabants. It was their wives who rushed to Luxus to buy the pricey fashionable sweaters.

Of the rest of the *nouveaux riches*, many are peasants. Traditionally far poorer than industrial workers, the economic reform has increased peasant fortunes dramatically faster than anyone else's. In 1970 their average income equaled that of the workers for the first time. By now it is so much higher as to cause considerable resentment among the workers and has only intensified their dislike of their country cousins and comrades whom they had hoped to have left behind.

Collectivization did not initially make for efficiency. By 1965, 86 percent of the country's total land area was operated by state farms or cooperatives. The other 14 percent was in tiny private plots and this minute area produced almost half the agricultural share of the national income. This clearly had to be changed and it was. Now Hungary has a remarkably successful agricultural system.

Most Hungarian peasants now officially operate in an almost completely free market; their cooperative farms are far more democratically controlled then ever before: they elect a management annually, and they are now allowed to produce whatever they want and sell everything except basic foods at whatever prices they can get. Most of them prosper, and since 1968 they have been attracting skilled industrial workers away from factories at a rate that causes industrial managements some alarm. Twenty percent of clerical workers, 50 percent of all workers, and 70 percent of unskilled workers already live in the villages because of the underurbanization of the early fifties. Suddenly thousands of the country's one million commuters are finding that rather than travel up to one hundred miles on lamentably slow and uncomfortable buses and trains to factories and offices in Budapest or other big towns, they can find much better paid and more enjoyable work in their own villages where the collective farms are converting garages, cowsheds, and barns and are setting up small light industrial workshops. With the freedom to fix their own prices, the collectives are able to pay labor its true value—unlike state enterprises.

The most rational way to stem this flow away from the towns would be for factories also to raise workers' wages to their true value. They have not done so and, instead, the government has introduced a labor tax to be levied on the collectives—in the same sort of spirit that the Labour government introduced the Selective Employment Tax to penalize the British service sector. This is, of course, an "administrative" method which goes against the spirit of the reforms. But there are not a few Party officials in Budapest who consider that the peasants themselves are flouting that spirit in no small way. Their worries are demonstrated by what has happened in the village of Soltvadkert. It can now boast thirty-three "millionaires": thirty-three peasants, that is, who earn over $35,000 (1 million forint) a year. That's twenty-eight times what the average worker is paid, a differential which even Rezso Nyers would consider excessive.

Soltvadkert is a winegrowing village in flat, open, drab country some one hundred miles south of Budapest along the country's most dangerous main road. It has eight thousand inhabitants, almost all of them involved in the wine industry and most of them members of the village's one cooperative. It is this organization which is the secret of their success.

In 1961 most peasants actively resisted collectivization, but the inhabitants of Soltvadkert were more canny and agreed immediately upon its suggestion and therefore got themselves the best possible terms. As a result their land is still their own—only the means of wine fermentation, bottling, and selling are socialized. This has meant that those peasants who started off with a little money, often acquired from illegal distilleries and watering the wine, have ever since got richer and richer.

There are 950 members of the cooperative. Each has to pay it one-tenth of his production, the rest he can sell either privately or through the cooperative. The co-op will give him the best price and to earn a million forint he needs to sell seventy thousand liters a year. Easily within the grasp of the "Big 33."

One of the aims of nationalizing agriculture was to rid the mass of poor peasantry of exploitation by the rich peasants, the *kulaks*—like Janos Czermanik's father, Janos Kressinger—on whom they had previously been almost totally dependent for employment and income. But in Soltvadkert the old system has returned: the poor peasants are once more employed by the rich. Not that they do so badly. The rich peasants come and pick them up by car in the morning (so that they have longer to work), pay them $7.50 (200 forint) a day, give them three meals and five liters of wine—all of which they drink while working.

The village is, as a result, totally divided into rich and poor. Every Sunday morning the rich peasants crowd with their families into the Espresso café and order sticky cakes, beer, and wine; no poor peasant would dream of venturing anywhere near the place. But that is the only break in the week; otherwise work is the supreme ethic by which the rich peasants live. The pattern of acquisition reflects this totally. Most Hungarian peasants live in little one-story, whitewashed houses with perhaps a main kitchen-cum-living and sleeping room and another bedroom which doubles up as the best parlor. The back of the house usually leads into a small fenced farmyard. Not so in Soltvadkert. There seem to be more new buildings there than in Budapest itself, and dozens of the houses are two-story, very few of them only two-roomed. Many of them look more like villas in an expensive French suburb than the homes of peasants in a socialist country of Central Europe. All have enormous storage space and wine cellars.

His house built, the Soltvadkert peasant does not yet buy furniture. More important is a car. Not for tourism, not for prestige, but to make him more money. He uses it not only for fetching poor peasants from neighboring villages to work his land, but also for carrying produce to the market in the nearby town of Keskemet. Schnapps, for example, costs him $1.20 (thirty-five forint) a bottle to produce and he sells it for over double. The smallest, cheapest, East German car, the Trabant, can carry at least one hundred fifty bottles a trip. In Hungary that's excellent money.

It's only when he's earned enough from the sale of schnapps that he thinks about buying furniture (of the most expensive kind), and, last of all, a television. In Hungary, as almost everywhere else in the world, far more families have televisions than cars. But not in Soltvadkert; there the peasants think they don't have time to watch it. And, as one very rich peasant admits, "I'm rich enough to travel all over the world, but I haven't the time. Round here we believe the traveller is a bad manager."

This is a man whose daughter is at agricultural college and planning to come home and work on the farm. He and his wife, both over fifty years old, are also taking correspondence courses in winegrowing. They reckon that when they have the diplomas to hang on the wall they will be able to make still more money. They both work enormously hard on their vines and they are as rich as he is fat. Their six-room, ranch-type house has all its cellars and its outhouses filled with nine-foot-high casks brimming over with white wine, and in his garage are two cars, one of them a Volvo. His house is sparsely furnished—but with pieces that are heavy and expensive and ugly. In his glass-fronted cabinet in the dining room are a whole series of books on the history of Africa: each book the size of one volume of the *Encyclopaedia Britannica.* He says he has never looked at them. He and his wife sit a visitor down at the table to discuss their business. Most Hungarians are enormously hospitable and friendly and never fail to produce coffee, wine, cognac, and cakes on such an occasion. That thought never occurs to these two; it would be a waste.

Every village in Hungary has a Culture House run by a permanent poorly paid official whose job is to stage plays, musical evenings, and the like. All over the country attendance is usually bad, and the culture house is tatty, run down, cold, and depressing. But in Soltvadkert it is worse than elsewhere: the peasants don't believe they have any time to spare. The only way the culture director can get them to come is to sell them season tickets in advance; they then think that to stay at home would be a waste of money, which, to them is an even greater crime than a waste of time.

Soltvadkert is an extreme example, but all Hungarian cooperatives are now making more money than ever before and are producing everything from buttons to electric motors at prices most state-run factories cannot hope to match. In 1971 the government had to legislate to end an extraordinary abuse that followed from this. Workers were being bought and sold by agricultural cooperatives like stocks and shares. A cooperative would first offer a worker a higher salary than his factory was paying him. In order to keep his labor, the factory then had to pay the cooperative a still higher sum, not out of its labor fund (that was illegal) but out of its special project fund. Thus the worker stayed in the factory, but was now technically the employee of the cooperative and with a higher salary; it was just the factory that came off badly from the deal.

Given such phenomena it is hardly surprising that Andras Hegedus, George Lukacs and others worry about the country's "New Morality." But most Hungarian economists, Party officials, and other apologists are at constant pains to convince the Western observer that the economic reform does not in any way affect the basis of the socialist system in Hungary. It is designed, they explain patiently, only to introduce new techniques of *guiding* that system, and is therefore not a reform of socialism but simply an overhaul of certain planning methods. Enterprises do now have a much wider opportunity for making decisions themselves. Just as during the nineteenth-century period of industrialization owners of large enterprises appointed managers to run the day-to-day business for them, so now has the state designated authority to Hungarian managements. This, of course, involves the creation of a very new type of manager. No longer can he be simply a party official who has distinguished himself by long service to the local organization, nor can he simply be a friend of a friend of a man in the ministry. He has to be a technocrat.

That is why, in an ugly modern building, on an ugly, muddy boulevard, twenty minutes out from the center of Budapest, the managers of Hungarian industry are going back to school. And that is why, among the literature they are studying is the book *New Decision-Making Tools for Managers,* edited by the Harvard Business School.

The school was set up in 1968 after thousands of Hungarian managers found themselves quite unable to meet their new responsibilities. It runs courses of between two and four weeks on all aspects of modern business management in a socialist economy. To begin with, attendance was voluntary but in 1970 the government made it compulsory for every manager in the country down to the rank of personnel manager to take a course before 1975 either at this school or at one of the other four business schools in Hungary. There is no precise figure of how many people this will involve, but the "managerial class" down to shop-floor supervisors numbers 120,000.

The Budapest school is run by Dr. Gyula Berczi, plump one-time miner, agricultural worker, economics student, bureaucrat, and—after attending a course run by the YMCA in New Brunswick—now management expert. He has a staff of 186 which is to be increased to 250 by the end of 1972. Over half the teaching is done by visiting lecturers—sociologists, economists, and civil servants. To cope with its expansion, the school is buying a new British computer.

Apart from computer training, the school also runs courses on sales techniques, personnel selection and training, price fixing—indeed, on almost everything which might help managers to raise the productivity and increase the profits of their enterprises. On the reasonable assumption that all socialist economies have, in the past, been overburdened with dogma, management theory gets a very minor place in the syllabus. Most of the courses are taught on the basis of case histories—in classes of around thirty the students examine specific problems that individual Hungarian enterprises have had to try and overcome in meeting the demands for efficiency that the reform has imposed upon them.

Civil servants and Party officials have found the pressures of the reform almost as exacting as managers. Instead of simply issuing written instructions and expecting them to be fulfilled without discussion, they are now called upon to advise and help the people they once just ordered. This calls for unprecedented human contact and so Berczi's school has been asked to set up four-week courses to instruct apparatchiks in the delicacies of human relations.

Over black coffee and cognac, the grind of the trams outside, Berczi agrees that for many managers the principles of management are very hard to understand. He says that the main problem his teachers face is that under the old system managers had absolutely no incentive to learn; the habit of idle ignorance dies hard. He reckons that national output could be increased by 50 percent if only management were more efficient. Indeed, in a speech in 1971 on the problems of the economy, Prime Minister Jeno Fock cited the "sluggishness" of managers and their idle refusal to seize the opportunities the reform offered them to improve their products and increase their profits as among the main causes of the country's continuing economic problems.

Older managers, the men whose promotion had previously depended on the speed of their fulfilling ministerial decisions and on their loyalty to the apparat, tend to find the courses at the school both unpleasant and very difficult. But competition for places sooner rather than later is very stiff among the younger middle-rank managers, many of whom believe, with good reason, that a month at the school will be worth far more to their careers than a decade of diligent attendance at every meeting of the local Party cell. For the criterion by which they will be judged is the profit they make—part of which is shared out, in unequal portions, among employees. Nyers defends this profit-sharing system by saying that "the entire profit serves public interests or those of the collective units. The increase in enterprise profits is today in the interest of socialist society and it would be wrong to view it as something damnable."

Damnable or not, it clearly allows for the inequality of workers' incomes according to the performance of their particular enterprise. This is just what Nyers wants to encourage in the belief that in the fifties and early sixties there was so much equalization of incomes that individual effort no longer played any part in determining the size of a man's pay packet; no wonder men did not work as hard as they might, he says. He points out wryly that although the principle "Equal pay for equal work" is accepted as a laudable socialist objective, its corollary, "Differing pay for differing work," is less often quoted.[10] If one assumes that there is within a socialist society no possibility of a literal equality between individuals and that that can be attained only "in an age of abundance, under communism" (not yet even over the horizon), then the only equality which can now be enforced is that of opportunity. Or so the Hungarian leaders argue.[11]

At present most top managers receive between three and three and a half times as high a salary as the worker; the average monthly income of skilled workmen is 22 percent higher than that of the unskilled worker, the employee with secondary professional training gets almost half as much again as the unskilled laborer and the university graduate 70 percent more. These disparities are not enough, says Nyers.[12]

Many of the attacks upon the "New Morality" induced by NEM are in part based on the fallacious theory that in the early days of socialist construction, life in Hungary was more "meaningful," more "socialist," and thus less "selfish" than it is now. True that there were some, perhaps many thousands of genuine Communists who then believed that they were about to create a new socialist man and that in just a few years' time egoism, individualism, greed, envy, and their related emotions would no longer be known in Hungary. "In our country labour means honour and glory" was a slogan which some undoubtedly believed, and which many more certainly professed. Fewer believe it, though some still profess it today. Perhaps it is true, as one Hungarian writer put it, that "only hit songs can recapture what was beautiful in the past" and that too much nostalgia should not, therefore, be indulged for the old ideals of yesterday. To reconcile themselves to the change, Hungarian officials tend now to talk with reverence for Lenin's New Economic Policy, and they quote him: "Let us not build directly on enthusiasm but, with the help of the enthusiasm created by the great revolution, work with the help of personal interest . . . this increases production which we need at any price." [13]

It is true that the reform has introduced the opportunity for personal profiteering on a scale which never before existed in a socialist country. Hungarians now can and do spend a great deal of time, energy, and material resources on transforming themselves into all (or almost all) consuming consumers. To deduce from this, however, that Hungary is abandoning the principles of socialism for the individualistic spirit of capitalism is superficial. The aims, at least the published theoretical aims, of the Hungarian government remain what they have always been—to establish a "socialist" and then eventually a "communist" society. The new economic reform has not changed that; it has only introduced new methods by which it is thought (at least in public) that those aims may be best and most quickly achieved. It is no more true that Hungary is becoming capitalist because of its use of the profit motive than it is true that Great Britain is becoming communist by its use of planning.

It is obvious, however, that some of the by-products of the reforms—the most blatant examples of getting rich quick and decisions about what to do with your riches when you've got them—will continue to cause distress among many Party members, especially in the conservative provinces. And much of what is happening is anathema to Kadar himself. He is a man of puritanical temperament, imbued with the ethic of work, distrustful of the flesh, disapproving of easy success. In 1970 he personally ordered the banning of striptease. Under the incentives of the NEM, dancers had been enthusiastically taking off their clothes for their own and others' profit in bars and restaurants around Budapest. Kadar found it degrading, unworthy of Socialist Woman and now Hungary is one of the few East European countries where a publicly naked breast is almost never to be seen except on the screen.

Nevertheless the problems that Hegedus raises, of the slide into an "acquisitive society," remain unsolved. "The development of the socialist prototype of man and a socialist public mentality on a moral level is one of the main conditions for the final construction of socialism," declared the guidelines of the Tenth Congress, reasonably enough. "We have to strengthen the conviction that the individual can succeed only in alliance with society against egoistic, petit bourgeois views of life and attitudes."

How can this be achieved? There are very few answers. In an otherwise intelligent and sensitive analysis of the problems raised by income differentiation and financial advancement, Istvan Foldes, the editor of *Nepszabadsag,* is reduced to recommending lamely,

"We have to form a workshop outlook in which the good worker, the outstanding engineer, and an efficient staff are the factory's pride." How? Well, Foldes suggests that "it is a pity that in many factories the names and pictures of the production competition winners have disappeared from the notice boards." [14]

Since the end of 1970 the distressing unoriginality of such suggestions seems to have been replaced by a genuine concern of government and Party leaders to meet the criticisms that are made of the NEM from both its supporters and from those who fundamentally dislike its material values. In February 1972 Kadar declared that the development of the petit bourgeois spirit was the most important and most harmful phenomenon with which the Party now had to deal. And although part of his concern undoubtedly reflects an anxiety to assure his Soviet allies that Hungary is not straying too far along the path of capitalist business tendencies, there is no reason to doubt his basic sincerity.

Some steps have now been taken to curb the profits of private enterprise—no artisan is now to be allowed to earn more than about $35,000 (100,000 forint) a year, and land speculation has been curbed by restrictions on property ownership—but no solution to the basic dilemma has yet been found by Kadar or anyone else sympathetic to the aims of the reform. The Maoists and other New Left groups have their own final solutions and so, of course, do the Stalinists: all believe that the reforms should be abandoned. They argue that in his desire to appease the people and raise its standard of living Kadar has already sidetracked Hungary off the narrow road to communism down along the wide and greasy slope of consumerism.

Kadar himself once declared that "one simple provision taken in the interests of increasing productivity is more effective in our class warfare than hundreds of anti-imperialist slogans" [15]; now he makes a few more qualifications as to the exact nature of the increase. Perhaps he is beginning to realize that the influence of the Party tends to decrease in exact proportion to the rise in the standard of living as the demands of the economy take precedence over those of ideology in molding government policy. It is a problem that almost all East European regimes are beginning to face. But as the standard of living has developed further and faster and as personal freedoms are more extensive in Hungary than elsewhere in the bloc, it is the Hungarian Communist Party which faces the dilemma most immediately.

Ten

Kadar is the son of two peasants and he is fond of pointing out that so is almost everyone else in Hungary, whatever his job today. When the Communists took power in 1948 their most obvious and immediate aim was to overturn the Hungarian class structure. Semifeudalism was to be transformed overnight into socialism, the aristocracy annihilated, the gentry dispossessed, the bourgeoisie destroyed, the workers and the peasants exalted. It was not so much the development of an open society that the Communists sought, but one in which all emphasis was placed on the upward mobility of workers and peasants.

This involved not only glorifying the work that these two classes pursued, but also promoting many thousands of their members into posts of greater responsibility and power within the transformed administration of the country. With the creation of the vast Party apparat, which was filled almost exclusively by workers and peasants, and under pressure of the other changes in government, this aim was achieved: apart from the feudal characteristics of some aspects of Rakosi's Hungary already outlined, the power transformation of Hungarian society in the early fifties certainly deserves to be called revolutionary. As a result of it, today two-thirds of the country's executives are children of peasants and workers. And a token of the move upward from the land to industry (until recently, it was always thought to be in that direction), is that half of the present-day workers had peasant fathers.

But rejuvenating as this process undoubtedly was in the fifties, it has now become somewhat less exciting. The Party has achieved its purpose: after ten years of intensive movement, the upward flow from class to class began to slow down in the early sixties and has now almost entirely ceased. Hungarian society is today once more as static, it not as stagnant, as it was in the 1930s. There is now a new, reduced peasantry, a new enlarged working class, and a new, also enlarged, middle class of Party workers, government officials, intellectuals, petits bourgeois, and industrial executives. The aristocracy and the gentry have certainly gone for good (though their attitudes continue to permeate Hungarian life), but the other three classes still bear much the same relationship to one another as they did forty years ago. Kadar and his colleagues are now keenly seeking methods by which to keep society fluid and classes mobile.

Some sociologists argue that it is possible because urbanization is a continuing process in which only the first stage has yet been completed. Peasants have been transformed into workers: over the last twenty-five years every second peasant child has taken this step. The next step is the move to town. This has not yet occurred on as large a scale as it might—partly because of the underinvestment in the infrastructure already described. If the Hungarian government does wish to continue the process of social mobility then clearly the urbanization of those workers who still live in peasant surroundings is one solution. The next step up can be in one of two directions. It might simply be within their trade up to the rank of foreman. Or it can be onto the rungs of the Party apparat. This used to be the way in which they would most certainly assure themselves a complete break with their parents' worker-peasant past and a continuously rising standard of living, as well as ever increasing prestige. But since the introduction of the NEM, even this is not so certain. For, although no apparatchiks have yet been known to lose their jobs, those jobs are losing their importance as responsibilities are decentralized to enterprises and the apparat is being thinned by natural wastage. A career in the Party does not offer a less certain future than ever before, but it is one that is open to fewer people and it is also one that carries increasingly less prestige as the role of the Party per se shrinks in an otherwise expanding economy and maturing society.

One of the possible solutions currently being considered is in educational reform. After 1948 the school system was totally overhauled and redesigned to destroy rather than perpetuate cultural differences in the country. School became compulsory for the child till the age of fourteen, and up to the beginning of the sixties the proportion of working-class children continuing on to secondary education constantly grew against that of children from the professional classes. But ever since Kadar abolished class criteria for university entrance in 1962, Hungarian education has limited rather than encouraged social mobility in the country. As in several countries of Western

Europe, so in Hungary today, the proportion of working-class and peasant children who benefit from the educational system is constantly falling.* One of the most urgent public debates in Hungary at the moment is over how to reverse this process.

Worker-peasant parents tend to rationalize their reluctance to send their children to secondary school in two ways; they claim either that they cannot afford it or that the child doesn't do well at primary school. The second is more important, for most parents claim that they would be prepared to make financial sacrifices if they thought their child would benefit from them. But of those workers' children who do get to university, a tragically high proportion—24.1 percent—drop out. Over half of all student failures are children of manual laborers. In 1971 Dr. Karoly Nagy, rector of Lorand Eotvos University, Budapest, attributed this in part to the feelings of inferiority which working-class children often developed when they came into contact with middle-class children for the first time. (Their local schools have often been almost exclusively working-class or peasant).[1] This means that the children of peasants now tend to stay on the land or move up only into unskilled labor jobs; unskilled workers' children often advance no further than to skilled working jobs and the children of the middle classes (both new and old) retain the power and influence that their birth confers upon them. These are problems similar to those faced by most in-

* Three-quarters of the children who now leave primary school are from manual worker families, but only 25 percent of them apply for secondary school. Among the intelligentsia the picture is quite reversed: 75 percent of their children apply for secondary education. Whereas at the beginning of the sixties 44 percent of university students were from working-class or peasant homes, by the end of the decade, the figure was only 39 percent. In 1970 only 3.2 percent of the applications for places at Budapest University were from the children of peasants.

dustrialized societies, but politically rather less easily accepted in a socialist society than under capitalism. Almost everywhere in the world there is a clear contradiction between the educational and social functions of the school. The children who are easiest to educate benefit far more than the slower learners. The search for a solution is now being conducted in Hungary with some haste. Kadar has publicly renounced the easier alternative of regressing to the pre-1963 system of class admission to the universities, and in 1971 the government set up twenty commissions of teachers, sociologists, and social psychiatrists to study every aspect of education in the country and to find a way of improving it. In the belief that by the age of eight his cultural background has already almost completely determined the path of a child's future development, the emphasis is currently on the reform of primary education.*

The commission's report on primary education has not yet been published, but it recommends that education should begin at the age of two in crèches provided by the factory or cooperative and that from the ages of four to five the children should attend state-run kindergarten. At the moment there is an acute shortage of kindergarten places—there is room in them for only 57 percent of the country's children—and a frantic building program is under way. But even this will provide only 43,000 places by 1976 and 120,000 are needed. Now.

The commission also suggests that there should be far more elasticity in the age at which children begin primary school. They say that the present compulsory starting age of six is the correct time for only 30 percent of all children and believe that the child should

* As of June 1973.

be able to start at any age between five and seven. At the ages of nine and thirteen a backward child should have the chance of entering a revision class for a year. This would not involve streaming, for after twelve months he would simply rejoin the normal class of the year below him.

To alleviate both educational and many other problems of socialist Hungary one of the vital changes the government needs to make is in the distribution of housing. The shortage of accommodation in Budapest and other Hungarian cities has reached a crisis point, partly because of the destruction between 1944 and 1945 and in 1956 but largely because of the underinvestment during the 1950s. (At one stage investment plans for housing were abandoned in favor of a two billion forint investment in a new underground railway system meant to serve as an air raid shelter as well as an underground military warehouse.) But not only is housing scarce; what is worse is that such housing as does exist is distributed totally undemocratically. Indeed, the working class is as grossly discriminated against in the Hungarian housing market as it is in England, or was in Hungary before 1948.

In 1969 the sociologists George Konrad and Ivan Szelenyi delivered a paper to a sociologists' conference at Balatonfured. It constituted, whether they meant it or not, a terrible indictment of communist housing policy. After a study of four hundred homes in Budapest and Pecs, they concluded, "It becomes quite clear from the data we collected that allocation by the authorities systematically favours the higher income groups." And since 1949 "the higher income groups had to pay less for housing than the lower income groups had to pay for housing of a poorer quality."

The Hungarian city-dweller has today (if he is

lucky) the choice between privately owned or built and state-owned accommodation. The cheapest form of housing is that owned by the state. But these homes are occupied mostly by the rich. Szelenyi and Konrad also found, to their distress, a somewhat unattractive attitude of "God bless the Party boss or manager and their relations and keep us in our proper stations." As they diplomatically put it, "Although their housing was worst they [the poor] are a long way from being the most dissatisfied." [2]

If their figures are correct, the Hungarian regime has much to be ashamed of in the way it has allocated housing over the last twenty years. The housing shortage is still acute, and Rezso Nyers admitted in an interview in 1970, "The home-building rate is higher in most other socialist countries than in ours . . . . We have every reason to be dissatisfied with the rate and must do better in future." He agreed that whereas in Europe as a whole eight apartments per one thousand of the population are built every year, in Hungary it was only six. He reckoned that four hundred thousand apartments were needed then.

That's exactly the number scheduled to be built under the new Five Year Plan (1971–75); so even if the plan is fulfilled there will still be a shortage of accommodation in 1975. Of the new apartments half will be built publicly—from state and local council budgets and from enterprise funds; the rest will be constructed privately.*

* Up until 1971, rents were remarkably low in Hungary, as indeed in all socialist countries. Whereas in Great Britain a tenant may spend up to a third of his income in rent, in Hungary the average worker spent 150 forint of his 2,500 forint salary on housing in 1969. These low rents only met about 40 percent of the cost of maintenance and as a result Hungarian apartments fell to pieces much faster than necessary. The annual obsolescence rate is 1 to 2 percent on an estimate average life span of between fifty to one hundred years. To put this right thousands of surveyors spent

To alleviate the shortage of accommodation, the government is now doing all it can to encourage the middle classes to build their own homes. Mortgages are very cheap, though not so very large by Western standards: it is now possible to borrow 140,000 forint ($4,800) at 2 percent for thirty-five years. On top of that the government will lend you, if necessary, through the state building society, OTP (*Orszagos Takarek Penztar*), another 30,000 forint ($1,000) at 6 percent for thirty-five years. It is, however, not possible to get a mortgage to buy old private property, though for a flat which is less than thirty-five years old you can take over the previous owner's OTP mortgage.

It is unclear how effective these measures will be in stimulating the growth of the housing market in Budapest. It is most unlikely that they will be drastic enough to make the necessary difference. But until that market does grow enormously, some of the country's many serious social problems will remain unsolved.

Today, Hungary has the highest suicide rate in the world. It also has one of the highest abortion rates. These statistics are seized by some Western commentators who conclude that Hungarians must therefore be among the world's unhappiest people and that since 1956 the noxious Kadar has totally failed to

most of the autumn of 1970 examining apartments to determine how far rents could and should be increased. On the basis of their reports, the government published a decree reforming the housing regulations in 1971. It set out the amount of space each individual should occupy: one person or a couple can have between 1 and 2 rooms; a family of three can have between 1.5 and 2.5 rooms and one of four, 2 to 3 rooms. Anyone who presently has much more than this amount of space (i.e. a widower or a pensioner) will now have to move to a smaller flat. The decree also authorized an increase in rents, partly to encourage redistribution, partly to improve maintenance. This was large (often up to 300 percent) but many categories of people can obtain subsidies to meet all of the increases, and the new regulations applied only to state and cooperative-owned housing.

make communism acceptable to them. That is not a conclusion easily sustained, but it is nevertheless true that both phenomena cause Hungarian sociologists, psychiatrists, and, not least, politicians some concern. During the 1960s, the country's birth rate fell to levels only previously touched in the war. And this was achieved by the efficient use not of contraception but of abortion, which was legalized in Hungary in June 1956. Before that it had been virtually outlawed by a measure passed in 1953 known as the Ratko Law after the then minister of health, Anna Ratko. Mrs. Ratko was celebrated in Hungary for her proclamation that "for an unmarried girl to give birth is a glory, for a wife a duty." Her nephew is a talented but officially slightly suspect poet who lives in an ugly, comfortable sprawling flat in Szabolcs, in the poorest region of Hungary. He once described, at some length, and in verse, the amazing meanness with which his aunt treated him as a child.

Her law was mean too. It was designed to compel, not just encourage, women to indulge in their "glorious duty" and procreate. It did so by improving the tax advantages of pregnancy and childbirth, by imposing special taxes on childless men and women at 4 percent of their income, by declaring merciless war on all abortions—illegal abortionists were sentenced for up to eight years in prison—and by banning the sale of any contraceptives.

It was a drastic measure and it showed immediate results. Between 1953 and 1954 births rose from 19.6 to 23 per thousand of the population. But like so much of the sweeping legislation that was passed under Rakosi, very little attention had been paid to its broad social and economic consequences—let alone to its effect upon individual human happiness. Housing, maternity clinics, post-natal-care facilities, nurseries, kindergartens, schools—all these were already totally inadequate before the Ratko Law was passed, and little was done to improve them.

Following Rakosi's first political demise, the law was eased: hospital abortion committees were allowed to consider a woman's social condition as well as her health in hearing abortion applications and in 1955 the Ratko Law was abolished and the decision on abortion placed solely in the hands of the expectant mother, after the Presidium of the Supreme Soviet had passed a similar resolution. The next year the Ratko Law was described by Radio Budapest as a "hard rule" born out of sectarianism and not inspired by any understanding of human destiny, and after the Revolution the Kadar regime pledged itself against any return to her regulation: "an inhuman rule which compelled mothers to bear children against their will and regardless of the social consequences . . . the result of the soulless sectarian spirit which overplanned everything, setting a forced schedule even for the growth of population."

Since then it has been virtually impossible for any woman to be refused an abortion. She simply has to apply to the local abortion committee at her hospital. This committee has three members: a doctor, a representative from the council, and one from the trade unions. The committee is able only to try and persuade the woman to change her mind by reminding her of the risk to her health or future fertility. She can be refused the abortion only if she is more than twelve weeks' pregnant.

Any Hungarian woman granted an abortion on grounds of poor health receives the operation and postoperative treatment free. If her reasons are social or personal she has to pay the equivalent of between twelve dollars for the operation itself, two dollars fifty cents for each further day in the hospital; the recommended stay is three days.

In 1956 the Stalinist policy on contraception was reversed, for it was hoped that it would be contraception, rather than abortion, which would help couples to control the size of their families. In fact, despite a massive publicity campaign, contraception has still not caught on in Hungary. In 1963 women workers interviewed at a Budapest pharmaceutical factory did not know that the Timidon pills which they made and packaged were in fact contraceptives.

One reason for the lack of the pill's popularity is that the Hungarians have still not been able to manufacture a safe and efficient one. The side effects (increasing weight, sickness, dizziness) of both Timidon and its successor Infecundin rightly dissuaded most women from using them. Another reason is undoubtedly expense. The buyer has to pay the full cost of the pill, which works out at about twenty-nine forint, just under $1.20 a month. For most women, the pill is therefore much more expensive than an abortion.

Hungary is not the only East European country to have a birth-rate problem, but the situation is more extreme in Hungary than elsewhere; in 1969 there were 201,000 abortions and only 154,419 live births. In Czechoslovakia, on the other hand, there were approximately 200,000 live births and only half as many abortions that year.* By 1971 abortions in Hungary were running at one and a half times the birth rate and only about 400,000 women were reckoned to be using the pill effectively. The previous year the

* Abortion is available on demand in all East European countries, except Rumania, where it was virtually outlawed in 1965 under legislation similar to the Ratko Law. Divorce was restricted in Rumania at the same time. In 1964 there had been 36,194 divorces, in 1967 there were only 48. As a result of these measures the birth rate doubled for a time, but the number of people who thought it advisable to get married fell.

increase in population had fallen to 3 per thousand and in 1971 it was only 2.6 per thousand.

In an already overpopulated world, it might be thought that Hungary was in a fortunate position. But partly because of the country's growing labor shortage and partly for ideological reasons the low birth rate is a matter of enormous concern to the government, and the debate on the moral, political, social, religious, and sexual values of the freedom of abortion is intensifying. On only two things are the various protagonists—doctors, party ideologists, demographers, psychiatrists, and women—agreed: there should be no return to the blanket inhumanity of the Ratko Law, and it would be in the public interest to devise some method of encouraging women to have more children. This, of course, presupposes the discovery of why it is that so many women do not at present want more or indeed any children.

There is no complete study of the reasons for Hungary's particularly low birth rate, but such evidence as there is suggests that latterly it has been not unconnected with the ever improving standard of living in the country, especially since the beginning of NEM. According to Dr. Egon Szabady, president of the Hungarian Demographic Committee, only one-third of eight thousand women who ask for an abortion plead poverty as their reason. Usually they have decided, along with their husbands, that before they want babies, they want a TV, a refrigerator, or a washing machine. As cars become more easily available in Hungary, so more and more people, who previously would have considered it quite out of their reach, are beginning to save for one. And that often means no baby. Some women have also been known to need an abortion in order not to spoil their holiday plans.

All of which makes it unsurprising that at the Tenth Congress in 1970 Kadar should have talked to the delegates about the problem. He considered that "if someone is weighing, according to his or her own conscience, the choice of buying a T.V. set or car, that is his or her business. There are no compulsory laws on the subject." But he did draw the line at mockery of pregnant women. "We communists must oppose this. The noble traits of human nature cannot be scoffed at . . . . There are women who think that giving birth to a child will spoil their figures. This may be so, but they will be more beautiful in a human and general sense."

But his only solution to such attitudes and the only cure offered for people who value material objects not as "the tools but as the aim of life" is, predictably enough, relentless "education." Children should be taught more forcefully in school that their aim in life is the creation of a large and stable family. Married couples should be convinced that society despises those who purposely remain childless. The desire for children is a "matter of world outlook." [3]

In one attempt to raise the birth rate new maternity benefits were introduced in the sixties and in another a marriage bureau has been set up "to help lonely people" of whom there are thought to be 320,000 in Budapest alone. The trouble is that for every lonely man there are three lonely women, so even if the bureau is 100 percent successful, there will still be some 160,000 ladies lingering in the cake shops and cafés of the city. [4]

The bureau was conceived by the sociologist Pal Locsei after a study of divorce and loneliness. Applicants have to answer personal questions and state their sexual experience, if any. After that they must talk to a psychiatrist or sociologist. Fees are charged on an adjustable scale according to income. The agency has a computer, somewhat old-fashioned but a computer nonetheless and it issues every applicant with three chances of love. During its first six months it brought together seven hundred lonely people; a few months later thirty-five of these couples were still coexisting and five of them had actually married.[5] Not a phenomenal success rate but who knows, perhaps it has saved a few people from the national disease of suicide.

But that we are unlikely to be told. For although Hungary has a higher suicide rate than any other country in the world, it probably talks about the problem less than any. Until recently the subject was hardly mentioned in the press at all, and still today it is only very rarely discussed; if anyone prominent commits suicide, his death is simply described as "tragically sudden." This reticence is a hangover both from Catholicism and from the Stalinist era when the status of suicide changed from a sin against the spirit to a near-crime against the state. After 1945 the government even refused to publish any statistics on the subject, and this policy was not abandoned until Kadar came to power.

There are now some signs that the government is at last beginning to speak about suicide slightly more openly, that it is finally being recognized as a social as well as an individual problem. But only very slowly. In November 1969 Mihaly Gergely, a colorful writer who has also been a soldier, clerk, and factory hand, published an article on the subject in the literary review *Kortars*. He complained of the ludicrous secrecy with which the problem was still surrounded. In one hospital in the town of Szeged he presented his credentials and letters of introduction to the chief physician and asked to talk to him about the problem. "He studied the signature for several moments (his assistant had already informed him of my request) then returned it and our short but illuminating talk began. He cited his Hippocratic oath . . . and the regulations which made it impossible for him to reply to my questions, to talk of his experiences or even to show me his department. . . . He was very polite but he showed me the door within 5 minutes."

Gergely pointed out that the doctor got rid of him probably because he was frightened of trouble if he gave his opinions on such a "delicate issue," and one which, largely by default of the regime, still has undertones of anticommunism in many people's minds.[6]

It is easy to suggest that Hungary's high suicide rate is indeed a reflection of the people's disenchantment with socialism. Easy but incorrect. For some reason which has never been fully explained, (perhaps the country's landlocked puszta and wastelands are especially depressing), Hungarians have always killed themselves rather more enthusiastically than most other people. In 1892 the figures for what is Hungary today show that already over 20 people per 100,000 were committing suicide. The figure has dropped below 20 only twice in this century, but it has very often been much higher. In 1932, the depth of the economic depression, the figure reached a peak of 35.1 per hundred thousand and it was over 30 per hundred thousand for most of the thirties.

Nevertheless, some Hungarian sociologists have sought to explain the high postwar figures in terms of the stress of the revolutionary transformation of Hungarian society. Ivan Kemeny suggests, "The road uphill is a tiring one and is full of problems. Getting stuck on the way is even more painful. Exchanging cultures is often associated with a feeling of suffocation. The familiar world is left behind and the new one is friendless, bleak and awe inspiring. Rising socially is often accompanied by loneliness."

All of that may well be true, but unfortunately the figures do not prove that "rising socially" in Hungary also leads to suicide. In fact suicide fell markedly during the Rakosi period of the construction of socialism, when social mobility was most rapid. The period between 1946 and 1956 was characterized by enormous social upheaval and individual suffering, yet only once, in 1952, did the suicide rate exceed twenty-five per hundred thousand. Perhaps this is explained by the very fact of those upheavals; in those days the individual could shift all failures and misfortunes from his own shoulders onto the rump of the Party machine and any sense of personal responsibility was practically destroyed. At the same time, among the ordinary noncommunists, a certain unity was forged; sometimes it was one of defiance, more usually one of resignation, but either way there was a consciousness that problems were shared not peculiar to oneself.

The 1956 Revolution did not immediately affect the suicide rate, which remained below twenty-five per hundred thousand during 1957 and 1958. But the following year it shot up and for most of the sixties it was above thirty per hundred thousand. In 1970 it was 34.9; that year in the United States only 11.0 and in the United Kingdom only 6.5 people in every hundred thousand people killed themselves.

Interpretation of suicide statistics is fraught with danger at the best of times and with the incomplete information issued by the Hungarian authorities more so than usual. But the Central Statistical Office has tried to make some breakdown of the deaths, dividing them according to motives. Unfortunately their methodology is not revealed, so it is difficult to guess how reliable the figures are likely to be; they are, however, still of considerable interest.

During the 1930s one of the main motives for suicide was some form of financial crisis: money or, more usually, the lack of it accounted for 20.1 suicides per hundred thousand of the population. The Hungarian government can congratulate itself on having largely banished the specter of the workhouse: now only 3.7 suicides per hundred thousand are financial.

Today the single most common motive for suicide is family conflict. Three times as many people kill themselves because of difficulties with one or another of their relations than do it for straightforward nervous causes. More alarming is the fact that family conflict is almost as much a killer for children as it is for their parents. Among ten- to fourteen-year-olds suicide is the most common form of death after accidents and tumors. Among teenagers from fifteen to nineteen years old it is the most frequent cause of death bar none. These child suicides are three times more frequent than the average for European countries. But then the problems of Hungarian youth are rather particular.

Eleven

I have seen wide trousers, narrow trousers, then wide trousers followed again by narrow ones. Fashions come and go; it is not a vital matter. But whatever the fashion it must be brought into harmony with health, beauty and cleanliness. We have no use for people in drainpipe trousers. But our youth will not be like that. Those who have long hair will cut it in time.

J. Kadar
January 1, 1968

In the late fifties, Kadar once related a rather prim little parable in which he played the hero. Just after he joined the Party in 1931 he met a young Communist worker who was having difficulty in enrolling new members to her cell. She told Janos Barna, as she knew him, that this was because the girls were not interested in serious things like politics or economics, only in "movies, make-up, pretty clothes and boys." That was shocking enough, but worse was to come. Kadar relates that "she also said something—in a very upset tone—about their morals not being quite unimpeachable. In fact she used a much stronger expression."

Janos Barna, Kadar admitted, didn't know what to say to that. "I just stared ahead and thought for a while." He finally came up with the idea that the young should not be judged on outward appearances and told the girl from the silk factory that before she had joined the Party six months ago she had been just like the girls she now described, interested in boys, movies, and clothes. But not only. Not exclusively. For in that case she could not have become a Communist at all. Well, surely the other girls were like that too? Underneath the lipstick and the fancy shirt were not they also seeking the truth that only the Party could provide?

He recalled with evident pleasure that at this the girl became quite ashamed of her intolerance and within no time at all had succeeded in enrolling several new Party members. All of which led Kadar to deduce that it was necessary for Party workers to encourage and develop the latent socialist aspirations in even those who seemed to have the most superficial values.[1]

It's hardly surprising that this is a philosophy he continues to stress, for who is to lead the Communist party, the vanguard of the working class, along the road to full communism in twenty, thirty years' time if not the youth of today? There's little point in struggling toward socialism now if there will be no one to carry on the fight in the future. But, at the moment, Kadar has little cause for joy. The average Party member is now forty-four and getting older all the time; despite the achievements of Kadar's regime, Hungarian youth show a startling lack of enthusiasm for the works of the Party.

Like young people in many different Western countries, young Hungarians often express cynicism for orthodox forms of political organization. Students, young journalists, and intellectuals are skeptical about the role of the Party and often dispute the Party's own claim to be the only true and faithful guide to communism. Because, for all Kadar's attempts to allow noncommunists into important positions, many students feel that Party membership is still the quickest way to guarantee a successful career and they therefore tend to dismiss those of their friends who do join as opportunists.

In fact many of those who join out of opportunism are unwilling to take any real part in the Party's business. Often they join, just join, because they think it will ensure them a quiet life.

In many factories, for example, the chief engineer is only thirty. He is a Party member, but he joined only after being especially asked to do so. He attends Party meetings when he has to, but if he speaks it is to give his expert opinion rather than any ideological interpretation. He never takes any Party initiative; he is an engineer and an engineer he wishes to remain, he has no desire to meddle in politics. He is earning the equivalent of between $70 and $170 a month, and gets a share in annual profits of up to $1,900. He has a good private flat, a car, and is building a cottage in the country. When it is finished he will buy a second television, a second frigidaire, maybe even a second washing machine for it. He knows all about the factory and its Party cell and he knows which of its little Napoleons are intriguing against which of its Bonapartes. He does not want promotion. He knows that he would only earn another $20 a month and doesn't think it worthwhile. To move up the factory's executive ladder would involve him in much more negotiating with the Russians (he already has to do enough of that) and it's always possible that he could make a mistake which would later be held against him. Ambition is a risk. Better the quiet life.

In an effort to encourage young people to join, Kadar has lowered the age of admission from twenty-one to eighteen and abolished the probationary membership period. Both these reforms infuriated the old Party stalwarts and many local organizations protested bitterly to Budapest, but few young people seemed very interested. Kadar attempts to take cheer in the fact that most of the people who do now join are under forty and 35 percent of them are under twenty-six. But a statistic which he quotes less enthusiastically and less frequently is that over the period of 1966 to 1970 the proportion of pensioners increased from 9.3 percent to 12.3 percent. Like many young people everywhere the prevailing political emotion of the Hungarian young appears to be apathy—not anticommunism, for most of them would probably call themselves socialist—but sheer lack of interest.*

In 1968 the students of many countries arose. In the U.S.A., in France, in Yugoslavia, in Poland, and, in a more complicated fashion, in Czechoslovakia. But not in Hungary. At the University of Budapest there were no riots in the Philosophical Faculty, no debates in the Faculty of Letters, no demonstrations at the Political Science Department. All was calm; the calm of the post-1956 generation of young intellectuals whose memories of childhood include the tanks, the shooting, the dead bodies in the streets; theirs was the muteness of boredom, the boredom of having seen so much already through innocent uncomprehending eyes and of gradually growing up to understand the futility of effort. This apathy does not imply supine satisfaction but rather the conviction of impotence. The Hungarian regime continually stresses, and with excellent reason, that "things are really going quite well now and are much better than ever before." So they are, for people of thirty, forty, or fifty who remember Stalinism, the war, and the Horthy regime. For them, things are incomparably

* The best description of the complex attitudes of youth in Eastern Europe is Paul Neuburg's excellent book, *The Hero's Children*, London: Constable 1972, New York: Morrow, 1973.

better. But many Hungarian students remember well only 1956, and for Hungarian youth 1956 is in some curious, traumatic way both the beginning of political consciousness and the end of political interest.

Many of the most intelligent of them find it difficult to comprehend that the struggle in 1956 was really over the building of present-day Hungarian society. Their parents are happy, eager to accept the rise in the standard of living, the political compromises, the economic pragmatism, the easy life that Kadar has given them. Many students, however, seem to expect more from the crushing of the uprising than just this. Was this really worth fighting for? they ask. Was it *all* that was fought for? But continually impressed that "everything is in order," they see little chance of radical change in the Hungarian regime's present political and economic ambitions, there is no point in rebelling against the system which has been built for and without them. At the same time, however, today's under-twenty-five year olds, who remember the Revolution much less clearly—if at all—than their elder siblings, are beginning to show much more independence and spirit than those aged between twenty-five–thirty-five. But even this does not mean their active interest.

In November 1971 the Ministry of Culture disclosed that in a survey it had just completed, only 61.5 percent of twelve hundred secondary school students questioned had "precise positive knowledge about the difference between the contemporary and pre-liberation (ie pre-1945) social systems of our homeland."

Perhaps even more extraordinary, since they have been educated in an atmosphere of total dedication to communism, the students betrayed almost equal lack of understanding about the leading role of the working class and knew still less about the work of the

Party: "Several students even hypothesized several parties here." Because many of the opinions on the Party were unfavorable and decried the existence of corruption, inefficiency, and nepotism among Communists, the ministry commented that it was clear that their knowledge was very superficial.

The survey also showed that very, very few secondary school students knew just what the Communist Youth Organization (KISZ) was supposed to do. In twelve hundred interviews "there was not one answer which mentioned the relationship between the Party and the youth movement." [2]

Perhaps the main fault and failure of KISZ is that its task is first of all to organize campaigns and to commemorate anniversaries with suitable marches and parades. It finds it easier to remind people, at periodic intervals, of its militant past than to try and find a consistent and progressive solution for the problems that young people face today. It is old, narrow-minded, and bureaucratic.

Kadar himself is aware of the problem. In May 1969 he spent a day and a half talking to students at Budapest University. It was a fairly informal and useful session, covering questions ranging from China to the salaries of the teaching staff. For the record, at any rate, Kadar declared afterward that he had met with "a mature social sense of judgment amongst the majority of students." As for KISZ, he told them, "It is built on the fundamentally correct principles of democratic centralism. However, it evidently has some bureaucratic distractions which must be eliminated." [3]

Fine words, but not acted upon. Two years after his descent into the university, KISZ was banning from the Youth Park in Buda (about the only open-air place in Budapest where young people can con-

gregate and relax) anyone wearing either jeans or
long hair.

It took not the promises of Kadar but the indignation of an intellectual to induce KISZ to rescind this
rule. In an open letter to the KISZ Central Committee in July 1971 Laszlo Gyurko, distinguished play-
wright, critic, and author, condemned the ban as
quite unsocialist as well as unjust and stupid. He
maintained that it was ludicrous to judge young
people on their appearance rather than behavior
(sentiments of which Kadar would approve) and
pointed out that the members of the band which
played in the park and which was hired by the committee all wore their hair long. Gyurko argued that
young people identify KISZ "with socialist power and
the socialist system, and every unwarranted measure
of this sort therefore causes them to distrust the socialist order." [4] His public attack finally induced the
KISZ to rescind its rule, and the band played on.

Pop music has been popular in Hungary since the
mid-fifties, but it was not till the mid-sixties with the
spread of transistor radios, with easier access to Western records, and, above all, with the Beatles joyfully
spreading their music across the world like limitless
English peanut butter that it assumed a new and, to
some Hungarian ideologists, sinister political significance. Those of them who shrilly upbraided the Beat
Craze saw it as a new cloying attempt at subversion by
the West and, because of a few ill-judged moves to
suppress the phenomenon it did begin to acquire, for
some teenagers, a spirit of defiance which was not
originally in its essence but has subsequently become
indistinguishable from it.

The most popular of the indigenous pop groups is
the Illes band. They have won both fame at home and
considerable financial success abroad. But they have

also had their political problems. During a tour of West Germany and England in early 1970, the group agreed to give an interview to the BBC's Hungarian Service. That was a mistake in the first place because although no foreign broadcasts to Hungary are now jammed, their work is regarded officially with more than a certain skepticism in Budapest. Nevertheless, the Illes group proceeded to use the BBC as a medium for criticizing the state of pop music in Hungary. According to the official Hungarian youth paper, *Magyar Ifjusag*, they said:

> There is no light music whatsoever in Hungary. The young people—with very few exceptions—have no clubs where they can meet and listen to beat music. Under such circumstances bands can very rarely achieve fame and are not appreciated financially or otherwise. Those who wear their hair long are automatically branded as immoral. But those to whom long hair is a problem are in fact primitives who have no idea of life and the world in which they live. Youth can, however, demonstrate with long hair against bald old age.[5]

Well, if that's what they really did say, and perhaps they were high at the time of the interview, it is hardly surprising that they should have come in for some criticism at home. Their punishment was a restriction of appearances: they were banned from radio, television, and playing in Budapest, but were still allowed to perform in the provinces. This was despite some sort of explanation of the interview—and self-criticism.[6]

It was not to prove an extended exile, perhaps because the Party considered it unwise to annoy the young by an unnecessarily protracted punishment of the musicians. In an effort to improve its own image, their Budapest comeback was staged at Christmas

1970 by KISZ, and in the early new year the group was once more on television and making records. Its first LP after their return from the wilderness of the Hungarian puszta was called "Human Rights." It had been recorded before their fall from grace, but when it appeared the sleeve bore the slogan "For Angela Davis" and contained a postcard photograph of her. She was unknown when the songs were recorded and the lyrics do not mention her at all: they are more concerned with freedom of speech and travel. But she was, of course, very fashionable in Eastern Europe by the time the record was released.

For several years in the mid-sixties the most popular radio program among Hungarian teenagers was called "Teenage Party." This two-hour afternoon program of music and news was broadcast not by Radio Budapest but by Radio Free Europe in Munich. In order to counter the "pernicious" influence of such "hostile propaganda," the Hungarian government was forced to compromise with its own fears about the dangers of pop music and so, rather as the Labour government encouraged the BBC to introduce Radio One to replace the outlawed pirate stations, allowed Radio Budapest to begin its own pop music show. Called "For Young People Only," it has been very successful and, partly because reception is so much better, has superseded "Teenage Party" and is frantically tape-recorded by teenagers all over the country.

Pop music has been associated with hippie culture and the Hungarian media have, since 1965, paid considerable attention to the Western and especially American hippie movement. It is, therefore, hardly surprising that this should have had an imitative effect upon Hungarian youth, despite the terms of contempt in which official reporting of the Western phenomenon is almost always expressed. A program on Radio Budapest in December 1968 denied that there was any social basis for a Hungarian hippie movement but proceeded to show that such a movement nonetheless existed. "I am completely indifferent to my mother and would like to annihilate my father," declared one sixteen-year-old girl interviewed. The radio's reporter also disclosed that hippies often sell their girl friends to "straights" and asked one unidentified girl whether she didn't think it disgusting to make love for the equivalent of one dollar. She replied, "Shit. I've got to do something to get the money," and pointed out with some asperity that she was anyway paid about seventeen dollars, not, as the reporter ignorantly and insultingly suggested, only one; just as well, since she had to share her earnings with her boyfriend and his friends. "Disgusting, reactionary and imitative of sick Western values," declared the radio reporter with glee at the end of his not un-enjoyable program.[7]

In February 1970 there was a court case in Budapest which received a considerable amount of attention in the press, perhaps because of the very bizarreness of its defendants—the ten members of the Big Tree gang—who were charged with "continuous incitement of the general public." More precisely, on July 7 and 8 of the previous year, they, together with about one hundred other juveniles, had allegedly marched along the streets of Budapest singing. Among the songs they were supposed to have sung were a German Nazi tune "Erika," and they greeted the bemused citizens they passed with cries of "Heil Hitler" and "Kitartas," which was the slogan of the Hungarian Nazis—the Arrow Cross—and means "keep on." They marched past the Party headquarters to the Basilica of St. Stephan's Cathedral, where they tried unsuccessfully to celebrate a beat mass in requiem for Brian Jones, a member of the Rolling Stones who had just died in a swimming pool. Thwarted, they proceeded toward the American Embassy (with unknown intentions) where they were arrested.

The members of the gang were united by their sense of alienation from their environment and their self-confessed aim was to "bother the bourgeois," their well-to-do new middle-class parents. For this, chorused the press, their families, schools, youth organizations, and work places must bear a great deal of responsibility.

According to one paper they indulged in hostile political discussions and even wrote poetry.[8] Or rather, the leader of the gang wrote poetry—most of it distinctly flavored not only by antisocialism but also by misanthropy. They also had religious aspirations. Several of them wore large crosses on chains and one Catholic newspaper speculated on whether it might not be possible to encourage this flickering need for spiritual comfort toward the more orthodox church.[9]

The leaders of the gang were sentenced to three years' imprisonment and the others to terms ranging between eight and fifteen months. These were light sentences (statutory punishment for incitement is from two to eight years in prison), which are explained perhaps by the youth of the defendants—the oldest was only twenty-one.

Although the hippie movement is minute in Hungary and although the proportion of young people who demonstrate their disgust with the system is also tiny, the attitude of the young toward society nevertheless causes enormous, perhaps even disproportionate, anguish among the older generations. Old

Communists seem to be quite unable to accept that the new generation might be able to succeed them. Antisocialism is not an important political emotion of students, but while Marxism retains a broad allegiance among those few who still claim a degree of political interest, there are many different interpretations of the philosophy. As many, indeed, as there are elsewhere in the world, and ranging from a hopeful trust in "socialism with a human face" through the militancy of Mao and the romantic legacy of Che. All three of them represent philosophies which are officially anathema to the Kadar government, perhaps because in all three doctrines there are elements against which that regime finds it difficult to struggle with conviction; all three, in different ways, are specters which haunt Kadarization. "Socialism with a human face" is a reminder that in Czechoslovakia total restructuring of Party and society, not just Kadarist piecemeal reform, was considered quite essential if the spirit of Stalinism was to be exorcised and truly destroyed. And its failure is a reminder of Hungary's own client status in Eastern Europe. The lure of Guevarism is much the same to Hungarian youth as it is to the young of Western Europe, but it shows the Party leaders that the Hungarian Communist party has already lost the ethos of romantic idealism which, in the thirties at least, was so important an incentive to its membership, tiny though it was. And the rigid puritan ethic of Maoism is a constant reminder that there is a successful and, apparently, popular form of socialism in which profits, incentives, television sets, moneygrubbing, and cars are not necessary prerequisites to satisfying the people.

As in the West, many young Hungarian "revolutionaries" are children of the middle classes and

prominent among those who have turned to Maoism
are children of the most committed Stalinists of the
Rakosi era. In 1967 a group of Budapest students
founded the Solidarity Committee with Vietnam.
They were initially supported by KISZ, the Young
Communist League, but the police, nevertheless,
began to take an interest in their activities and found
that they were producing leaflets denouncing what
they called "The Red Bourgeoisie." These leaflets,
which they stuck between the pages of library books,
complained of the evils of revisionism; they bewailed
the fact that Hungarian workers no longer controlled
Hungarian destinies (they did not realize, or ignored
the fact, that Hungarian workers never did) and they
declared that the U.S.S.R. should be fought, if necessary, at gunpoint.

The police, inevitably, arrested them. And among
the leaders who were taken was Gabor Revai, son of
Joszef Revai, Rakosi's cultural commissar. Gabor was
a Maoist, a young man as dogmatic as his father, a
young man who would only smoke the cheapest ciga-
rette available in Hungary—*Munkas,* which means
"worker." The trial was in strictest secret, and Revai
himself was not prosecuted—his father's name
stopped that. One of his co-defendants was Anna Szi-
lagyi, daughter of the vice minister of culture at the
time. She too went free but her husband Bambino
Por, who had no high-placed relative, was locked
away.

The regime is now beginning to recognize that one
of the causes of disillusionment among the young
could be that they are subject to too much political indoctrination at school. In its August–September 1970
issue, *Tarsadalmi Szemle,* the Party's theoretical journal, admitted that by the time students get to university "their political reactions are almost paralysed."

There should be much more free debate in school, said the writer, but added that this must be kept within the bounds of Party policy—a somewhat contradictory provision. He nevertheless deplored the fact that young people felt it safer not "to stick their necks out"; it was terrible that students felt that to express criticism or even to query some aspects of Party policy could endanger their career and that they therefore preferred to talk politics only among close friends. The paper declared that this was totally undesirable; schools must learn to trust the "debating spirit of young people." They must not be suspected of "destructive" views if they dared criticize wage anomalies or conditions in a state institution. They should be encouraged to speak against corruption and the machinations of moneygrubbers. But not against the existence of the Party.

This is hardly likely to be enough to improve a situation in which Mihaly Sukosd, a brilliant thirty-seven-year-old writer and the coeditor of *Valosag,* the sociological weekly, is able to declare with no fear of contradiction that the trouble with Hungarian youth is that they have absolutely no political or ideological beliefs. The paradox is as Sukosd pointed out: "Today our youth is not in the least oppositionist but totally loyal. Unfortunately, however, there is nothing to be gained from this loyalty, because it has become the soil of indifference, disinterest, and individualism." [10]

The apathy of young people is explained partly by the fact that their horizons are artificially much more limited than those of many Western young because of the restrictions that the government continues to place upon their right to travel. It is probably safe to say that at any rate among students the inability to go where they want when they wish is the single oppressive characteristic of the regime that they resent the most. And this is a resentment shared by many of their parents.

Travel within the socialist bloc has recently become much simpler, though individual Hungarians are still not allowed to travel as tourists to the Soviet Union. Not that many wish to do so: tolerance of their own Communist party has led few Hungarians to tolerance of the Soviet Union; Russians are disliked more intensely today in Hungary than they have ever been.

The Iron Curtain is still barely torn for Hungarians who want to travel to the West. A decree law of the presidential council laid down in 1970 stated that "every Hungarian citizen has the right to obtain a passport and go abroad provided that he complies with the conditions stated in the rules of the law." Unfortunately, however, those conditions are somewhat severe and freedom of travel is not one of the rights guaranteed by the 1949 constitution.

It is easy enough to obtain a passport, valid for five years. But to leave the country, a Hungarian also needs an exit visa. This is more difficult to obtain. There are two ways in which the ordinary Hungarian citizen can obtain such a visa (commonly known as a "window") to travel privately to the West. In theory every two years he can have a visitor's pass. But this is issued only if he has a written invitation from someone in the West who guarantees the costs of his stay, and the invitation has to be accompanied by the envelope in which it was sent from the West. With such a pass he is allowed to take only the $5 in hard currency out of the country and is therefore totally at the mercy of his hosts. It is illegal to export forint and they are, anyway, valueless in the West.

If he has no friends in the West, he can apply only every three years for a tourist visa, with which he is allowed $100 in hard currency. He can have this visa more often if he has his own private sources of foreign exchange—if, for example, relatives in the West send him dollars via the Hungarian State Bank. Permission to hold special hard currency accounts was given in 1969 and there are now some four thousand people who do so. It is, however, probable that many of them are officials of one sort or another.

There are over three million Hungarians living in the West (a third of the present population of the country itself), but some of them left Hungary illegally either by escaping across the barbed wire and minefields of the frontier or by simply staying on after their tourist visas expired. The relations of such people still in Hungary are not allowed to receive money from them and will probably find it difficult to get a visa themselves. No Hungarian citizen is allowed to visit illegal émigrés and although the Amnesty of 1963 pardoned all those who had left the country since 1945, there has been no similar pardon since.

Hungarians can also be denied a visa if they have previously lost their passports, and even after a visa has been given it can be withdrawn at the will of the police or customs officials. It is still not uncommon for a Hungarian to be taken off the train to Vienna as it is thoroughly checked at the border station of Hegyeshalom or to be told at the airport passport control that things are not, after all, in order and that he will not be flying today.

It is difficult for a Westerner to understand the degradation of not being allowed to travel at will. Young Hungarians are bitterly rueful at the way in which their Western friends can blithely come and go to Budapest while they themselves may, for some bureaucratic mistake or vendetta, or for no reason at all, almost never be allowed to leave the country.

It is possible that were Kadar his own master he would allow Hungarians to travel abroad much more freely. The present maintenance of the Iron Curtain is, on one level, an absurd demonstration of the government's lack of confidence in itself. Absurd because if Kadar now allowed genuine freedom of movement to and from the country, as Tito does, perhaps very few Hungarians would defect. Certainly the size of the emigration would be more than offset by the enhanced prestige that the regime would gain, both at home and abroad.

But it is unlikely to happen. Not because the government cannot afford the risk and not because it cannot afford the hard currency (it cannot, but this is not a fundamental reason for the restriction). The barbed wire and watchtowers and minefields and machine guns and dogs will remain on the frontier because the Kremlin regards them as an integral part of the western seams of the Warsaw Pact. To remove them at the same time as easing the travel restrictions between the socialist countries would be far too dangerous. For although not many Hungarians might now want to flee, probably a great number of Czechs and Slovaks, now suffering the deprivation of Dr. Husak's barren rule, and perhaps many East Germans and Rumanians also would be only too delighted at this new escape route offered them. In the past, Yugoslavia has proved the easiest way for East Europeans to escape to the West. But Yugoslavia's open borders are not subject to Moscow's control. Hungary's are.

In 1970 a film which portrayed the young's confusions was released in Budapest. It was called *Kitores—Breaking Loose*—a title strangely prescient of the Czech film by Milos Forman called *Taking Off*. It was directed by Peter Bacso and the script was written by

George Konrad, the brilliant young sociologist and novelist whose book *The Visitor*, published in 1969, dealt with the rejects of society and was hailed as a masterpiece.

Breaking Loose tells the story of Laci Fonyad, a gifted young worker whose parents are rapidly accepting the "bourgeoisification" of modern Hungarian life. But because adequate housing is not yet a part of that process, Laci is unable to entertain his girl friend at home in his parents' tiny flat. Instead they have to make love in the trees of the hills of Buda, above the city. Arrested *inflagrante delicto* and charged with "offenses against public morals," Laci decides to chuck it all in and make illegally for the West. But he has no passport and his attempt to escape is discovered; he is arrested and sentenced. On release, he finds a job in a factory where he meets Anna, a sociology student who is making a survey of the workers. They fall in love and only later does he discover that she is the daughter of the factory's director; she is also a Guevarist and a would-be philosopher who despises her father as a bureaucrat.

Laci is then taken up by a go-ahead economist called Pray (portrayed by the real life economist, Tibor Liska, whose ideas have been quoted above). Liska is, in fact, almost playing himself in the film and he does it well. He is employed in the computer laboratory, attempting to streamline the factory so that it can be run more efficiently—just as the New Economic Mechanism demands. Predictably, the computer shows that several senior executives are fulfilling no useful functions at all; their posts are just sinecures. Alarmed, these men mount a campaign against Pray. This arouses the interest of the media and in a television interview Laci sides with his elder colleague. He has to leave the factory; Anna follows him, they move into a half-finished house and feed pigs. But Laci goes to pieces and so Anna goes home to daddy. Finally Laci meets Pray once more; he is now working in another factory and invites Laci to join him again. He does so. The last scene of the film is of gasping, choking fish.

Peter Bacso explained that his hero, Laci, was not trying to break loose from society, but just from a social structure which restricted him, a distinction which not everyone in Hungary would consider valid. He maintained that the film showed honestly, if not ruthlessly, some of the anxieties, problems, and conflicts inherent in the present development of Hungarian society. He thought such problems should be discussed openly rather than disregarded. Only in this way could a diagnosis be made and a cure perhaps be found. He believed this to be quite in harmony with the current political overtures of the Party leaders, eager to generate a dialogue with the public.

In a plea for better adult understanding of the problems of Hungarian youth, Vera Varga, a twenty-year-old journalist, declares, "I don't think that our aim should be to understand the past as our parents, who lived in the past, understood it." In *Elet es Irodalom*, a paper very popular among the intelligentsia and the young, she claims: "We have enough trouble—indeed it represents a life's work—to understand the present, which is indirectly and directly influenced by the past, since our present was created by those who were formed (and sometimes deformed) by the past." [11]

The article expresses well the dilemma of a generation unable to decide how far the crimes of Stalinism —in which so many of their present leaders and in which the entire framework of the country was involved—should affect its own political loyalties. It reflects also the difficulty that many people feel in reconciling the rhetoric of their government with the reality of its policies. Constant exhortations about the solidarity of the proletariat and the power of the Communist party—the vanguard of the working class—about the all-embracing influence of socialist morality, about the Marxist-Leninist approach to trade union reform, all these tend to jar slightly when it is abundantly clear that the Party's influence is all the time decreasing in a society that is growing fat on the same bourgeois consumer values that sleeken the West.

Government spokesmen and other propagandists spend considerable energy on trying to convince the young that nonetheless the Revolution continues apace. In an interview in July 1969 just after Kadar's descent on the Lorand Eotvos University, Lajos Mehes, forty-two-year-old leader of the Young Communists (KISZ), vainly tried to persuade young people that these times were just as revolutionary as the years immediately after 1945 or 1956. It was just that the needs of the Revolution had changed. Then it had been necessary to hold meetings, demonstrations, to beat up black marketeers, and to smash shop windows. That was how you showed a good class spirit. Nowadays, however, young people could show their commitment simply by the success of their work. It was less glamorous and, for that, probably more difficult, but nonetheless necessary.

Such protestations carry little conviction when young people juxtapose them with the way in which the government actually treats most displays of political enthusiasm. Because of her membership in the American Communist party, Angela Davis is an official heroine in Eastern Europe in a way that a noncommunist American Marxist revolutionary never is and never could be. She is also a spontaneous heroine among the young, quite independent of the Party's endorsement of her cause. Nevertheless, when the Students Union of Budapest University sought to march to the American Embassy in Budapest in protest against her detention, they were refused permission. Instead, they were told they could write a letter to the youth paper: the American ambassador would undoubtedly see it and pass it on. Similarly, students have been forbidden to demonstrate against the American involvement in Vietnam: send a petition to your paper was again the dampeningly drear reply. When a regime which constantly proclaims its burning revolutionary commitment demonstrates such extreme conservatism (in the worst sense of the word) it is hardly surprising that the young should be politically apathetic or Maoist.

In all, the effect of a lifetime of Marxist indoctrination has not been very profound. Not many young Hungarians seem to think in terms of the class view of history; several surveys have shown that the instruction of teachers lurks way behind the counsel given by parents. And on the whole, parents still seem to impart traditional nonsocialist attitudes to their children. A poll conducted among working-class and student youth in 1968 showed that the virtues they considered most important were honesty, truthfulness, helpfulness, love for fellows, and loyalty. The worst crimes were murder, theft, hypocrisy, compromise, and cheating. Thirty-two percent said they believed in God, most of the others described themselves as materialists, over half of those examined thought in terms of a traditional (i.e., Western Christian) value system, and only 14 percent professed Marxist and socialist ethical views and values. Not a very high percentage of people to lead Hungary further along the road toward communism.[12]

The real problem for the Kadar government is to try and combine an exciting atmosphere of constant development with the conservative caution that its relations with the Soviet Union impose upon it. This is a problem which Kadar—simple, pusillanimous, unadventurous and, for all his cautious enlightenment, hardly charismatic—is perhaps not best suited to solve.

Twelve

In a speech on November 7, 1961, Enver Hoxha, the Albanian leader, indiscreetly and, one suspects, with no little pleasure, quoted from a letter the Albanians had somehow obtained. It was written by Khrushchev to Tito on November 9, 1956, two days after the Kadar government had been established in Budapest. The letter referred, *inter alia,* to the fact that on November 4 Imre Nagy and about twenty friends, including George Lukacs and Mrs. Rajk with her son Laszlo, had sought refuge in the Yugoslav Embassy from the Russian tanks and from the NKVD men. "We consider it possible to agree with your view," wrote Khrushchev, "that no particular importance should be given now to the question of whether or not the Yugoslav Embassy in Budapest acted correctly in giving asylum to Imre Nagy and his companions." [1]

Nicely put, but both Khrushchev and Tito in fact considered that the future of Nagy was a matter of considerable importance. In determining just what that future should be, Kadar played a role which is still not entirely evident but which, even through the mists of lies and apologia, appears at least unattractive.

After he announced the formation of his government on November 4, Kadar tried to make clear that he wanted a reconciliation with Nagy. His program at that stage was, after all, not that dissimilar. On November 11 he declared over the radio, "I, who have myself been a member of Nagy's Government, hereby state that according to the best of my knowledge, neither Nagy nor his political group has willingly supported the counter-revolution." Later he told an official delegation of workers that Nagy was not under arrest. "Neither the Government nor the Soviet troops wish to restrict his freedom of movement. It depends entirely on him whether or not he participates in politics."

Five days later he was still making much the same promises. "Let Imre Nagy return to Hungarian territory and then negotiations and agreement will again become possible." [2] But, although there were those among the meek little agriculturalist's entourage who were doing their best to persuade him to try and make a political settlement with Kadar, Nagy himself was unwilling to compromise with a man whom he had never much liked and who, he rightly considered, had absolutely no legitimate claim to the office he was now occupying. Before he left his Yugoslav sanctuary, Nagy wanted a foolproof guarantee of unrestricted liberty for his entire party. Anxious that he should be given it, Tito sent his deputy foreign minister, Dobrivoje Vidic, to Budapest to negotiate with Kadar. For the Yugoslavs and for Nagy there were two possible solutions to the problem. The refugees could quite simply be guaranteed free movement within Hungary and thus just leave the embassy for their own homes. Or if this was impossible for Kadar to accept (and surely with all the offers of political cooperation that he was making, it should not have been), then the Nagy group should be given safe-conduct to travel through Hungary to Yugoslavia.

But that was not a solution that Vidic suggested with any great enthusiasm: Tito was, after all, still hoping that his relations with the Russians would continue to improve, and the presence of Nagy on Yugoslav soil could hardly be considered a catalyst to such friendship. For Kadar himself the idea was equally distasteful: whatever restrictions Tito placed upon his guest's activities, by the great majority of the Hungarian people Nagy and his followers would be seen as the legitimate government in exile. And who was now to say that if Soviet-Yugoslav relations ever deteriorated again, Tito might not decide to encourage such recognition? Both Hungarian and Yugoslav governments were thus anxious not to help Nagy seek exile in Yugoslavia and were determined to find their solution in a simple safe-conduct to his home. On November 21 Kadar wrote to Tito:

> In order to settle this affair the Hungarian government, in conformity with the proposal contained in the Yugoslav government's letter to me of November 18 1956, repeats here with the assurance already given several times by word of mouth that it has no desire to punish Imre Nagy and the members of his group in any way for their past activities. We therefore expect the asylum granted by the Yugoslav Embassy to this group to be withdrawn and that its members will return to their homes.

Whatever their misgivings, Nagy and his friends were induced by Vidic to accept this assurance. What then happened is best described by G. Altman, the correspondent of the Yugoslav paper *Borba:*

> Imre Nagy and his friends thanked the Yugoslav government for having granted them right of asylum and took their places yesterday evening, November 22 at 6.30 p.m., in the bus placed at their disposal by the Hungarian authorities, which was to take them home.
>
> In front of the Embassy building, at the corner of Heroes Square and the former Stalin Avenue, now Youth Avenue, a Soviet officer got into the bus. A Soviet police car drove alongside and another one followed behind. All three vehicles soon turned in the direction of the Soviet headquarters in Gorky Street. When the two Yugoslav diplomats who were in the bus protested, they were unceremoniously ejected, just in front of the Soviet headquarters.
>
> Upon the two diplomats protesting that the Russians' behaviour was a violation of the Hungarian-Yugoslav agreement, the Soviet officer replied that the agreement was no concern of his and he had his orders to take the passengers in charge. The two Yugoslavs then registered their protest to the Soviet officials against the intrusion by a third party into an agreement between the Yugoslav and Hungarian Governments guaranteeing the safety of Nagy and his friends—an intrusion which stultified the agreement.
>
> The two police cars were replaced by two armoured vehicles and the bus with Nagy and his friends set off for an unrevealed destination.[3]

That destination remained unrevealed. Their friends and relations, gathered at their homes, waited uselessly for the return of the refugees from the Yugoslav Embassy. Even reporters from the Party

paper tried and failed to find out where the bus had
gone. It was not until the following evening that
Radio Budapest answered all questions with the following curt communiqué:

> Imre Nagy, the former President of Council, and
> some of his companions, as it is known, requested
> and obtained right of asylum in the Yugoslav Em-
> bassy in Budapest. This expired on November 22.
> More than a fortnight ago, Nagy and his com-
> panions requested permission from the Hungar-
> ian government to quit the territory of the Hung-
> garian People's Republic and to go to some other
> socialist country.
>
> The government of the Rumanian People's Re-
> public having given its assent, Imre Nagy and his
> companions left on November 23 for the Ruma-
> nian People's Republic.[4]

That was the first public mention of Rumania in the
affair. The next day Vidic complained:

> The Yugoslav government is entirely unable to ac-
> cept the account that Mr Nagy and the other
> Hungarian personalities left for Rumania of their
> own free will. The Yugoslav government was
> aware that they wished to remain in their own
> country; it also knew that while they were in the
> Yugoslav Embassy at Budapest they had rejected
> the proposal that they should go to Rumania.[5]

The abduction was widely deplored by the Yugoslav press and the Yugoslav government later made a
formal protest. But, relieved as Tito undoubtedly was
at being able to wash his hands so simply of his em-
barrassing guests, we do not know how sincerely this
protest was actually felt. From the Yugoslav Embassy,
the bus was taken to the Rakoczi Military School and
there the kidnapped men and women and children

were visited by Ferenc Munnich, the man who had first gone over to the Russians with Kadar.

According to one of the kidnapped, Munnich told him, "I don't know why you've been brought here, but we will try and get you out as soon as possible." But another now remembers that the purpose of Munnich's visit was to see if Nagy and his colleagues had not finally been frightened enough into dropping their former obstinacy and coming over to join Kadar.* This seems a more plausible explanation.

Nagy had not been frightened enough; he and his friends still refused to associate with Kadar, and Munnich went away empty-handed. After five days in the school the "counterrevolutionary leaders" (as they were soon to be called) were ordered back into the bus and then, as one of them now recalls, "With a Soviet tank in front of us and another behind us, we were driven off into the night. After a long drive, the bus left the road and bumped over a field. I thought we were all going to be shot. In fact it was an airfield and we were flown to Rumania."

There Nagy was separated from some of the others who were given villas in which they lived unmolested for the next two years. How well Nagy himself was treated is not known. It is thought that further attempts were made to get him to recant. Whether torture was used to this end has not been revealed.

Kadar "explained" the situation to two Swedish journalists who managed to interview him in December 1956. Nagy and his friends, he said, had "dissociated themselves from the Hungarian problem by expressing a wish to leave the country. For a certain period I consider it more expedient that they do not reside in this country—not for ever, but until the sit-

* In private conversations with the author in Budapest.

uation is more normal." Talking to the Swedes, Kadar made little jokes (which they did not appreciate) about how he would order his own arrest if he thought methods of terror were being used in Hungary. The Swedes described him as very "grey"; "wearing a grey suit, over a grey pullover, above it grey cheeks." His eyes were "small and grey, with a look that does not flutter, which is dead. Deep down they have an eternal uneasiness about them." [6]

His own motives and exact role in Nagy's abduction are not self-evident. Did he or did he not know at the time of giving the promise of safe-conduct that that promise would be broken? There is no consensus: not among those who survived the enforced holiday in Rumania, not among those who have prospered in Hungary since the Revolution, and not among those who have written of the Revolution from exile.

Whenever he has been asked by an inquisitive Western journalist, Kadar himself has always claimed responsibility for everything that happened to Nagy after his departure from the Yugoslav Embassy. The evidence that he was not in fact responsible and that he was initially horrified by the news that his pledge had been broken is again based largely on what is known of his character and is circumstantial. Endre Marton, the AP correspondent in Budapest at the time of the Revolution, is one who is quite convinced of Kadar's innocence: "All my sources, including one who was personally very close to Kadar, told me how desperate Kadar had been when Nagy was abducted and when he was executed eighteen months later." [7]

But this charitable interpretation of his role in Nagy's abduction is not without problems. If he genuinely expected Nagy to return home, how on earth did he think he would deal with him? The Hungarian people were still in a totally unsettled mood and unless Nagy agreed to join Kadar's government, he would constitute (far more than in Yugoslav exile) a very dangerous symbol of resistance. Whether he wanted it or not, his house would become a place of pilgrimage and his presence in it would have given Hungarians real hope for change; every time he walked down the street, his bowler hat roundly above his walrus whiskers, he would appear a tangible and pragmatic reason for continuing their resistance to Kadar's regime.

But perhaps Kadar really did believe that Nagy could be induced to collaborate with him. And perhaps, indeed, he could have, for Nagy was an inconstant, irresolute, and malleable man. If he had joined Kadar, then many of the hardships and persecutions of the next few years could have been avoided, Kadar could have wooed the people straightaway, and the alliance policy of 1961 could have been forged much earlier. But Nagy, of course, though weak, was honest.

Over the next eighteen months the language in which Kadar and his colleagues spoke publicly of Nagy grew ever fiercer and more uncompromising as it became ever clearer that Nagy would never recant, as such a recantation anyway became increasingly useless to the new regime and as relations between Tito and Khrushchev once more deteriorated and the need to appease the Yugoslavs by treating Nagy well diminished. By mid-1957 he had been labeled unequivocally the leader of the "counterrevolution," despite Kadar's earlier, more charitable descriptions of him.

On June 16, 1958, a short communiqué was broadcast first from Moscow and then from Budapest: "The Hungarian legal authorities have concluded the proceedings in the case of the leading group of those persons who, on 23 October 1956, started a counter-revolutionary armed uprising." The People's Court of the Supreme Court had declared the defendants guilty and passed sentences of death on Imre Nagy and three of his associates. Others were sentenced to terms ranging from life to twelve years.* The sentences were nonappealable and by the time the communiqué was issued they had already been carried out.

That, for the moment, was where the matter rested. Very little other information was released officially. Gradually those who had not been tried, like Mrs. Rajk and her eight-year-old son Laszlo, Kadar's godson, were allowed to return to Budapest, and some of those who had been sentenced to terms less than death were released in the amnesty of March 1960. For a long time nothing more was known about the trial except what was revealed in a White Book, an apologia published by the Kadar government and containing a partial "transcript" of the proceedings. Many Hungarians imagined that Nagy had probably just been summarily executed in Rumania.

Little more was said until on February 19, 1964, *Le Monde* published an interview which Kadar had just given André Fontaine. Fontaine asked him if the complete minutes of the trial would ever be published and whether Nagy would ever be rehabilitated. The answer was no: "The question is completely closed . . . it's better not to talk about it." That was Kadar's prepared reply to a previously submitted question. He then added, ostensibly off the cuff, "At that time things were not quite normal, because of the hysterical attitude of international opinion towards Hungarian events. My feeling was that, in such circum-

* Another, Geza Losconczy, who had been imprisoned with Kadar, died—or was possibly murdered—in prison.

stances, it was not sensible to have an open trial. But I can assure you that the proceedings were legal in every way and that only Hungarians took part. A lot of lies have been told about the trial—even that it didn't take place in Hungary. Come with me." Kadar then led Fontaine over by the arm to the window and pointed out across the river to the High Court: "That's where it took place. . . . Despite Western attacks, everyone in Hungary knows that they were sentenced because they had broken Hungarian laws. . . . We [i.e., the state] intervened only to grant an amnesty. . . . In no way were we inspired by feelings of revenge."

That last remark at least is almost certainly true. Whatever his weaknesses and his unreliability, it is hard to believe that Kadar derived any satisfaction from the execution of Nagy. Indeed, disappointment and self-disgust may have been his predominant emotions. A few days after the execution he reportedly told a group of officials at Budapest airport, "Comrades because we entered on this course on November 4, it was necessary to go to the very end." [8] These were not the words of a man confident that the right decision had been made, that justice had really been done. Quite apart from his personal feelings, he must also have realized in 1958 that the execution would do nothing to heal the country's wounds and could serve only to augment the distrust which so many millions of Hungarians still felt for him. He agreed to it only because Khrushchev compelled him to do so. And Khrushchev compelled him to do so largely because the Chinese and their close supporters in the Kremlin were putting increasing pressure on him for "a more Leninist" treatment of Nagy, "the traitor to the international working class."

Unable to refuse Khrushchev, Kadar submitted.

And so that wretched fat little "counterrevolutionary," that pathetic, inept, but honest agriculturalist who should really have spent his life in the study of the development of collective farming and never meddled with national emotions and revolts, that meek and mild-mannered Marxist was taken, in circumstances the loneliness of which we can only guess at, to his pointless death, a death which caused joy to no one except Mao Tse-tung.

For Kadar, it was the old, old argument, the same that he had used to convince himself at the time of the Revolution, the same he had to use in 1968, the same used by collaborators and politicians everywhere, "If I don't do it, I will be replaced and someone else far worse will do it instead." Because he genuinely wanted Hungarians' lives to improve and because he really thought that he himself could achieve this quicker and more completely than any other leader and because, of course, he also preferred power to dismissal, he compromised, sacrificed the short term, the means to the end, the individual to his concept of the nation. It happens often.

Pragmatically he was right: the execution of Imre Nagy, like the death of Laszlo Rajk, is no longer an issue which exercises the Hungarian people at all. That fact, extraordinary as it is when set against Nagy's popularity through the 1950s and especially in 1956, is perhaps the best measure of Kadar's success at healing the wounds of the uprising.

But what *is* of concern to Hungarians today is their country's relationship to the Soviet Union. The execution of Imre Nagy reminds them that the Kadar regime exists by Soviet pleasure and that Kadar's government is a weathercock registering the Kremlin wind; the slightest shift is instantly recorded: the personalities of his government pop in and out, like children's rain and sun men, as the change in the atmosphere demands. Decisions, and especially foreign policy decisions, are implemented in Budapest, but very often only in the light of other decisions already taken in Moscow. Nothing brought this limited sovereignty home to Hungarians more sharply than the invasion of Czechoslovakia in 1968.

Hungarians are sometimes suspicious and resentful toward Czechoslovakia—not least because in 1919 the Treaty of Trianon accorded to Tomas Masaryk so much Slovak territory which they considered still rightfully theirs. There has never been the same sympathy between Budapest and Prague as between Budapest and Warsaw. The poet Petofi once declared, in a poem which every Hungarian school child can recite, "In our hearts, two peoples, the Polish and the Hungarian, are mingled. If both set themselves the same objective, what destiny can prevail against them?" In October 1956 both did set for themselves the same objective but destiny, a Soviet destiny, nonetheless prevailed against Hungary and, in the long run through the bankruptcy of Gomulka's 1956 promises, against the Poles as well.

Unlike the Poles, in 1956 the Czechs were among the most orthodox of Hungary's neighbors and the quickest to condemn its attempts to alter its communist system. In 1968, therefore, sympathy for the Prague Spring was not unreserved in Budapest.

That is not to say that there was not great understanding of many of Dubcek's aims. Indeed, not only were the plans of his main economic adviser, Ota Sik, for the overhaul of the Czechoslovak economy similar to those of Rezso Nyers, the two schemes were actually designed to work in conjunction with one another. When the Czech reforms had to be abandoned after the invasion the Hungarians lost what was to have become one of their most crucial partners. Together the two economies would probably have both advanced much more quickly than the Hungarian alone, and leading Hungarian economists readily admit today that many of their economic problems are caused by the way in which, since April 1969, Dr. Gustav Husak, Dubcek's successor, has systematically destroyed the Czechoslovak reforms.

As Soviet and East German alarm at the Czechoslovak experiment "to give socialism a human face" increased through the summer of 1968, so did the anxiety of Kadar and his closest colleagues. Not because they shared Ulbricht's and Brezhnev's fundamental disgust with the liberalization on which Dubcek had embarked, but because they feared that Soviet determination to crush revisionism in Czechoslovakia would involve also the end of Hungarian aspirations for political and economic change. Kadar was alarmed lest the rash, spontaneous, and unplanned enthusiasm of the Prague Spring would encourage the Kremlin to destroy the freedom of all East European reformists, notably himself.

He was fond of Alexander Dubeck, the gentle, timid, honest, and slightly bewildered Slovak who seemed to be, and was, so much more agreeable a partner than Walter Ulbricht or Wladislaw Gomulka. Throughout the summer of 1968, as Moscow's temper worsened, Kadar took on himself the role of honest broker and endeavored to persuade Dubcek to slow down the headlong process of reform in Czechoslovakia. They talked together often that summer and they met secretly at least three times—before the July Warsaw meeting at which Czechoslovakia's allies publicly condemned her, before the Czech-Soviet confrontation at the little Slovak border town of Cierna-nad-Tisou, and finally on August 17. On

each occasion Kadar apparently tried to persuade
Dubcek to make some concessions to Soviet demands,
to restrict the uninhibited freedom of the press, to
ban embryo opposition groups, for otherwise (and he
emphasized his own experience) he dreaded what
might happen. He did not succeed; like so many
others, Dubcek believed that things had changed
since 1956, that the Russians could no longer afford
to behave as they had then. But it wasn't so.

Their last encounter, on August 17, was only four
days before the invasion. They met in a villa outside
Komarno, the border town through which Borbala
Czermanik had passed south so many years before.
Dubcek drove over from Bratislava, Kadar up from
Budapest, and Kadar told the anxious Czechoslovak
leader that although he himself had little against the
Prague Spring, the Russians were angrier than ever,
that they reckoned the agreements Dubcek had made
three weeks ago at Cierna were being broken and that
the situation was hence more serious than ever before
and might well result in the Russians' insisting that
the Warsaw Pact countries invade Czechoslovakia.
But however strongly he may have stressed the
danger, almost all of the available evidence suggests
that he did not tell Dubcek categorically that the invasion would take place the following Tuesday. For
one thing, it is not even clear that the Russians had at
that stage taken the final decision to invade that day.
And even if they had, they might not yet have transmitted it to Kadar.

On the other hand, Kadar had said on Radio Budapest on August 4, after his return from the Warsaw
Pact conference in Bratislava, which had followed the
first Czech-Soviet confrontation at Cierna, "It is not
certain that everyone will understand at this moment
the meaning of the Bratislava declaration, but think-

ing men will understand it—and others will do so after a week, a month or longer."

This could suggest that Kadar already knew that the Russians were even then determined to invade and that the Cierna and Bratislava confrontations had each been a meaningless deception. But immediately after their August 17 meeting, Dubcek told his friends he could not understand why Kadar had wanted to see him at all, and in his moving, passionate speech of self-defense to the Central Committee of the Czechoslovak Communist party in September 1969 he maintained that even after meeting Kadar the invasion came as a total, shocking surprise to him. In other words, even if Kadar had known of it, he did not tell Dubcek it was about to occur. There is no more reason to doubt Dubcek's sincerity on that issue than there is on almost anything else he has ever said or done. Indeed, one can go further: it is impossible to believe that Dubcek was told in advance of the date of the invasion. Had he known of it, his behavior would have been utterly different.

Whether Kadar had known about it or not on the seventeenth, on August 21 Czechoslovakia was invaded and Hungarian troops were among those who rolled in tanks and armored cars across four borders toward Prague.

Despite their previous misgivings at the pace of Dubcek's reform, horror at being party to such a crime was widespread in Hungary. Although felt most keenly in intellectual circles, in Budapest at least the shock spread right across the classes; people inevitably identified their army's role in Prague with that played by the Soviets in Budapest in 1956; shame focused on Kadar himself: Why could he not have kept the Hungarian army out of the invasion as Ceaucescu had done for the Rumanians? people asked, in shops and cafés, in hairdressers and in parks, in annoyance and sometimes in whispers.

According to *City on the Danube*, a clandestine Czechoslovak radio station, Hungarian workers staged protest strikes in several factories and the invasion was condemned openly in the streets of most towns. Another Czechoslovak resistance radio (*Kukoricavaros*) declared that the Hungarian troops in Slovakia kept out of the towns and tried to be as self-effacing as possible, and *Zemedelske Noviny*, a Czechoslovak agricultural paper, described their conduct as quite unlike that of the Soviet occupation troops: "They are sad, indifferent, walk around with their heads bowed and do not like to look people in the eye. Some of them understand Slovak and they just nod when our people explain to them the situation in our country." [9]

Kadar had agreed to allow Hungarian troops to take part because he was convinced, rightly or wrongly, that were he to refuse, his own leadership and therefore Hungary's own reform program would be totally destroyed. It may be that Brezhnev had even threatened to invade Hungary once more if the Hungarians did not show socialist solidarity and march resolutely into Prague alongside their Warsaw Pact comrades. The Soviet leader could easily have argued that this was an excellent moment for destroying all revisionism in the camp, even that which had been contained within hitherto acceptable limits. In any case Kadar certainly understood that his own position was not as secure as Ceaucescu's and that whereas the Rumanians could defy the Russians successfully, he Kadar could not. For at that time, and still today, it seemed that the Russians were prepared to allow each of their allies to pursue either a measure of political reform or a relatively independent foreign policy, but never both.

Ceaucescu, true to the spirit of Rumanian nationalism, had chosen independence and had consistently and harshly clamped down upon all internal discussion and dissent. Kadar had long since chosen the opposite way and, sacrificing Hungary's right to make any foreign policy initiative, had attempted to make life within the country itself more tolerable for its citizens. August 1968 was no time suddenly to reverse this policy or to try to get the best of both. There were, after all, four Soviet divisions stationed in Hungary. Noncooperation with the Russians over Czechoslovakia would inevitably have brought at least the end of the NEM, so Kadar reasoned, and he may well have been correct.

Nevertheless, agreeing to take part in the invasion was, in a sense, Kadar's darkest hour since 1956. And he knew it. For the next two months he virtually retired from active politics, canceling all his public appearances, making no speeches, attending no rallies. "Sulking in his tent," the *Guardian*'s columnist Victor Zorza not unfairly called it. He left it to his lieutenants, principally Lajos Feher and Istvan Szirmay, to explain and try to justify, to a skeptical and disillusioned people, the invasion.

He did not reappear until the beginning of November. In an interview with the *New York Times* published on November 13 he explained his long absence by saying that because of the Czech crisis in August he had had to postpone his holiday that year and that since then he had simply been on vacation. This was quite untrue; it is known that he was in Budapest for most of September conducting discreet official business—among other things he saw off

Hungary's first ambassador to the United States, Janos Nagy, and, more importantly, received Marshal Yakubovsky, commander in chief of the Warsaw Pact. According to one unconfirmed report he also flew to Moscow at the beginning of October—a moment at which the Russians were angered by the continued intransigence of the Czechoslovaks and their refusal to accept the logic of the invasion—to plead that Dubcek be given more time to "normalize" the country.[10] The usual annual announcement of the start of his holiday was never published because it did not take place. He disappeared not to bronze his skin but to hide his shame.

After his eventual return to public life he justified the invasion when required to do so but far less often and less enthusiastically than his colleagues, Ulbricht, Gomulka, and Brezhnev. In one of his first speeches he tried to make a joke of the situation: "In those August days, somewhere in Czechoslovakia, even Hungarian tourists were regarded as 'occupiers' and 'invaders.' What sort of invaders are we? We have not brought back a single potato; normally, invaders are those who loot." Shades of the Red Army's conduct in Hungary in 1945; everyone laughed. Perhaps his true opinion was expressed most clearly in May 1971 at the Czechoslovak Party Congress in Prague. By now the official orthodoxy accepted by the new Czech leaders as eagerly as almost everyone else in the pact was that the invasion was a fraternal act of help rendered absolutely necessary by the danger of counterrevolution in Czechoslovakia. And as such all applauded it. All except Kadar who declared, to some surprise around the hall, that in his opinion the Czechs themselves would have been quite capable of dealing with the situation in 1968 if they had been left alone.[11]

In some ways the three men, Kadar, Nagy, and Dubcek, are very similar. All of them are honest. All of them are Communists who have sought to humanize communism in Eastern Europe. And all of them are weak. But both Nagy and Dubcek were dominated and strengthened by their honesty in times of crisis. The opposite, say his enemies, seems to happen to Kadar. In times of stress, they claim, he always shows himself to be a coward, a man who is unable to stand up for his convictions; his normal everyday honesty fades and he is left weaker than ever, prey to whatever external influences are the most powerful—at four crucial moments in his life to Rakosi, to Khrushchev, to Khrushchev and to Brezhnev.

But the weakness of all three men is not just a function of their own particular characters. It is also a function of their relationship to the Communist parties which they have tried to change but of which they are all (Nagy the least) creatures. And insofar as they are the creatures of their parties, so are they the creatures of Moscow, for the training which they were accorded in their youth and in their early years in the apparat—Kadar as Janos Barna before the war and as apparatchik after—consistently emphasized nothing so much as the ineluctable supremacy of the Soviet Union. There was no such thing, they were taught, as Czechoslovak or Hungarian national interests: there were only the interests of the U.S.S.R., mother and father of all the world's Communist parties. What was good for the Soviet Union was by definition very very good for their own countries.

This training is not one that is easily sloughed, but in their supreme moments of crisis both Nagy and Dubcek have been able to see suddenly the untruth of the argument. Kadar has not been so fortunate. It is impossible for him ever to see any other truth than that of current Soviet orthodoxy, or ever to have confidence in his own opinion. Whenever he has betrayed himself, or seemed to do so, it has been for the sake of what the Soviet Union at that particular moment believed to be its own interests. He has sacrificed his own conscience for the greater good of the Union of Soviet Socialist Republics. This is just one of the many reasons why—from Moscow's point of view—Khrushchev's choice of Kadar as the man to save socialism in Hungary was so inspired; one of the Soviet leader's most successful gambles in his games with Eastern Europe.

But however pragmatic that choice may at first have been, the relationship between Khrushchev and his creation, Janos Kadar, soon developed into much more than that rather servile pattern that so often obtains between Warsaw Pact leaders and their Soviet comrades. The two men became warm friends. Indeed, although Czechoslovakia's ruler, Antonin Novotny, was also very fond of Khrushchev, the relationship between Kadar and Khrushchev was probably more intimate and more trusting than that which had ever before or has ever since existed between two ruling national Communist party leaders.

Although Kadar had always to respond to and reflect the twists in Khrushchev's political pirouetting, their personal relationship was never harmed. In May 1959 Khrushchev cut short a visit to Albania, explaining in a speech at Korce, which could hardly have flattered his hosts, that he wanted to go to Budapest to see "one of my best friends, Janos Kadar." Kadar himself constantly used to tease Khrushchev, whom he called *Atyai Baratom* ("my old friendly protector"). At the Hungarian Trade Fair in Moscow in 1960 he pointed out to Khrushchev that there was one thing that the U.S.S.R. could never achieve. "What's that?" asked Khrushchev in alarm. "It's something that the U.S.A. will never manage either," replied Kadar to a somewhat reassured but still curious Soviet leader. "Well, come on then, what is it?" demanded Khrushchev again. "You'll never make ties like the Italians," said Kadar. Bad joke, but laughter all around.

Atyai Baratom was a term used not only in jest. In September 1960 they traveled together on the *SS Baltika* to a session of the United Nations in New York. It was the first and only time that Kadar has visited the States (the only time he has been to the West, indeed) and the recollection of it still sears him. From beginning to end he was surrounded by the almost total hostility of both public and politicians. At that time his regime was still completely non grata in many Western countries; it was not until 1962 that the General Assembly resolved that the Hungarian question was closed and that Hungary should be treated in the General Assembly just as any other member.

When Kadar was there memories of 1956 were still acute and apart from the company of Khrushchev, the only remotely enjoyable aspect of the visit was the friendship provided by Cyrus Eaton, the eccentric founder of the Pugwash conferences, millionaire chairman of the Chesapeake and Ohio Railway, and longtime friend of Communist leaders.

Eaton had first met Kadar earlier that year when he had visited Hungary "to see for myself conditions." He decided that the American press reports of Hungarians' misery and starvation were nonsense; for Kadar "gave us a splendid reception with excellent food." When the *SS Baltika* arrived in New York, recalls Eaton, "The US Government would not permit the boat to land at any of the recognised docks, so it had to seek landing privileges at an old dilapidated wharf. The CIA had assembled a group surrounding the wharf to shout insults to the visitors. Although it was a rainy day and the dock was poor and leaky, Mrs. Eaton and I met the boat and greeted our old friends."

Eaton gave a lunch in Kadar's honor.

> It was attended by men of various callings who were in favour of reaching some accommodation with the communists rather than attempt to destroy them. Mr Kadar made a witty speech at the luncheon in which he referred to the organised attempts in New York to give unfriendly demonstrations against the Communist visitors. Each hotel occupied by a Communist leader was surrounded with groups of demonstrators who had been recruited, instructed and paid for by the CIA. The group outside Mr Kadar's hotel somehow missed their cue and shouted "Tito Go Home" when Mr Kadar left his hotel to attend my luncheon.[12]

That might indeed have afforded Kadar a wry laugh. But the rest of the visit was without amusement; he still speaks of it in horror and says that it was only the ebullient, devil-take-all attitude of the little Russian, Nikita Sergeivitch, which really carried him through the implacably hateful reception he was almost everywhere accorded.

Politically there is no doubt that the policy of alliance in Hungary was what Khrushchev wanted Kadar to pursue; indeed, Kadar would never have overcome his home-based Stalinist opposition had this not been so. Khrushchev was clearly quite delighted by the unexpected success of his protégé. In 1964 he demonstrated this in the most formal and obvious way by awarding Kadar one of the highest honors of the So-

viet Union—the Order of Lenin. At his investiture
Kadar, most moved, declared:

> It is part of human nature that one is not able to
> evaluate one's own activities and deeds exactly
> and properly; this must be done by others . . . I
> can only say that during the entire period of my
> conscious social activities I have endeavoured to
> serve the policies of the revolutionary party of the
> Hungarian working class, according to my com-
> munist convictions and my conscience . . . I shall
> strive to do so in future.

He concluded by saying, "let me add that it is a
splendid feeling to accept the decoration from
Comrade Khrushchev whom I have always looked
upon and honoured as a fatherly friend, an elder
brother, and will continue to do so." [13]

A few weeks later Khrushchev had his seventieth
birthday, an occasion celebrated with great pomp and
pride throughout the hierarchies of Eastern Europe,
all of them oblivious of how soon that pride would
fall. Every leader of the Warsaw Pact converged on
Moscow to mark the event, and each of them presented his protector with one of the highest honors
his nation could offer. Antonin Novotny, president
of the Socialist Republic of Czechoslovakia, first secretary of the Czechoslovak Communist party, and once
voted the best-looking leader in Europe by a Western hairdressing federation, proudly brought from
Prague the Order of the White Lion First Class. From
Sofia, capital of Bulgaria, Todor Zhivkov bore the
Medal of the Golden Star, the Dimitrov Order, and,
overdoing it as Bulgarians so often overdo, the title
"Hero of the Bulgarian People's Republic" besides.
Ion Maurer, prime minister of neighboring Rumania
presented the little Russian with the Star of the Rumanian People's Republic First Class, and, predict-

ably more orthodox still, the desiccated Walter Ulbricht brought from Pankow the Karl Marx Insignia
of the German Democratic Republic.

And Janos Kadar brought from Hungary a present
for his friend. But it was not, as everyone expected,
the Order of the Hungarian People's Republic First
Class, the most prestigious honor that the Hungarian
government can confer upon a civilian. Instead he
presented Khrushchev with the Golden Medal of the
Hungarian-Soviet Friendship Society, an organization whose duties are exactly what its name implies
and which is consequently disregarded by many Hungarians as simply an instrument for the dissemination
of Soviet propaganda. It has rather less significance in
Hungary than does the Anglo-Soviet Friendship Society in England and certainly its medal, even its golden
medal, is not a decoration usually thought to carry
enormous prestige.

Although Kadar also presented Khrushchev with a
delicate music box made by a Hungarian goldsmith,
the apparent meagerness of his formal gift caused
some murmurings of discontent among middle-rank-
ing Soviet officials, always quick to interpret any situation in the most uncharitable possible light. Hungarian journalists in Moscow were immediately asked why
Kadar had neglected to honor the Soviet leader in a
more appropriate fashion. Why this deliberate slight
to a man to whom he owed so much, indeed everything?

To these questions no public reply was ever given,
but Kadar explained the reason privately to a group
of those journalists who were themselves made anxious by the apparent discrepancy between Hungary's
gift and those of her allies. It was quite impossible for
him to decorate Comrade Khrushchev with the
Order of the Hungarian People's Republic, he said,

because it was only a few weeks ago that Khrushchev had given him the Order of Lenin. To return the honor in kind so soon would convince the Hungarian peasants that their leader and Khrushchev were engaged in a cliquish game of mutual self-congratulation of as corrupt a kind as that in which Rakosi and Stalin had so blatantly indulged. Of course, said Kadar, Khrushchev himself understood this perfectly and was not in the least offended by his gifts, whatever the reaction of petty bureaucrats.

The journalists laughed at the explanation and, though they found that most of their Soviet colleagues were unable to comprehend, let alone accept it, they understood Kadar's reasoning completely. It was quite typical both of his close relations with Khrushchev and of his sensitivity to the traditional characteristics of the Hungarian peasant that he should have acted thus.

But Kadar's easy relationship with the Soviet leadership was not to last much longer. That October Khrushchev was deposed by the collective troika of Brezhnev, Podgorny, and Kosygin. Kadar was in Poland at the time and until his return there was an uneasy virtual interregnum in Hungary as millions of people worried that his own fall was now inevitable. Among his enemies the reaction was of gleeful expectancy. Happy self-congratulatory telephone calls were made all over the Stalinist demimonde of the Party, toasts exchanged, new loyalties pledged. Within days dozens, if not hundreds, of people had resolved to abandon Kadar and Kadarization.

Kadar never travels by air if he can avoid it and on this occasion he kept to his usual routine and returned from Warsaw by train, perhaps in order to give himself more time to consider the implications of this sad and for him most disquieting news. Would it in fact mean his own downfall, the end of the policies of rapprochement which Khrushchev had urged him to pursue?

Finally his train arrived. A large crowd had gathered at the station, anxious to know his reaction to the coup. When he stepped out of the carriage Kadar kissed his wife (she always came to the station to meet him) and shook hands with those members of the Presidium who were lined up on the platform. Then he made a very short speech to the people waiting: "I am of the opinion," he said, "that Comrade Khrushchev displayed great merit in the struggle against the personality cult of Stalin and in the safeguarding of peace. Hundreds of Hungarians, recently in our country, were able to greet Comrade Khrushchev wholeheartedly as the representative of the great CPSU . . . and the untiring champion of peace." They were right to do so, he said, and even now there was no reason for any Hungarian to regret or be ashamed of the friendship he felt for Khrushchev. After which Kadar declared with more confidence than he can at that moment have felt, "The essential decisive fact is that the political structure of the HSWP and the Government of the Hungarian People's Republic has not changed one iota and will not change either." [14] Referring obliquely to the supposed cause of Khrushchev's resignation, he pointed out that he and his colleagues were in the best of health.

The crowd went away from the station more than happy. Just as the incident with the medals had reminded or convinced many of the journalists he spoke to of the basic honesty and simplicity of their Party's leader, so his tribute to the deposed Khrushchev enormously and instantaneously increased his standing in the country at large. For every one realized that his defense of his fallen friend was an act of considerable political courage.

Four months later, referring to the plots that had been hatched against him, often by ostensible allies, he said that "those autumn days" were "a good time to draw some conclusions about the opinions of men in general . . . how firmly they stand on their feet. . . . On the right they talked about resignations, the downfall of the Government, on the left, they were whispering of a return to a true militant hardfisted leadership." [15] That was easy for him to say later, but he had himself been concerned lest Khrushchev's fall would lead at least to a slowing down of the process of reform for the changes in the Kremlin had, after all, caused "definite unrest among wide circles of the supporters of socialism." [16]

He lost no time however, in trying to establish a workable relationship with the new leaders; in the twelve months after Khrushchev's departure, Kadar met Brezhnev seven times and was no doubt gratified to discover that the new regime did not intend to order an immediate and total reversion of Khrushchevian reform policies in Eastern Europe. Nonetheless, his relationship with Brezhnev has none of the ease of his friendship with Khrushchev.

Whatever the original source of the friendship, it was deep. And, true to his character, Kadar never forgot the debt he owed Khrushchev, even after his railway station speech. When the old man died in 1971, Kadar was the only East European leader who sent his wife and family a telegram of condolence.

When Khrushchev had awarded him the Lenin Prize in 1964, Kadar wept with gratitude and emotion on television. Afterward he is said to have told Khrushchev again and again, "You are like a father to me." In a political sense it is true; Khrushchev was his mentor (whereas Brezhnev, if anything, is only his keeper). But it was also true in a more personal sense, for, as has been shown, as a child Kadar never knew his father, indeed he didn't even know his father's name.

That chance discovery, at the age of sixteen, of the letter to his mother cutting off her tiny allowance had taught him only that somewhere he had a father who was either very poor or very mean. He learned nothing more from his mother at that stage. It was not until after the war, when he became deputy chief of the Budapest police, that the Party made inquiries to find out who he really was. It was only then that he discovered that he had been born a bastard in Rijeka and that his father was Janos Kressinger, a peasant of the village of Pusztaszemenes.

In fact his father was, by peasant standards, rich and had almost certainly been well enough off to support his old girl friend and his son. In the twenties he had had seven acres of land and, in addition, worked as bailiff to the local lord, Count Szechenyi. As such he was responsible for the harvesting, on which he took a cut and, more importantly, was the dominant influence in the lives of some twenty peasants.

Janos Kressinger had had three sons by the wife he married after he left Borbala Czermanik pregnant and alone in Rijeka—Janos Kadar's half brothers, Lajos, Adam, and Janos.

Kadar likes his half brothers well enough; indeed, so easy is he with them that when they are in Budapest they think nothing of calling on him unexpectedly at his office or in Parliament. But typically enough, and unlike Rakosi whose most distant cousins were all given money, houses, and sinecures in the Party machine, Kadar has not used his influence to get his brothers jobs. In fact, just as no one in

Hungary knows anything about Kadar's personal life, so no one knows of and few will even believe in his brothers' existence. Lajos is now a cowherder on the cooperative farm which stands on the land the count once owned and his father once managed; Adam is the village barber; and Janos, the only Party member of the three, was until recently the manager of a radio building enterprise in nearby Kaposvar and now works in Budapest.

Kadar had also a fourth, even more obscure, half brother. At some point in the 1920s, when he and his mother were living together in Budapest, a new lover moved in with her. It is not known whether this was a permanent liaison or not; in a newspaper interview in the 1950s Kadar himself, attempting to give the gloss of normality to his childhood, declared, "There was very little room in my parents' flat and they often wanted us out of the way." [17] "My parents" means his mother and her lover and the "us" refers to the other half brother who was born to Borbala and her unknown friend sometime in the early twenties. This half brother was called Jeno, but he has proved impossible to trace.*

* One story has it that Jeno was a member of the Communist secret police after the war and was murdered (defenestrated, say some) in the late forties: this has never been publicly admitted. Another tale is that he emigrated to Canada during the 1930s. During the 1956 Revolution a farmer called George Kadar from Calgary claimed that he was one of the brothers of Hungary's new ruler and began trying to telephone his alleged sibling in Budapest. But a few days later George's undisputed brother, also an émigré to Canada, decried the story. Considering that Janos Kadar only assumed that name in the Second World War, George Kadar's claim to brotherhood does seem, to say the least, improbable. Kadar himself has done nothing to relieve the mystery. Apart from the occasional oblique reference to "our" parents, he has mentioned the fact that he had a brother in Budapest as little as he had talked about his half brothers in Pusztaszemenes. The only certainty is that whoever Jeno's father was, like Janos's father, he neglected to marry Borbala.

It was characteristic that when Kadar got to know his father for the first time after the war, he bore him no resentment for the way in which he had treated his mother. He used to delight in visiting him occasionally until his death in 1965 and would sit at the top of the table in the kitchen of the little cottage listening to the old man's stories. When his "Old Dad," as he called him, died, he sent a wreath and a telegram saying "My father died after an honest worker's life." But he had no time to come.

In some ways Kadar's life and personality bear a remarkable resemblance to those of Jozsef Attila, the prewar poet whom he had so much liked and whom he so deeply admires. Both were the children of a housemaid and a peasant, both therefore, in Attila's words "the son of the land and the street." Both their mothers were deserted by their fathers.

Jozsef Attila's father was in fact rather more interesting than Kadar's. During his wife's pregnancy he dreamed that his son was to conquer the world and therefore insisted that he be named after the Hun. Nevertheless, it was not that misplaced; Jozsef Attila did not conquer the world, but he certainly conquered the hearts of most Hungarians. Fatherless, both Kadar and Attila were devoted to their mothers, each of whom had to struggle so hard as washerwomen and concierges to bring up their children. Attila wrote several poems in praise of his mother; these passed immediately into the heritage of Hungarian literature so that she has now become a folk-heroine. One of them:

> For a whole week I've thought only of Mamma
> The whole day long. She carries
> Her loaded creaking basket,
> And, light on her feet, climbs before me.

In those days I was all of one mind
I never let off screaming and howling
That Mamma should leave the washing to others
That instead she should carry me up to the attic.

But she hung out the gleaming linen
And climbed without a rebuke, without a glance,
Intent on her washing which, on live wings
Whirling, swelled in the darkness.

Today I scream no more.
It's too late. In my eyes my mother grows colossal,
Her grey hair streaming across the heavens
She rinses the blue in the skies above.

Kadar too was obsessed by his mother. It was she, after all, who had devoted a lifetime to caring for and helping him and not only at home in their tiny flat; whenever he had been imprisoned in the thirties she had risked her livelihood (a Communist son could mean the sack) to bring him food in his cell. After the war he never told her that he had discovered his father's identity and it was only after she died in February 1949 that he finally married Maria, the plump dark-haired girl with whom he had been living, on and off, since the beginning of the war and who had worked with him in the illegal underground. He had previously refused to marry her for fear of upsetting his mother who, by this time, was as dependent upon her son as he had always been on her.

During her husband's imprisonment during the early fifties great pressure was put upon Maria to accept the accusations made against him and denounce him publicly. All over Eastern Europe similar pressure was put upon the wives of other "Titoists" and many of them succumbed to it. But Mrs. Kadar refused to believe the charges and has stood by her husband ever since.

They have no children and live alone together in a large comfortable house in Buda, the traditionally smart, hilly area of Budapest overlooking the Danube and the Parliament on its other bank. They can sometimes be seen walking together in the district and occasionally they dine out at the *Matyas Pince* restaurant, one of Budapest's best. She works at the state publishing house and their life is remarkably simple—as was Jozsef Attila's.

Like Kadar, Jozsef Attila hated pomp, distrusted the middle classes, and was determined to alleviate the misery of the people with whom he so closely identified and whose feelings he reflected so minutely in his verses.

Just before he died, George Lukacs—sitting shrunken in his musty, dirty book-lined flat which had not been painted for fifteen years, writing and reading high above the Danube and facing the Soviet war memorial on the hill across the river, sipping tea from chipped cups at a grubby kitchen table—remembered Kadar with great affection. At their last meeting they had talked about their different backgrounds. Lukacs claimed that as he came from a middle-class family he knew all about the bourgeoisie and they held neither interest nor attraction for him. In fact, he said, they made no impression on him at all. Kadar countered that as he had had a working-class upbringing, "I know the working class from within and therefore do not make the mistake of thinking that every worker is a revolutionary." Lukacs considered that this was very typical of Kadar and that it was, indeed, one of the secrets of his appeal to the people and of his success in uniting the country. He pointed to Kadar's speech at the station after Khrushchev's fall as one of the few really great moments of rapport between a leader and his people that he had ever witnessed.[18] It is certainly true that Kadar is able to relax with and relate to ordinary people in a way which many party leaders, including Dr. Husak, Walter Ulbricht, Richard Nixon, and Edward Heath, never managed.

Both Jozsef Attila and Kadar lacked confidence in themselves, perhaps because of the extreme reliance that each placed on his mother, fatherless as he was. Attila was a schizophrenic. So, figuratively, is Kadar, whose life is made up of a series of tragic incidents each of which reveals another and often very different angle of his many-mirrored emotions. Attila was a suicide. He tried to kill himself by drinking poison at the age of nine; he succeeded when he threw himself under a tram in Balatonszarszo in December 1937. For Kadar the betrayal of Rajk, of the Revolution, of Nagy, and (to a lesser extent) of Dubcek all involved a negation of himself, a partial moral suicide.

He claims that such betrayals have not caused him undue suffering. In 1971 telling Henry Shapiro of UPI what were his greatest achievements, he said:

> Of course, anyone can suffer disappointments. As for me, I was never spoiled by life and this always compelled me to think realistically; so I was able to endure inevitable disappointments fairly well. I never had any special plans for myself and I don't have any now. Long, long ago I became wedded to an ideal and, by and large, have done all that service to that ideal calls for, or permits me to do.[19]

It is difficult to believe that he was not disappointed by the way in which Rajk and Nagy died, the way in which Czechoslovakia was invaded; nonetheless, it is probably true that his perpetual feeling of inferiority gave him few expectations from life. In the event he has not been able to give the Hungarian people all to which they are entitled but he has achieved rather more than many people, perhaps even he himself, expected in November 1956.

Thirteen

In May 1972 Kadar's colleagues gave him a sixtieth birthday party. He was pleased—families should celebrate anniversaries, he thought—but he was nonetheless unused to it: "Comrades, I am embarrassed by this anniversary and these celebrations, they bewilder me and leave me confused." [1] After lunch he made another of the homely, largely unprepared speeches at which he is so practiced and told his friends and his comrades a good deal about the philosophy of life by which he is guided, or which, at least, he would like other people to imagine guides him.

He spoke modestly and warmly and said that he was grateful that while still a teenager he had understood that if someone wants "to find a place in the sun," he can do it "only together with others: one cannot be human or happy alone." And it was not only other people that an individual needs—but also a raison d'être and a moral code by which to live. "Some do live without ideologies and ideals but theirs is not a human life, at least not in my view. I am a Marxist and profess to be a Communist, but quite understand if someone is not a Marxist and not a Communist, so long as he does have some sort of general human ideology which guides him."

His work in the Party had shown him that his first wild dreams of instant communism were a little unrealistic. Life had, he considered, taught him almost nothing as much as the need to compromise. "What we need [are] decisions which take into consideration the real situation and which help us to progress towards our ideals and goals." His goal was the continued and effective rule of the Communist party; after 1956 he worked out very well just what the real situation was and adapted his plans accordingly.

And with what result? To see how far he has fulfilled the demands of the Revolution, one can look again at the resolution adopted by the students on October 22, 1956. Their sixteen points included the removal of Soviet troops, the dismissal of all Stalinists, and the return of Imre Nagy to power. Kadar has done none of these things. Also included was that Matyas Rakosi and other prominent Stalinists must be tried; that did not really happen either, but Farkas and a few other jailers were imprisoned, and after the Revolution Rakosi was exiled to the Soviet Union: in 1971 Kadar denied his last request to come home to die.

The students also demanded general elections with the participation of many parties; they have not got them, but they were eventually given a new electoral law by which candidates can stand against the Party's choice—the one which allowed blind Zoltan Szep to come to power. Workers have now been given at least a limited right to strike, in special circumstances, and relations with Yugoslavia have, as the students asked, been revised on the basis of almost complete equality. But this last concession no longer means very much.

The economy has been reorganized and rationalized as they demanded and foreign trade figures are now published. But the vast deposits of uranium around the sleepy little town of Pecs are still loaded in closed trucks and wagons and sent straight to the Soviet Union at ludicrously low prices. The Stalinist trials have not been completely examined or explained and it is therefore impossible to say that their victims have all been fully rehabilitated. No deportees have been returned from the Soviet Union; indeed after the students' resolution was published, thousands more were carried off there.

The statue of Stalin no longer stands in Budapest—it was destroyed by angry crowds during the Revolution, not removed by Kadar after it. There is still no complete freedom of expression or of opinion and although there is no preliminary censorship, the press is still fettered.

In terms of that particular list of demands, Kadar's success is obviously limited. The crucial demand that he has not been able (and could not even try) to satisfy was, of course, for equality with the U.S.S.R. If today the Russians are a little more tolerant of Hungarian ambitions, if they do give fewer direct orders to Kadar than they did to Rakosi, if their control over Hungary has relaxed at all, this is only because it is useful for them to behave thus. Certainly they may respect the Hungarian temper—they do not want a repeat performance of 1956—but little credit for their concessions is due to Kadar himself; all improvements that Kadar has made in Hungary he has made slowly, cautiously, each time with Soviet approval, never despite his comrades in the Kremlin.

The opposite course was chosen by Alexander Dubcek. He and his colleagues decided in 1968 that the conservative, semi-Stalinist society which they wrested from Antonin Novotny needed a total overhaul to enable it to survive. Piecemeal Kadarist reform was not enough. Indeed, they specifically rejected the Kadarist example. Hungary seemed to them in January 1968 a tired, apathetic, dreary, apolitical society without élan, without impetus, without perhaps even a future.

They saw there a Communist party which was accepted certainly but not embraced, a Party which had won legitimacy but not kindled enthusiasm. It was a Party still compromised by its past, a Party which had never told the truth about the Stalinist period, which was indeed still partly staffed by men responsible for the trials. It was, therefore, a Party which could never ask or expect the unconditional support of its people. That, thought the Czechs, was not what they wanted.

With Dubcek nervously at their head, the Czech reformers decided that only a complete break with their Party's past, such as Kadar had never attempted, would enable them to regain their people's trust. In effect they began to try and fulfill in Czechoslovakia all the demands that the Hungarian students made in 1956 and which Kadar has been unable to meet, principally the complete overhaul of their relationship with Moscow.

But Moscow, of course, refused to allow this to happen. The Prague Spring failed precisely because it was revolution not reform, exactly because Dubcek dared to broach those problems and suggest those solutions which Kadar knew the Kremlin would never tolerate.

As a result, Czechs today live with far less liberty than Hungarians. Dubcek's runaway enthusiasm has been punished; Kadar's cautiousness, seemingly, still pays off. And yet the Czechs have had for a few short months a relationship with their Party and with their leaders which the Hungarians have never had and probably never will have with Kadar. The Czechs also have had a glimpse of what might have become a completely new socialist society; the Hungarians have never seen that: Hungarians live in a state which is more advanced, more tolerant, and in all ways more liberal than the Soviet Union, but which is nonetheless still patterned on the Soviet model and which still takes its example from only Moscow. It is difficult for Western visitors and journalists to say which is better for East Europeans: the bored comfort which Kadar provides, or the short, exciting adventure which Dubcek gave them, but for which they have, almost inevitably, suffered.

George Lukacs had few doubts. Despite his admiration for Kadar's self-effacing modesty Lukacs, in common with most Czech and many Hungarian intellectuals, feared for the future of Hungarian society. He felt that the New Economic Mechanism risked leading the country in the wrong direction; not only, indeed not primarily, because it introduced seemingly capitalist values and spurs—such as competition and profit—into the society, but because it neglected and covered up the real problems of Hungary today, principally the need to democratize the system. Lukacs felt that all Eastern European societies need to offer the worker much greater control over his life and his work, not consumer durables and inequality of incomes.

Just a few weeks before he died in 1971, Lukacs agreed to meet a French intellectual, Yvon Bourdet, in a house deep in a forest outside Budapest. For an hour and a half Bourdet put frank and provocative questions to the old man who answered or deflected each of them with all his usual quiet courtesy. His replies really amount to his last testament and they constitute a fairly devastating indictment of all Eastern European socialist societies, Kadar's Hungary among them, by Eastern Europe's greatest contemporary philosopher.

Lukacs feared that the communist organizations in all these countries were still so bureaucratic as to alienate almost all their potential working-class supporters. This was explosively dangerous—in Poland, he said, an explosion had indeed occurred when, in December 1970, the workers rioted and secured the removal of Gomulka. He thought that the Polish experience might be repeated all over Eastern Europe even, though he did not say so specifically, in sedentary Hungary. When Bourdet pointed out that any such uprising would, as before, be crushed by the Red Army, Lukacs merely replied that "a system that is based on having us sit on bayonets is not a solid system. Thus it can be considered that all the countries of Eastern Europe are transitional regimes in which economic problems necessitate economic reform. But a true economic reform can only be achieved through a democratisation of the daily life of the workers." Nothing else would break down the barriers between rulers and ruled which Rakosi had built and which, though perhaps lower and narrower today, are still obstacles to understanding.

By Lukacs's standards little effective democratization has occurred in Hungary, but given Moscow's absolute refusal to tolerate the philosophy of the Prague Spring, Kadarization—the theory that people who have washing machines and cars and a limited freedom of expression don't need or want political participation—is the way in which most East European governments will probably continue to develop. It was at Budapest (and to East Berlin) rather than at the ghost of Prague 1968 that Edward Gierek gazed intently when he was brought to power after the Polish riots of 1970. But it is unlikely that this slow partial process of change will ever enable Hungary to develop a society that other nations, outside the socialist bloc, might want to emulate. Dubcek's Czechoslovakia might have grown into a scheme of government worthy of copy and many Western Communist parties, especially the Italian, saw in the Prague Spring the most exciting socialist development since the war. While they approve of Hungary, they are not thrilled by it. No one is.

The Hungarian mood today is much as it was in the 1860s. Concessions have been made by the Soviet Union since 1956, just as concessions by the Austrians followed the crushing of the 1848 Revolution. And on both occasions the people concentrated on the pursuit of enjoyment rather than ideals. Freedom lost, comfort sought. Older Hungarians are willing, if not anxious, after their experiences during the Nazi occupation, the Soviet liberation, Stalinization and the years of terror, and finally the Revolution, to sacrifice much for a quiet life. And many of the young (those with memories of 1956) see little point in overtly demanding change. Kadar is acceptable because many Hungarians seem to be becoming like him—conservative, unambitious, safe, steady, quite sympathetic but unexciting, and growing fatter and older all the time. It's a far cry from the dashing romantic Hungarian nobleman/warrior/lover of popular historical fantasy.

Lukacs considered the implications of this easing of the Hungarian girth disastrous. But he did not either doubt or impugn Kadar's honesty. Nor does Kadar.

"Considering everything I feel myself lucky and also happy in the sense that under every circumstance I lived according to my convictions and was able to work and struggle for a cause for which I have always felt a special affinity," he told those who attended his birthday party.

But he realizes that conviction of one's own honesty is not automatically shared. Perhaps thinking of his relationship with Rajk, he declared, "There are situations where one has to do something which is understood only by a few at the time. Yet it has to be done in the hope that they will understand one's motives later on." And then, maybe with the Revolution and his desertion of it in mind, he said he was happy to see the day when "even millions understood what he had to do in another situation."

In fact Hungarians can still not agree on just what the fighting in 1956 really was. Was it a revolution or, as the Russians and the Hungarian Communist party have claimed ever since, a counterrevolution? Individual noncommunists of all ages seem to be divided according to their own personal experiences during the autumn of 1956. Many of those who were shocked by the shooting of Imre Mezo, for instance, now tend to agree that it was a counterrevolution. Those who remember mainly the plans of Nagy, revolution. It can be called a counterrevolution because it was intended to overthrow the communist system which Hungary had experienced since the Revolution of 1948. But the followers of Nagy exclaim that that's just why it was revolutionary—Rakosi's tyranny had nothing to do with real socialism and had to be removed. Perhaps Kadar has the most sensible answer to a rather meaningless semantic dispute. Counterrevolution, he says, is the "scientific definition" of what happened in 1956. "But there is also another concept which we might all accept: it was a national tragedy. A tragedy for the Party, for the working class, for the people and for the individual. We lost our way and the result was tragedy."

He said the same thing to William Rogers, U.S. Secretary of State, when Rogers visited him in 1972. Rogers was impressed by Kadar's humility, by his unpretentious, spartan office and above all by his sadness. Kadar repeated over and over what a terrible tragedy the Hungarian people had suffered since the war. He seemed intensely involved in it himself. Rogers came away thinking that Kadar was a decent, melancholy and simple man who understood his people well and was doing all he could for them.

To help people forget or at least overcome that tragedy, most of Kadar's policies since 1956 have been designed as sedatives, not stimulants. He has tried to convince people that the Revolution was already won, the dictatorship of the proletariat ensured, and the main tasks now left were the milder ones of consolidation and consolation. He has—with periodic fluctuations—been concerned with playing down the importance of ideology; he has tried to appear undogmatic and pragmatic in his judgments and has encouraged his colleagues to do the same.

Many older Party members complain that this is the reason why young people will no longer join the Party—it just isn't exciting for them anymore. "There is nothing like the old revolutionary days," they moan. "We have become too soft. Everyone travels by car. We complain when the shops occasionally fail to provide an adequate choice of sausages, portable radios, winter coats, or even motorcycles." They profess sympathy for young people who cry, "We can't be revolutionaries anymore."

The problem Kadar and his colleagues face is to

convince people, and especially young people, that the cause can and should still be helped. As one writer put it, "Today there are no barricades to storm and we do not have to offer our bodies to the volleys." But think, he says, of the pleasure to be derived from the simpler, less glamorous tasks that now face revolutionaries. "Countless thousands are satisfied if a bakery succeeds always in baking appetising products . . . and trains that run on schedule ease the life of tens of thousands of people." He asks, "Could there be a more splendid or greater honour for a revolutionary than the contentment of the majority of the people and a general condition of rising prosperity? It is for this that people died on the barricades."

Many young people ask, reasonably enough, whether this is really so: Did men die to have the trains run on time and the cream cakes properly filled? They argue that the fact that Party apologists even make such suggestions shows that Hungarian Communism is in a state of considerable crisis; it is a crisis that is beginning to affect many Parties in Eastern Europe and which might eventually engulf the Soviet Union also.

This crisis is the paradox that the greater the Party's success, the more extensive its social achievements, the less essential does its work become, and the more irrelevant do its ideological strictures seem. The mammoth work of the Party has been done; traditional feudalism, poverty, and ignorance have been destroyed in Hungary—and although the old individualist attitudes toward life have survived and are still far stronger, even among the young, than collectivist credos, the framework of a new society has been constructed.

In an attempt to flesh out that skeleton, the Party is now committed to the surrender of much of the power that it had clutched jealously when it first seized office and began to build itself into an irresistible force for change. The huge apparat which it needed to transform society and to sustain itself is no longer necessary. Indeed, it is a hindrance to reform. Compulsion is now being replaced by economic persuasion and as theology gives way to consumer durables, the theologians themselves become expendable. Lukacs is right: the more emphasis that is placed on indicators of economic development, the less influence will remain for ideology as a guiding force in society.

But ideology is not dead in Hungary—there are still bitter arguments over the effects of the reforms. Many workers, all Maoists, all neo-Stalinists, and several others claim that the growing inequality of incomes is deplorable in a socialist society and that washing machines have nothing to do with Marx. The dispute really centers on the question of what a socialist society is meant to be and meant to do for its members. Should it be more concerned with moral values or material aims?

When one remembers the appalling misery of the masses of the people before the war, it might seem a tribute to the Party's success that today the main argument in Hungary should be over the size of individual incomes. Certainly Party spokesmen like to praise their own achievement in turning Hungary from a nation of impoverished peasants into one of fattened workers. But the price at which that has been achieved—eight years of cruel terror, the brutal suppression of a national uprising against arbitrary dictatorship, fifteen more years of less inhumane but nevertheless narrow-minded and unimaginative government—is a price which no nation would ever willingly pay and which none should be asked to pay.

What makes it worse still is that it was quite unnecessary. Stalinism and Kadarization are not the only ways in which Hungary could have been transformed. Under a bourgeois democracy its sibling Austria has suffered none of the horrors that Hungary has had to endure—it has actually progressed much further and faster than Hungary in terms of *economic* development. The Austrian experience is immensely important to both Hungarians and Czechs. It is according to the successes of the Karntnerstrasse and the standard of living in Graz that they measure their own countries' achievements. In 1968 the Czechs were infuriated by the fact that the Austrians had a higher standard of living: in 1914 it had been higher in Prague. Despite all that they have undergone, many Hungarians still today think in much the same way as their Austrian neighbors. The peasant from Pecs and the worker from Miskolc are not yet as rich but they are just as petit bourgeois as their siblings from the hills of Carinthia and the streets of Linz. This is not reprehensible, but nor is it what the Party intended.

Because there is still no real freedom of speech in Hungary it is difficult to assess accurately Hungarians' real attitudes toward their rulers today. On the one hand it seems not only an irony but an insult that the people should be told that the events of the fifties—the suspicion, the fear and the hatred that Stalinism deliberately fostered to keep them cowed as their lives were rescheduled, the Revolution and its destruction, the carnage and disullusion which followed—that all this was worthwhile so that now in the bakeries the bread should properly rise.

Nevertheless, from this author's own very limited observation, it seems that although most people profess total disinterest in the Party and its values, complain of the restrictions it places upon them and revile the Soviet Union, probably a minority would consider themselves out and out anti-communists. Indeed, given what they have suffered at the Party's hands, the tolerance with which most of the people interviewed in the course of this research judged the Party was rather remarkable. For this reconciliation most of the credit must be given Kadar, whose own assessment of the Party's success is limited to the belief that "on the whole our people have been taken up with communism."

Kadar had enjoyed his sixtieth birthday party. A rather old-looking man for his age, some thought, his face more than ever like a deflated football bladder, his skin paler than before, a little unsteady on his feet and in his voice, not so much from the toasts of Georgian cognac he had drunk as from the heart attack he had recently suffered. His cheap, thin plastic glasses pushed crookedly on his nose, his ill-fitting suit bulging at the pockets, his hand fumbling with his fork, he looked more than ever like an impoverished grocer's assistant on a weekend at the seaside, an unsuccessful and far from smarmy brush salesman, almost a pavement artist with a sudden windfall—an old jacket that was no longer good for someone else but was better than best for him.

As he came to the end of his speech, which had been received well by those of his hosts and their guests who were his friends, noncommittally by the rest, he seemed a little moved: "We know each other, more or less," he said to them. "Today is a date in the calendar. Tomorrow it will be the 26th, and the day after the 27th; life will go on and there will always be work to do. I won't change any more at my time of life. I am the same person I was last week, and will be the same person next week and afterwards. I will remain the same as I have been up to now."

But what did he consider the consistent part of himself? Who is "the same" Kadar? Is it the poor little bastard minding the pigs in Kapoly and then selling papers in the cold outside the glow of the huge houses and the hotels of Budapest? Is it the naïve and idealistic young Party member who fell in love with a girl just because she was the first female Communist he had ever seen? Or is it the pragmatic Party worker?

Is Kadar the underground fighter who had a good comrade in the war called Laszlo Rajk, whose comrade's wife, Julia, suffered excruciating torture by the Nazis rather than reveal his whereabouts? Is it the friend whom the Rajks trusted so much that they later asked him to be godfather to their son in the belief that he would protect him should anything (not that they expected anything) happen to the two of them? Or is the real Kadar the Party loyalist who, despite all these things, obeyed the orders of his superiors and told his friend that if he confessed he would live?

Is Kadar the Hungarian who was the ally of Imre Nagy or is he the Communist who destroyed the Revolution when the Russians asked him to? Is he an opportunist who always seizes the main chance for preserving himself at the summit of an insensitive, totalitarian Party, or is he a pragmatist who sincerely believes that Hungarians will be happier under communism than under any other social system and that concessions to the reality of the moment are therefore justified? If he is to remain, as he says, the same, does that mean that he will in fact continue to change? Will he be as susceptible to pressure next week, next month, next year as he has proved in the past? Or is he now set, set firmly, in the mold of the quiet, modest, uncertain, self-effacing, timid, and unbrilliant bureaucrat, a man who remembers that in his life he always did as he was told and who probably thinks he usually did right, who considers that in the short term at least he has consistently tried to improve his people's fortunes?

In 1965 Ferenc Vali, an exiled commentator on Hungarian affairs wrote, "The greatest barrier preventing the Kadar regime's popularity drive from becoming a real success is the person of Kadar himself . . . Kadar has been thrust upon Hungary by an invading foreign army . . . the mark of Cain will continue to plague him."

Mr. Vali is using "the mark of Cain" in its popular, pejorative sense. It is easy to understand his distaste for Kadar: his past is not attractive and of course it is true that in, say, the British political context, one would hope not to find a man with his history as a leading politician.

But if Abel is the entire Hungarian people betrayed in 1956, Mr. Vali's parable is inapt. As has been shown, many Hungarians doubt Kadar's resolution to withstand Soviet demands and perhaps few have total confidence in the future, but it is nevertheless in the person of Kadar that any such confidence does lie.

In Budapest the story is told that when he heard that a county Party secretary had the local swimming pool emptied of people every day at noon so that he could practice his diving undisturbed, he had him sacked at once. On another occasion he went shooting with a group of local Party officials in Transdanubia. They all went out to lunch in a pub and at the end of the meal Kadar pulled out his purse to pay his own bill. Many of the other apparatchiks were somewhat embarrassed; they had expected to get a free meal and had come without money. Either or both of these stories may be mythical. What is important is that they exist; they show the attitude that people have come to expect Kadar to take. Some say they think of him as Honest Janos in the spirit of their great king, Honest Matyas.

At least twice a year he makes a pilgrimage of one of Hungary's nineteen counties to show himself to and be greeted by the people. Although painfully shy, he always tries to appear as homely and as easy as possible. And despite his reticence, he succeeds very well, making a much more sincere and effective whistle-stop tour than most American politicians manage, stopping off here for a beer, there to see the new cowshed, in the pub for a dirty joke (which he does not like telling but which he realizes helps his image of a man still close to the earth). On these occasions he also gives formal addresses in the factories he visits and attempts to take his listeners into his confidence, explaining to them what are the particular problems that the country faces at the moment and how best they can be overcome, what sort of help he needs right now.

He possesses an understanding of and a sympathy for the national mind and mood (insofar as such a phenomenon can be conceived) not shared by many politicians in either East or West. For instance, he can fly into rages if he is photographed with his wife, Maria, while on official business. In vain do the photographers argue that the Hungarian people are interested in seeing his wife: he retorts that he will not allow it because the Hungarian peasant will say that it's a disgrace that Mrs. Kadar should travel at the expense of the state. His great good fortune is that he is a home-grown politician whose Marxism is of an entirely practical kind, learned all in Hungary. Unlike both Rakosi and Nagy, he owes nothing to a Moscow education; perhaps as a result he is rather more sensitive than either of them. As a result an appalling but popular joke circulates in Budapest of an anxious husband who accompanies his middle-aged wife to the doctor. Taking him aside, the doctor whispers, "You know that there are going to be some important changes?" "Good heavens," says the husband in terror, "You don't mean that Kadar is going to be replaced?" "No, no, of course not: your wife is having her menopause."

Till now there has been little sign of Kadar being replaced—for one thing he has groomed no successor. Till now he has managed to persuade his dogmatist colleagues that for the Party to maintain its supremacy it must sacrifice some of its unessential powers. But there may come a time when even Kadar realizes that those sacrifices have already been so extensive as to threaten the Party's continued overall control of society. It is from the economy, not from new politicians, that the threat will come. The Party is now finding that the process of decentralization is rendering it powerless, like many Western governments, to control wage and price rises, inflation, productivity, the balance of payments, and the general standard of living. This process will continue and at any moment the Party's leaders might, in alarm, try to seize back some of the influence over men's lives which they are now losing to technocrats, to cooperative farms, and to the ordinary people who have become, over the last few years, their own bosses. If such a nervous reaction does set in, it could hardly be other than extremely unpleasant for all Hungarians and might be bitterly resisted.

Throughout 1973 there were also unwelcome and

unexpected signs that the course of liberalization might also be slowed or even reversed by the process of East West detente. The last two years' rapprochement between President Nixon and Chairman Brezhnev had not, as had once been hoped, done anything to improve conditions of life in the Soviet bloc. Indeed, in the Soviet Union itself it had been accompanied by an unrelenting campaign against the civil rights movement and such critics of the Soviet bureaucracy as Alexander Solzhenitsyn and Andrei Sakharov. The message was very clear: peaceful coexistence between the world's greatest military powers was in no way intended to lead to the "convergence" of the systems which East European intellectuals had once hoped to be the main result of detente. At the beginning of the decade Hungarian intellectuals had agreed with Sakharov that in increased trade and contact with the West lay the best hope for the liberalization of Soviet society. By mid 1973 it was very clear that the Brezhnev-Nixon deal was to do nothing of the sort. Predictably enough, the Kremlin's new harshness toward its domestic critics was reflected in Hungary not only by such arbitrary acts as the expulsion of Hegedus and his colleagues from the Party but also by an officially imposed mood of greater than usual caution amongst Budapest's writers and intellectuals.

This was immensely depressing and demonstrated once again the limits of Kadarization. But whatever the eventual outcome of Kadar's experiment (and any outcome will be determined by developments in Moscow) almost all Hungarians are now a great deal better fed, clothed, and schooled and less restricted than they have ever been. Kadar has, in almost every way, extended the limits of the freedoms his people can enjoy.

In the village of Kapoly where Janos Czermanik was brought from Fiume, the pigs still squelch along the muddy street, the rain still comes in through the roofs of the thatched cottages, but there is always work in the cooperative farm, either on the surrounding green, hilly fields or in the buildings near the village. The peasant women still wear their traditional dress; their children play in the road, and that road is certainly more dangerous than ever before as herdsmen and threshers and milkmen drive past in their new cars, but unlike Janos Czermanik those children no longer have to work all day as midget farm hands to earn enough to eat.

The two tall churches still stand at either end of the street but they are falling into disrepair. The Protestant priest has given up altogether, so disheartening did he find the empty pews: every Sunday morning his parishioners crowd into the tiny pub a hundred yards away, slapping their glasses down on the zinc counter, demanding more and more beer, another schnapps, and laughing loudly. Across the road, in his own freezing and drafty church, the Catholic priest, wearing under his cassock his overcoat and under his overcoat his patched trousers and under them his pajamas, shivers with the few old women who still come to pray. When Janos Czermanik lived there, both churches were almost always filled, but in those days it was the priests alone who went home afterward to large hot lunches; today it is only the priest whose home is as cold as the church, who cannot afford a huge meal with much to drink, and who wraps a blanket over his cassock as soon as the service is over.

In the hazy drunken Sunday afternoons the villagers speak well of Kadar, proud that he once lived there. Theirs, of course, is a vested interest, but although Hungarians still speak of "them" and "us," that sympathy for him seems to be shared across the land. This pleases Kadar himself, for he is a man who still needs popularity to boost his confidence. He is not a happy man. "As you know," he told those who attended his birthday party, "my personal road was not simple and smooth." He is a strange man, difficult to understand, weak, uncertain, and unoriginal; he is a dedicated and well-instructed Party worker who will accept, unquestioningly, his Party's orders rather than an individual who is able and eager to make his own decisions. But, perhaps because his own life reflects so nearly the tragedies that have overtaken his country, he has gone a long way to fulfilling the ambition he expressed in 1962. "Whenever our comrades speak about communism and socialism being a superior system" he then said, "the reactionaries shout 'What about Hungary?' We want our friends to be able to answer back: 'Yes what about Hungary, indeed; let's talk about Hungary.' "

Source Notes:

Chapter One

1. See, for example, The United Nations *Committee on Hungary Report,* 1957.
2. See, for example, the biographies of Kadar in his two Party-published books of collected speeches, articles and interviews: *Socialist Construction in Hungary, 1957-61* and *On the Road to Socialism, 1960-64* (Budapest: Corvina, 1962 and 1965).

Chapter Two

1. Interview published in *Budapest* Magazine, 1957.
2. Ibid.
3. *Magyar Ifjusag,* May 2, 1957.
4. Ibid.
5. This and other personal stories about Kadar were told to me in Hungary by Hungarians close to him who, for obvious reasons, do not wish to be named.
6. *Ifjusag,* op. cit.
7. Ibid.
8. Ibid.
9. Ivan Berend, *Contribution to the History of Hungarian Economic Policy in the Two Decades following the Second World War* (Budapest: Hungarian Academy of Sciences, 1967).

10. *Ifjusag,* op. cit.
11. Ibid.
12. Ibid.
13. Ibid.
14. Speech at Ganz Mavag Works; *Collected Speeches 1960–64* (Budapest: Corvina).
15. George Paloczi Horvath, the *Sunday Times* (London), March 24, 1957.
16. Ibid.
17. *Ifjusag,* op. cit.

Chapter Three

1. Sandor Nogradi, *The Start of a New Chapter in History* (Budapest: Kossuth, 1966).
2. *L'Humanité,* January 6, 1963.
3. *Tarsadalmi Szemle,* April 1952.
4. Ibid.
5. Ibid.
6. *Szabad Nep,* February 7, 1951.
7. *Szabad Nep,* April 30, 1949.
8. *Vjesnik,* October 5, 1956.
9. *Nowa Kultura,* story by Wiktor Worosylski, November 1956.
10. *Vjesnik,* op cit.
11. George Urban, *Nineteen Days* (London: Heineman, 1957), p. 228.
12. Quoted in a private conversation with the author in Budapest, 1971.
13. UPI from New York, June 5, 1957.
14. *Vjesnik,* op. cit.
15. Bela Szasz, *Without Compulsion* (Brussels: Imre Nagy Institute, 1963), pp. 308–309. (Published under the pseudonym Vincent Savarius.)
16. Ferenc Fetjo, "Hungarian Communism," *Communism in Europe,* vol. I, ed. Griffiths (New York: Pergamon, 1964).
17. This story has been widely quoted. See, for example, Szasz, op. cit.

Chapter Four

1. *Il Giornale d'Italia,* November 2, 1956.
2. Bela Szasz, *Volunteers For The Gallows* (London: Chatto and Windus, 1971).
3. *Nepszabadsag,* December 8, 1959.
4. Ferenc Fejto, "Hungarian Communism," *Communism in Europe,* vol. 2, ed. Griffiths (New York: Pergamon, 1964), p. 197.
5. *L'Humanité,* January 6, 1963.

Chapter Five

1. *L'Unita,* December 1, 1969.
2. *Magyar Nemzet,* December 10, 1961. Quoted by William Juhasz in *A Hungarian Social Science Reader.* (Munich: Heller & Molnar, 1965).
3. Eighth Party Congress, 1962, *Collected Speeches 1960–64* (Budapest: Corvina).
4. Ibid.
5. Ibid.
6. *Nepszabadsag,* December 3, 1961. Quoted in William Robinson, *The Pattern of Reform in Hungary* (New York: Praeger, 1973).
7. See, for example, his interview with UPI, 1966.
8. Radio Budapest, July 21, 1970.

Chapter Six

1. Agence France Presse: December 6, 1961. Quoted in Ferenc Fetjo, "Hungarian Communism," *Communism in Europe,* vol. I, ed. Griffiths (New York: Pergamon, 1964), p. 273.
2. Ibid.
3. William Robinson, *The Pattern of Reform in Hungary* (New York: Praeger, 1973).
4. *Collected Speeches 1960–64,* p. 206.
5. *Nepszabadsag,* February 12, 1966.
6. International Commission of Jurists, February 21, 1966.
7. *Nepszabadsag,* October 29, 1966.
8. *Nepszava,* April 25, 1971.
9. *Partelet,* January 1970.
10. *Nepszabadsag,* February 18, 1969.
11. *Szabad Nep,* March 29, 1956.
12. *Nepszabadsag,* August 16, 1962. Quoted in William Juhasz, *A Hungarian Social Science Reader.*

Chapter Seven

1. See William Robinson, *The Pattern of Reform in Hungary* (New York: Praeger, 1973), for the most comprehensive account of economic reform in Hungary yet published.
2. *Pravda,* January 1, 1950.
3. Ivan Berend, *Some Main Tendencies of Industrial Development in Postwar Hungary* (Budapest: Hungarian Academy of Sciences, 1970), p. 274.
4. Ibid., p. 284.
5. Archive of the Institute of Party History. Memo on efficacy of investments, October 29, 1951. Quoted in Berend, op. cit.

6. *Magyar Statisztikkai Evkonjv,* 1962. Quoted in Berend, op. cit.
7. *Kozgazdasagi Szemle,* November and December 1957 and July 1958. Quoted by William Robinson, op. cit.
8. *New Hungarian Quarterly,* Budapest, no. 40, Winter 1970.
9. Ibid.
10. *Magyar Nemzet,* May 1, 1968.

Chapter Eight

1. *Nepszabadsag,* January 28, 1958.
2. Ibid., December 25, 1957.
3. *Elet es Irodalom,* March 13, 1959.
4. *L'Humanité,* January 6, 1967.
5. *New Hungarian Quarterly,* Budapest, no. 42, Summer 1971.
6. Ibid.
7. Joszef Revai, *The Situation and Tasks of Our Literature* (Budapest: Agitprop, 1954).
8. *New Hungarian Quarterly,* op. cit.
9. *Magyar Hirlap,* July 23, 1968.
10. *Kortars,* April 1969.
11. Quoted in East Europe, New York, June 1964.
12. *New Hungarian Quarterly,* Budapest, no. 35, Autumn 1969.
13. Ibid.
14. International Press Institute Conference Proceedings, 1970.
15. MTI (The Hungarian Press Agency), March 10, 1969.
16. *Nepszava,* February 10, 1971.

Chapter Nine

1. *Nepszabadsag,* September 15, 1966.
2. *New Hungarian Quarterly,* no. 40, Winter 1970.
3. *Elet es Irodalom,* September 13, 1969.
4. "168 Hours," Radio Budapest, September 4, 1971.
5. *Elet es Irodalom,* July 20, 1970, and *Figyelo,* May 5, 1971.
6. Ibid.
7. *Magyar Nemzet,* February 17, 1971.
8. *Nepszabadsag,* July 9, 1971.
9. *Figyelo,* May 5, 1971.
10. *New Hungarian Quarterly,* no. 40, op. cit.
11. Ibid.
12. Ibid.
13. *Kozgazdasagi Szemle,* no. 11, 1971.
14. *Tarsadalmi Szemle,* October 1970.
15. *Nepszabadsag,* November 21, 1963.

Chapter Ten

1. MTI, March 2, 1971.
2. George Konrad and Ivan Szelenyi, *Balatonfured Proceedings 1969* (Budapest: 1971).
3. Kadar to Tenth Congress, Congress Proceedings, 1970.
4. Radio Warsaw for Poles Abroad, March 10, 1969.
5. *Magyar Nemzet,* July 2, 1970.
6. Gergely subsequently published a book on suicide called *Magunknak Elunk* ("We Live for Ourselves") (Budapest: 1971).

Chapter Eleven

1. *Magyar Ifjusag,* May 2, 1957.
2. *Partelet,* February 2, 1971.
3. *Nepszabadsag,* June 1, 1969.
4. *Valosag,* July 1971.
5. *Magyar Ifjusag,* June 5, 1970.
6. Ibid., June 19, 1970.
7. Radio Budapest, December 3, 1968.
8. *Magyar Hirlap,* February 1, 1970.
9. *Uj Ember,* February 15, 1970.
10. *Magyar Ifjusag,* February 13, 1970.
11. *Elet es Irodalom,* April 24, 1971.
12. *Kortars,* November 1968.

Chapter Twelve

1. Ferenc Fetjo, "Hungarian Communism," *Communism in Europe,* vol. 2, ed. Griffiths (New York: Pergamon, 1964).
2. *Magyar Szo,* November 16, 1956.
3. *Borba,* November 23, 1956.
4. *Politika,* November 24, 1956. Quoted in *The Hungarian Revolution,* ed. Laski (London: Secker and Warburg, 1957).
5. *Borba,* February 25, 1956.
6. *Dagens Nyheter,* December 2, 1956.
7. Endre Marton, *The Forbidden Sky* (Boston: Little, Brown, 1971), p. 211.
8. Fetjo, op. cit., p. 252.
9. *Zemedelski Noviny,* August 25, 1968.
10. UPI, October 7, 1968.
11. Minutes of Czechoslovak Party Congress, Prague, May 1971.
12. Recalled by Cyrus Eaton in a letter to the author, July 8, 1971.
13. *Collected Speeches 1960–64,* p. 268.
14. MTI, October 18, 1964.
15. Quoted by Imre Kovacs, East Europe, New York, May 1965.

16. *Nepszabadsag,* February 12, 1965. Quoted by William Robinson, *The Pattern of Reform in Hungary* (New York: Praeger, 1973).

17. *Magyar Ifjusag,* May 11, 1957.

18. George Lukacs in conversation with the author, May 1971.

19. UPI, February 1971.

Chapter Thirteen

1. Yvon Bourdet, *L'homme et La Societe* no. 20, April–June, 1971, pp. 3–12.

Index

William Shawcross is twenty-seven. His first book, *Dubcek* was published in 1971. Since then he has worked for the *London Sunday Times* in Eastern Europe and Indochina. Nineteen seventy-three he spent in the United States as a Harkness and Congressional Fellow. He is co-author of *Watergate,* published in 1973. He is married to the writer Marina Warner.